Performance Golf

Performance Golf

Developing and Perfecting Your Golf Game

Gerald A. Walford and Gerald E. Walford

Van der Plas Publications, San Francisco

Published by

Van der Plas Publications

1282 7th Avenue

San Francisco, CA 94122, U.S.A.

E-mail: pubrel@vanderplas.net

Website: http://www.vanderplas.net

Distributed or represented to the book trade by

U.S.A.:   Seven Hills Book Distributing, Cincinnati, OH

U.K.:   Chris Lloyd Sales and Marketing Services, Poole, Dorset

Canada: Hushion House Publishing, Toronto, ON

Australia: Tower Books, Frenchs Forest, NSW

Cover design by Kent Lytle, Alameda, CA

Front cover and frontispiece photograph: Corbis photo agency

All other illustrations by the author

Publisher's Cataloging in Publication Data
Walford, Gerald. A. Performance Golf: Developing and Perfecting Your Golf Game.
Gerald A. Walford and Gerald E. Walford.
p: cm.   Includes index and bibliographical information.
1. Golf, manuals and handbooks.
I Walford, Gerald E. II. Title
Library of Congress Control Number 2001-131627
ISBN 1-892495-33-3 (paperback)

Table of Contents

About the Authors 8

Introduction 9

Part I. Golf and the Laws of Science 11

1. The Physics and Biomechanics of the Golf Swing 12
Inertia 12
Angular Speed 13
Torque 13
Starting the Downswing: Pull and Push Action . 14
Gravity 15
Distance and Accuracy 17
Wrist Cock 17
Slow Hands at Impact 18
COAM: Conservation of Angular Motion 18
Snapping of a Whip 18
Transfer of Energy of the Golf Swing 19
Sources of Energy 19
Principles of Force 20
Falling Back 20
The Grip 21
Harry Vardon and His Bent Elbow 21
The Set-Up 22
Relax 22
Loose Grip 22
Choking up on the Club 23
The Sweet Spot (Center of Percussion) 23
Speed of the Ball 24
The Single-Axis or Single-Plane Swing 24
The Palm Grip 24
The Wide Stance 25
Right Arm/Wrist Power 25
The Swing Arc 25
The Single-Axis or Single-Plane Theories . . . 26

2. The Physics of Golf Equipment 28
Club Face Inserts 28
Putters 28
Wedges 29
Irons and Woods 29
Swing Weight 29
Featherlight and Very Light Golf Clubs 30
Modality Synchronization 30
Shafts 31
New Trends 34
Golf Balls 35
Putting 36
Roll of the Ball 37
The Ball's Center 37
Compression 37
Durability 38

USGA 38
Dimples 38
Aerodynamics 39
Grips 39
Size 39
Clubheads 40
Center of Gravity 40
Clubface 40
Equipment Summary 41

Part II. Using the Senses for Learning 42

3. Evolution of the Golf Swing 43
Yesterday's Swing: 43
Early Modern Swing 44
The Late Modern Swing 45

4. The Role of Vision and Nonvision in Learning the Golf Swing and Putt 46
Feeling Versus Thinking 46
Three Stages of Learning 47
Kinesthetic Learning 47
Right Brain/Left Brain 47
Clubhead Focus 48
Visual and Kinesthetic Imagery 49

5. The Use and Misuse of Imagery, Reflexes, and Learning 51
Clear Mind 51
Feedback 52
Automatic Learned Reflexes 52
Pros and Cons of Imagery 53
Learning Skills 54

6. Neuro-Linguistic Programming and Golf 56
Learning the Skill 56
Anchors or Triggers 57

Part III. All About the Golf Swing 59

7. Mechanics of the Golf Swing 60
Centrifugal Force, Center, and Radius 60
The Golf Swing's Centrifugal Force: Center and Radius 61
The 90-Degree Swing Angle 62
Golf's Swing Problems: Center and Radius Changes 63
Body Weight Placement 63
Wrist Action 64
Shoulder Rotation 64

The Arm Roll 64
Lever-Powered Golf 65
The Only Necessary Movement 65
Power Turned on by Forearm 66
Impact 66

8. Learning the Swing 67
Making the Circle 67
Chevreul's Pendulum 68
Visualization 68
Scrape-the-Grass Drill Without Golf Ball 69
The Basic Swing 70
Nonvisual Practice 71
The Full Swing 71
The Backswing 71
The Weight Shift 71
The Arm-and-Hand Roll 72
Scrape-the-Grass Drill With a Golf Ball 72
Ball Placement 72
Swing Problems and Failures 73
The One-Leg Stork Stand Drill 73
The String Drill 74
Putting 74
Subconscious Putting 76
Lining up the Putt 76
Putting Distance 77
Chipping 77
Pitching 78
The Fade, Slice, Draw, and Hook 78
Learning the Skills 78
Keep it Simple 79
Learn Like a Kid 80
Be Natural 80
Playing Outside Your Own Rhythm 81

9. The Twin Pendulum 82
The Pendulum Analogy 82
The Single Pendulum 82
The Twin Pendulum 84

10. Science of the Short Game 86
Swing Speed and Distance 86
The Killer Bee "Stinger" Golf Club Method . . . 87
Chipping 88
Putting 88
Sand Shots 89
Short and Simple Method 89
Distance/Club Chart 90

Part IV. The Mental Aspects of the Game . . 91

11. From the Practice Range to the Golf Course 92
Mind Confusion 92
Do Not Try to Hit the Ball 93

How to Practice 93
Mental Strategies 93

12. Golf Strategy: The Percentage Game . . 94
Positive Thinking 94
Consistency 94
Equipment 95
Do Your Own Thinking 95
Club Selection 95
Off the Tee 95
Long Fairway Shots 96
The Approach Shot 97
The Greens 98
Reading the Greens 99
Scrambling 100
The Rough 101
Sand Trap Shots 101
Water Shots 102
The Weather 102
The Rules of Golf 103
Your Own Par 103

13. Mental Strategies for Golf 104
Strategies and Abilities 104
The Performance Phase 105
Self-Talk 106
Rational Thinking 107
Positive Thinking 107
Lessening Importance of the Situation 108
Perceptions 108
Mental Recall 108
Confidence 109
Anxiety and Tension 109
Routines 110
The Preparation Phase: Psychological Strategies for
    Use When Not Performing 110
Goal Setting 110
Relaxing the Body 113
Imagery 113
Imagery for Mental Development 114
Evaluation 114
Concentration 115
Hypnosis 115
Meditation 115
Reminiscence 116
Choking 116
The Five Stages of Accomplishment 116

Part V. Advanced Techniques 117

14. Does Your Golf Ball Know What Your Body Is Doing? 118
The Grip 118
The Stance 119
The Backswing 120

The Downswing 121
Contact 121
The Follow-Through 122
The Overall Swing 122
The Short Game 123
Putting 124
Summary 125

15. The Practice Swing Is Always Better . . 126
The Ball 126

16. Don't Aim 128
Alignment Obsession 128
Squareness on the Swing 129

17. Don't Hit the Ball Straight 130
The Most Difficult Shot 130
Learning the Straight Ball 130

18. Club Selection 132
Distance and Dispersion Pattern 132
Short Irons 133
Your Ego 134

19. The Role of the Right Elbow 135
Throwing Action 135
Lead with the Elbow 136
Right Shoulder Problem 137
Learning the Move 138

20. Analyzing Your Game 139
Computer Spreadsheet Analysis 140

21. Golf Drills for Feel 143

22. Practice Workbook 146

Part VI. The Spiritual Side of Golf 148

23. Golf and Life: The Final Stage 149
Practice 149
The Self 150
Zen Learning 150
The Moment 151
Breathing 151
Act "as if" in Control 152
Fear 152
Patience 153

24. Enlightenment 154
Mind Control 154
Obsession 155

25. The Tao: Nature's Flow of Golf 156
The Prime Mover 156
A Round Of Golf 157
The Ninth Hole 160

Appendix: The Rules of Golf 162
Chart 1. What a golfer may and may not do . . 162
Chart 2. Water hazard, lateral water hazard,
    unplayable lie, lost, and out of bounds . . . 163
. . . . 163
Chart 3. Obstructions–artificial/man-made . . 164
Chart 4. Lifting and cleaning the ball 164
Chart 5. Line of putt 164
Chart 6. Casual water, ground under repair,
    hole, cast, or runway 165
Chart 7. Lifts, drops, redrops, and placing ball 165
Chart 8. Loose Impediments, natural objects . . 166
Chart 9. Ball moved, deflected, or stopped . . . 166
Chart 10. Lie, area of swing, and line of play . . 167
Chart 11. Practice 167
Chart 12. Match and stroke play 167

Bibliography 168

Index 172

About the Authors

Gerald A. Walford, Ph.D. is Head and Associate Professor of the Physical Education Department at Alice Lloyd College, Pippa Passes, Kentucky. He received his Ph.D. from the University of Maryland with a dissertation on "Proprioceptive and Visual Feedback on Learning the Golf Putt and Golf Pitch." He has a wide range of experience in education and golf. His earlier publications include textbooks and magazine contributions on the subjecst of teaching golf, hockey, and baseball, as well as on the psychology of sports and teaching methodology. In addition, he has produced several television films on these topics and has performed extensive research on a wide range of related subjects.

Gerald A. Walford, M.Sc. is a school psychologist for the Hays Consolidated Independent School District in Buda, Texas.

Introduction

Golf is a simple game when you understand the laws of physics. In fact, all sport skills are based on the laws of physics or the laws of science. Break these laws and your skill execution cannot reach maximum potential. This book teaches the game of golf through the laws of science. If you learn the laws, practice the laws, and acquire the feel for the laws, then you will improve to your maximum ability. Good athletes have good execution of the laws. Great athletes have great execution of the laws, almost to the point of perfection.

Perceptions often interfere with correct execution. What you does is often not what one actually *do*. What you feel is often not what you think you feel. This often shows when a student is asked to take a backswing only to waist high. Almost always the swing goes higher than the waist.

Teachers often teach to their perceptions—what they *feel*. Their perceptions often are not in line with the student's perceptions. This book is not about perceptions. It is about facts, laws, and principles of science. As a student, you must learn these laws and apply them to your golf game, to your feel, and to your perceptions. Whatever your athletic ability, you can improve. The closer you come to correct execution, the better your skill. The better your skill, the better you score.

With skill improvement comes the coordination of the mind with the body. Most golfers realize the mental factor and how this factor can affect their skill level. After all, the mind controls the body. We move the body or parts of the body by signals from the brain. Skill execution is the harmony of brain and body. The two cannot be separated. This is what this book is about.

The book is divided into the following six parts and an appendix:

I. **Golf and the Laws of Science**: This part deals with the scientific background of golf. It covers the mechanics of the body, the swing, and the equipment.

II. **Using The Senses For Learning**: This part is about the senses of touch and feel, scientifically called the kinesthetic sense. Imagery or visualization is also one of the senses. The senses are a part of motor learning.

III. **Mechanics of the Golf Swing**: This part discusses the actual movements (mechanics) of the golf swing.

IV. **Mental Aspects of the Game**: This part is about the mental aspects of learning the swing and playing the game.

V. **Advanced Techniques**: This part contains observations about various aspects of the golf swing, how to analyze your game, drills, and a checklist on your learning and improvement.

VI. **The Spiritual Side of the Game**: Golf is life; life is golf. The comparisons are endless. The game has a mystique. The game has enlightenment.

Appendix: This section summarizes the rules of the game in an easily accessible form. In addition, there is an extensive Bibliography and an alphabetical index at the end of the book.

Part I
Golf and the Laws of Science

1

The Physics and Biomechanics of the Golf Swing

Athletic activity involves the creation and control of motion. The laws of physics, through the study of biomechanics, govern this creation and control of motion. By understanding the laws of physics you can better understand the golf swing and not be misled by your feelings and perceptions. What you feel and what you perceive does not always fall in line with the laws of the universe. Better knowledge can help you *feel* the laws of physics.

Inertia

Inertia is the reluctance of a body or object to change its present state, whether it is in motion or at rest. It is natural for a body to give resistance to inertia. Try and stop quickly when your body is running at full speed. The golf swing involves overcoming inertia by starting the backswing from a stationary position called the address or stance. Overcoming inertia is again repeated at the top of the backswing when the backswing motion stops going back in one direction and then moves forward in another direction called the downswing. Moving from a stationary position into a

smooth rhythmical movement often starts in a jerky manner. Overcoming inertia from this jerky start is not necessarily easy, but it can be done.

The golf swing overcomes inertia twice, at address and at the top of the swing. We get the swing going, stop it, and then get it going again to hit the ball. This stopping and starting can be difficult. Movements are often easier to perform when the body or object is in rhythm. The body does not really stop, it flows from one continuous movement into another continuous movement. This is much like a dancing or gymnastics routine. The small forward press sometimes helps to build up a rhythm to put the body into rhythm for the larger swing motion. This is like starting a small pendulum action that leads to a bigger pendulum action.

It is interesting to note that Conrad Rehling and Andrew Mullin teach the golf swing with no backswing. Scientifically, the backswing is not needed, as motion created in one direction, if stopped, has no bearing or advantage to motion in another direction. Scientifically this is true, but many teachers think the feel aspect of the backswing is important. Eliminate the backswing and you eliminate half your potential problems. Some claim the baseball swing has no backswing, only a little hitch sometimes. But, it is interesting.

The golf swing is *centripetal force*: a force toward the center of a circle—a center-seeking force. *Centrifugal force* is actually a misnomer as it is nothing but the natural laws of an object in motion trying to move in a straight line. A ball on the end of a string being swung in a circle is centripetal force. The string prevents the ball from moving out of the circular pattern. If the string breaks, the ball would continue in a straight line. This is Sir Isaac Newton's Second Law of Motion: an object in motion tends to move in a straight line unless acted upon by an outside force. The string is the outside force on the ball. The golf swing falls into this category as if the clubhead is the ball and the shaft is the string.

This centripetal force is controlled mainly by the arms being swung on a frontal plane (a plane of rotation in front of the body) and by the trunk of the body rotating on a transverse plane with an axis running from the head to the feet. Coordinating the two planes can be difficult.

Angular Speed

One of the most important laws of physics that applies to the golf swing is the law of angular speed. A pendulum swings to an angle. The bottom of the pendulum must swing twice as fast as the half way point of the pendulum in order to maintain the angle. This means that if the end of the pendulum swings at 100 mph, then the halfway point must swing at 50 mph to maintain the

angle. The golfer's hands are about halfway to the ball, halfway between the shoulder (center of the pendulum) and the clubhead (the end of the pendulum). If the hands swing at 50 mph, the clubhead moves at 100 mph to maintain the angle. This means that the shoulders must move at about 10 to 15 mph to maintain the angle. In golf, this shoulder speed creates problems by moving too fast, and often too soon, and results in destroying the angle. Maintain the angle and the body is in balance and the clubhead is moving fast.

Torque

Torque is the turning effect produced when a force is exerted on a body or object that pivots about a fixed point. The golf swing has five torques acting on it. They are:

1. the arms;

2. the wrists;

3. centripetal force;

4. gravity;

5. the golfer shifting toward the target.

Five torques. No wonder the swing is so difficult. Timing and executing these factors has to create great difficulty when swinging a golf club.

Trying to explain the scientific principles in a simple manner is extremely difficult. So many factors occur simultaneously and some factors overlap. It is hard to tell where to start and what sequence should be followed. It must be remembered that even physicists seem to disagree on their interpretations of what actually is happening or may be happening. But, despite their different explanations or perceptions, the laws of physics are never wrong. The laws are correct, we just have to interpret them correctly. In the remainder of this chapter we will take a look at the different aspects of the swing.

Starting the Downswing: Pull and Push Action

It appears that when the arms are above horizontal, the top of the backswing, the golfer makes a horizontal pull with the left shoulder to pull the

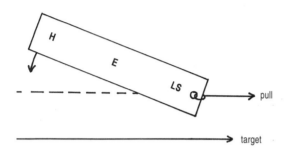

Fig. 1-1.
Ruler representation of push-pull action in the golf swing.

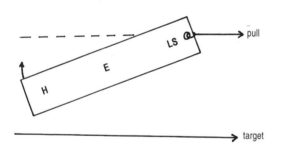

Fig. 1-2. (See text for details).

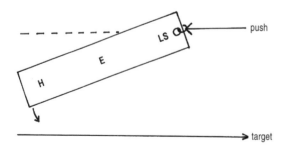

Fig. 1-3. (See text for details).

left arm into the downswing. The pull of the left shoulder on the left arm starts the swing down to the ball. This pull action produces a positive angular acceleration to help overcome inertia. The pull must not continue when the arms are past horizontal, because such action will cause the swing to decelerate toward impact. If the left shoulder continues to pull on the arm past horizontal a negative angular acceleration will have a lifting effect on the left arm and will slow down the arm and the club. Actually, once the arms are lower than horizontal, the left shoulder gives a little pushing action.

This pushing action stabilizes some of the left shoulder action to give the feeling for the common expression "hitting against a firm left side." This feeling of the push or stabilization of the left shoulder encourages teachers to instruct the downswing slowly. By starting the downswing slowly, all the large muscles have more time to be involved in the downswing. Using all the muscles gives the swing more mass to help prevent a weak-arms swing (explained in detail later). Also, it helps create advantageous torques in the downswing.

This pull-and-push action is complete at impact, but physicist T. P. Jorgensen explains this pull-push action in his book *The Physics of Golf*. In fact, he may well be the only person who has put this in writing. Jorgensen says that he has not seen it in print, although he has seen and heard expressions and sayings that may allude to this action.

The pull-push analysis is complicated and scientific, but the accompanying diagrams may help to clearly illustrate this action in simple terms.

Place a ruler on a smooth table (see Fig. 1-1). The ruler represents the golfer's left arm. Draw a line to represent the shoulder level (horizontal) and another line parallel to the first horizontal line to represent the direction of travel to the target. You are now looking at a golfer from the front. In the diagrams, the left arm and the clubhead represent the ruler. LS represents the left shoulder, E represents the elbow and H the hands.

Notice how when the ruler is pulled at LS (left shoulder) toward the target, the end of the ruler H (the hands) move down to horizontal to get in line with the pulling action. This pull overcomes inertia in a smooth and efficient manner and gets the swing moving from the stopping action after the backswing. Another advantage of this pull is that the arm moves in the direction of the pull. If the pull is in line with the target, the arms move down in line with the target. Sure helps accuracy.

Now place the ruler at an angle so that the H end is below the horizontal line (Fig. 1-2). Pull the ruler at LS toward the target, and it is readily noticeable how the CH end of the ruler moves up toward the horizontal level. In an actual golf swing the hands or clubhead does not move up, as the force of the swing down is too great, but this pulling action causes the arms to actually slow down and creates negative acceleration.

Now set up the ruler in the same position as in diagram 1-2. When you push the ruler at LS it helps create momentum at H toward the ball (Fig. 1-3). If the pull-push action is in line with the target, the arms will be assisted in swinging to the target.

Peter Croker has his pupils push the club to the ball with the right shoulder squeezing toward the stable left shoulder. The pupil does this by holding the body back in the coiled position of a completed backswing and then swinging or pushing the arms forward to the ball. This action gives the feeling of an early release, which he and David Leadbetter find acceptable and advantageous. As Croker says, this is more a perception than a fact, as the late release still occurs despite the feeling of an early release.

Slow backswing

Momentum or inertia created in the backswing must be overcome, so that the downswing can occur. It is easier to control and stop a slow backswing's momentum than it is to control and stop a fast backswing's momentum. Logically this is why the slow backswing makes sense. The golfer's strength is a strong factor in assisting this change of momentum. A longer golf club and/or a heavier clubhead has scientific advantages to the ball's flight, but only if the golfer can cope with

the momentum change. Naturally the longer the club and the heavier the clubhead the more the correct technique becomes a factor. Also as the club gets longer and heavier the golf swing will require more strength. The strength factor and mechanics are important for not only the application of force but the maintenance of balance when swinging the longer club and/or heavier club. Timing of the swing will also change and the golfer must cope with this factor.

Shorter backswing

Don Trahan, in an article in *Senior Golfer*, reported on research on the value of the shorter backswing. With his definitions, a long backswing was when the golf club was parallel to the ground when at the top of the backswing. The short backswing was when the club was positioned vertical to the ground. He found that the long and the short backswing both registered the same speed at impact but the short backswing had accelerating speed at impact while the long backswing was actually decelerating at impact.

With the club in the parallel position at the top, the clubhead has to overcome gravity to begin the downswing because the clubhead has to go up before it can come down. Trahan also stresses to move the backswing in line with the target line to give a more vertical or upright swing to help add speed to the club through the force of gravity. The flat swing plane does not take advantage of gravity.

Gravity

Another method of starting the downswing is by letting gravity initiate the action. Under this method, the golfer simply reaches the top of the backswing and then just lets the arms fall through gravity. As the arms fall, the swing action of the arms and body come into play. This means that the body seems to stop at the top of the backswing, the arms fall to the ground and the body then comes into action. This action is simple as it just lets the laws of gravity take their course to start the downswing. David Lee, in his book *Gravity Golf,* and Joe Buttitta, golf pro at Westlake Golf Course in southern California, stress this action.

Marc O'Meara, in his article "How to Make the First Move Down" (*Golf Digest*, September 1996) also uses gravity to start the downswing. He says, "you should start the downswing by letting the hands drop to about waist level." Marc likes this method because as the downswing begins, the arms have more distance to travel than the body. With many golfer's, the body rotates too fast or ahead of the arms, so the arms do not catch up with the body. By dropping the arms before starting body rotation, excellent timing and coordination of body and arms at impact is easier. If the body moves ahead of the arms or too fast for the arms the swing's power is destroyed or weakened, as well as the direction and control of the ball.

In an article in *Golf Magazine*, July 1997, they discussed research by Dr. Dave Williams in his book *The Science of the Golf Swing*, done on Bobby Jones' downswing. When Bobby Jones hit his drives 250 to 260 yards, his downswing was measured at the acceleration rate of 34 feet/sec². Gravity's speed or pull is 32 feet/sec². So Bobby Jones downswing acceleration was at about the speed of gravity. He simply let his arms and hands drop to the bal—no force, no effort, no strain.

In his book, Dr. Williams goes further in stating that the hands of Bobby Jones accelerate from zero feet per second at the top of the swing to 34 feet per second to about shoulder level. From here to impact, the hands maintain their 34 feet per second speed, but the clubhead gains speed so that at impact the clubhead is moving at 165 feet per second or 113 miles per hour.

Reaching his speed of 165 feet per second is not accomplished by wrist uncocking or hand leverage. Williams claims that since there is no bending of the shaft prior to impact the hands cannot be applying leverage. clubhead speed is accomplished by centrifugal force or the pulling action of the swing. Williams also emphasizes that when the hands swing from the top to shoulder height the hands must accelerate slowly with a gradual build up of speed. As we all know, and as he states emphatically, this is not easy. We want to reach full speed too quickly. We think this gives us more power. It does not. It gives us problems.

The weight shift

There may be some advantage to the weight shift in clubhead speed but it is small. An improper weight shift puts energy into the forward movement of the body rather than into the clubhead. Julius Boros said that he wanted his body almost motionless at impact. Boros was noted for his effortless and powerful golf swing. He was not going to let his body absorb any energy. All energy was to transfer to the club. This is explained in more detail in the transfer of energy section.

The shift

The shift toward the target can help accuracy if performed properly. As the club is swinging forward in an arc, the body shifts forward toward the target. This flattens the arc in the impact area to a straighter line. If the shift is toward the target, the swing path straightens toward the target. With no shift, the swing follows an arc, and the ball must be placed precisely on the arc to achieve the correct direction. The correct shift is to move the center of the swing toward the target and not let it

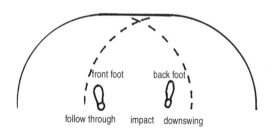

Fig. 1-4. Weight shift during golf swing.

rotate away from the target until the ball is hit. Moe Norman moves his left knee over his left big toe on the downswing and through impact area to prevent the hips from rotating away from the target. Moe, along with many others, also keeps his left knee well bent after impact to facilitate the clubhead staying in line with the target. This really increases the flattening of the arc.

Notice in diagram 1-4 how the swing arc is prescribed when the weight is on the back or right leg. Also, the swing arc changes when the arc is on the left leg. The weight shift moves the swing arc from the right leg to the left leg and gives a straight line between the feet. This diagram also emphasizes the importance to the proper weight shift of moving toward the target and not being pulled away from the target until after the ball is hit. It is best to finish the weight transfer over a bent left knee into the follow-through. This action helps in not only increasing the flattening of the arc but also helps to absorb the force of the swing by keeping the center of gravity low and over the base of support for maintaining balance.

Distance and Accuracy

Increasing the wrist cock angle at the top of the downswing can produce an increase in clubhead speed at impact. It is believed that this increase in clubhead speed results from the increased torque of the arms as a result of the larger wrist angle prior to the hit.

Golf is a game of distance and accuracy. Unfortunately, it is commonly held that the shorter backswing gives greater accuracy but less distance. This is not necessarily so. In the last 30 degrees of the downswing prior to contact, the clubhead speed varies very little. This means that the golfer can move his downswing 30 degrees ahead of the original position and still achieve his swing speed if the wrist cock and the torque remain the same.

The shorter backswing can give better accuracy with little or no loss of distance, however, when doing the shorter backswing the golfer must maintain his original mechanics. There is a

tendency, when learning and executing the shorter backswing, to force the arms forward, to push the arms forward, to rush the swing, all of which kills power and accuracy. These errors are easy to understand as the golfer's body tells the mind that the shorter backswing feels powerless. To get the feeling of power the golfer incorrectly makes these mistakes.

Wrist Cock

Back in the 1950's, someone called Ike Handy wrote a book with the premise that all you have to do to have accuracy is have the hands well ahead of the ball at impact. The right wrist cock angle at impact should be larger than zero. In a golf magazine, notice a still action shot of a top golfer at impact and you will see that the right wrist is not straight, it appears still cocked.

Golfers who try to increase clubhead speed by working the wrists or using wrist action will actually find that the action decreases clubhead speed. The mathematics and physics is astronomical but it boils down to that anything the golfer does with his wrists will decrease clubhead speed at impact. Wrist action counters the torque and centripetal force to weaken the swing.

David Williams, in his 1969 book *The Science of the Golf Swing*, analyzed the swing of Bobby Jones. He mathematically concluded beyond any argument that hand leverage or wrist uncocking has nothing to do with accelerating the clubhead in the hitting area. Cochran and Stobbs, as well as many pros, refuted this in their book, *The Search for the Perfect Swing*. It is interesting to note that lately Crocker and Leadbetter have also supported the theory that the "late hit" is not that important. If Williams is correct the action of centripetal force, not the wrists, is what creates the power . Ernest Jones, in his book *Swing The clubhead*, also advocates this philosophy.

Slow Hands at Impact

Its been claimed that the rapid rotation of the club toward the end of the downswing produces a torque back on the golfer's arms that slows down the hands at impact.

After one-tenth of a second into the downswing, the golfer relaxes his wrists so that he no longer exerts a torque at his wrists. The centrifugal torque of the swing helps gradually decrease the wrist cock, slowly at first and then very rapidly at impact.

The arm and wrists slowing down at impact, as just described, makes it seem as if the golfer is not accelerating and quitting on impact. It must be remembered that the hands are slowing down at impact, but the energy created by the swinging arms (centripetal force), is being transferred to the clubhead. The energy from the body is going into the club only if you let the swing occur and don't fight it or force it. Even though the golfer is trying to move the hands faster, the rotation and speed of the club produces a force on the golfer's hands that slows the hands at impact.

The torque on a golf club created by the swing is very large and powerful. It gives the clubhead high speed with no help from wrist/arm action. Try swinging a golf club with no uncocking of the wrist (hands stop) and you will notice the power in the impact area created by torque alone.

Ralph Mann, the former Olympic hurdler who is now a biomechanic, says that his studies show that Jack Nicklaus' hands are almost stopped at impact. Nicklaus was the best at this skill, as most of the pros slowed down but not as much as Jack. This means he was able to transfer most of his energy into the club. Also, Jack had plenty of body mass in his swing as his whole body is involved in his swing.

COAM: Conservation of Angular Motion

Other physicists emphasize that the COAM law slows the hands down in the impact area. Watch a figure skater spin. For a fast spin, the arms hug the body and to slow the spin they spread the arms out. This is similar to the golf swing. At the start of the downswing, the arms are close to the body. The left arm is almost hugging the chest and the right arm is folded and to the side of the body. As the hands swing down to the ball, the arms move away from the body and like the figure skater the spinning arms slow down. At the ball, the arms are at the farthest extension from the body and are at the slowest moving part of the swing. The clubhead is lagging behind the hands and is able to catch up with the slow hands in the same fashion as the bullwhip.

It is possible to stop the hands at impact (like Nicklaus) and achieve good clubhead speed, but it is not necessary, as the COAM law will take care of everything if you let it. Also, stopping the hands in the precise spot is difficult.

Snapping of a Whip

When a whip snaps, the sound is the tip breaking the sound barrier. The arm swings the whip forward with the larger mass of the whip being in the handle. Overcoming inertia of this larger mass handle creates momentum to the rest of the whip. Kinetic energy is now created in the whip handle and flows into the whip. Since the whip gets smaller toward the tip, the energy created in the body's mass and handle is transferred to the whip when the hand stops. The larger mass of the body requires lots of energy to move the larger body mass. This "lots of energy" cannot be destroyed, so the energy moves along the whip, increasing in power because of the narrowing of the whip. The power remains the same, but the less mass in the narrowing of the whip means that the narrower the whip, the more violent the action. The tip has the least mass and is the easiest to move fastest. The energy created to move a larger mass transfers into the smaller mass as the whip narrows. As the energy moves along, the whip moves faster and faster until the energy reaches the tip of the whip where the tip breaks the sound barrier of about 840 miles per hour.

This same action occurs when one snaps a towel. The energy from the larger mass of the body transfers to the smaller arms, to the smaller hands, and then to the towel until the towel snaps. Naturally, the hand must stop moving so that the energy can flow out of the body, through the arms, and into the towel. Swing a towel fast without stopping the arm action and the body will feel like utilizing lots of power. The body feels this power because the energy has stayed in the body and has not transferred out of the body and into the towel. This same phenomenon occurs in the golf swing. The golfer swings hard and feels a lot of power, but the golf ball goes nowhere near where it should. The energy was not transferred out of the body and into the golf club. This is why, when the proper swing is completed and the ball goes a long way, the golfer feels an effortless swing.

If you want to see an example of the transfer of energy from a large mass to a smaller mass, try this: Take a basketball (or a similar large ball such as a soccer ball) and a tennis ball. Drop the basketball on the floor or a hard surface and watch how high the basketball will rebound. Drop the tennis ball from the same distance to the floor and watch how high the tennis ball will rebound. Now hold the basketball again from the same distance from the floor. Place and hold the tennis ball on top of the basketball. Now release both the basketball and the tennis ball at the same time so that the tennis ball falls in line with the basketball and remains in contact with the basketball until contact with the floor. At impact, the tennis ball will bounce extremely high in the air. Much higher than when it rebounded off the floor by itself. The larger mass of the basketball creates "lots of energy" to move the ball, and this "lots of energy" is transferred to the smaller tennis ball, and so the tennis ball receives more energy than it can create itself. This makes the ball bounce higher than normal.

Transfer of Energy of the Golf Swing

The basic philosophy of the golf swing is to create energy in the mass of the larger body and then transfer the energy into the smaller mass of the

golf club. This is like the larger mass of the basketball creating "lots of energy" to transfer to the smaller mass of the tennis ball to give the tennis ball more energy. With proper mechanics and timing, the larger body mass can create great potential energy to transfer to the smaller mass golf club. Many feel that this is why women generally do not hit the ball as far as men. Less body mass, or body size creates less potential energy to transfer to the club.

The male golfer's arms are fairly heavy, about 15 lbs. each, and the golf club is fairly light. Like the bullwhip, the weight from the body to the arms and to the golf club gets increasingly smaller and lighter. The golfer's swing is like the bullwhip being snapped.

This same transfer of energy prevails with martial arts experts in the karate chop when breaking boards and cement blocks. At impact the karate expert is getting the mass of the body, to the shoulder, to the arm and to the hand (like the bullwhip) in a locked position to give power to the blow. The mass of the body flows out to the hand so that it is almost as if the body is hitting the target and not just the hand. This is the feeling a golfer has when he feels like he is hitting the ball with his whole body.

With proper use of the body's larger muscles, more mass is used to create energy. The muscles deliver about one-eighth horsepower per pound. The golf swing uses about two horsepower. This means you need over 30 pounds of muscle for power. Unless the mechanics are executed exactly perfectly, you'll need well over 30 pounds of muscle for the same effect. This is a lot of muscle. Keep in mind that for every muscle that is used an opposite muscle must relax. So to get your thirty plus pounds of working muscle we need a lot of muscle and good mechanics.

Sources of Energy

A golf club does not have energy. The golfer must create energy and transfer that energy to the golf club. The golfer's body coils to stretch the muscles to reflex into action. The various torques, as mentioned earlier, also give the body potential energy for the hit. By bringing the large muscles into play, more force for the swing can be created by generating more mass into the swing. As explained in the bullwhip's snap, this large mass is most advantageous in creating power through the transfer of energy from the mass of the body to the clubhead.

It is interesting to note that the coiling action over the years has changed. Mindy Blake, an engineer and physics professor, in his book *The Golf Swing of the Future*, tells how the coiling action has become more vertical in the modern era. Table 1-1 compares the old swing with the present swing and the swing of the future.

From the table, it is readily noticeable how the body coil is going more upright and less around the body. It appears that for a future golfer's backswing, the left arm is swung back so that a line from the left hand, through the left arm and to the left shoulder will point to the target. On the downswing, the right arm straightens through impact and continues to point directly at the target when the hands are waist high. This is what Moe Norman, perhaps the greatest ball striker ever, means when he says to grab the pin on the follow-through. If you have never tried this technique, it is well worth experimenting with. It produces straight and consistent shots. This swing is also explained later in this book under *The Twin Pendulum*. Many teachers are now having their students draw an imaginary line across their toes and onto the target. They then have their students swing so that the clubhead or hands do not cross this line on the backswing, downswing and follow-through.

Table 1-1. Old to modern swing

Type of swing	Hip turn	Angle between left arm and target
Old swing	70 degrees	75 degrees
Today	45 degrees	45 degrees
Tomorrow	10 degrees	14 degrees

Principles of Force

The maximum force of the golf swing is the sum of all the velocities of all contributing movements providing the movements are in one direction, in the correct sequence and with proper timing. At contact, the clubhead has a velocity almost equal to the sum of the velocities of the contributing levers. The golf swing has many levers to operate in such a short time. Actually, the body has 17 levers and the swing is usually less than 1.5 seconds. It is not hard to see why timing of the levers to achieve maximum force and power and with accuracy may be so difficult, darned difficult.

Falling Back

A common problem with many golfers is that with the arms and hands dominating the forward swing, the golfer will usually fall back on the shot. This action is a result of Newton's third law of action/reaction. Momentum forward by the arms (action) creates equal momentum backward (reaction). The recoil of a rifle is another example of Newton's third law. To prevent this recoil, the golfer must use all the available body muscles like the legs, hips and back, to stabilize the swing as well as adding mass to the swing. You can't shoot a cannon from a canoe.

The abdominal muscles play an important part in stabilizing the body for the golf swing. Marianne Torbert, in her book *Secrets to Success in Sport and Play*, says that for force to develop, some portion of the body must be stabilized as the stabilized part acts as a brace against which the moving parts can push or pull. With no stabilization, force is absorbed into the body and not into the swing. The abdominal muscles stabilize the hips and create an anchor point around which the swing and weight transfer takes place. Boxers know this when they throw a punch with their feet off the ground. The punch is not stabilized and is powerless.

The Grip

The grip raises many questions. According to the laws of physics, the research claims no advantage to any of the various grip styles. In the laws of science the grip is merely to hold onto the club firmly, as will be explained later, so that the swing can be executed despite the violent nature of the swing. The desired hand action or wrist action is nothing, meaning the hands or arms are swung with the wrists acting like a piece of rope by not being forced or manipulated in any way. From a scientific standpoint, the golfer simply holds onto the club so as to not interfere with the laws of motion. When beginning golfers hit that perfect shot, they often say, "It felt like I was just hanging on to the club" or "The club swung me." This is an accurate assessment. There is no feeling as to manipulation or force. It happens.

The question of feel may arise. The grip must feel comfortable, solid, and in control of the club. The pros all have different grips and the ten-finger grip is gaining in popularity, as is the Moe Norman palm grip.

Moe Norman uses the ten fingers and palm grip. The club's grip fits into the palm of the right hand and not in the fingers. The palm has more nerve endings than the fingers, so it is claimed that the palm is more sensitive to feel, especially in control of direction. The best use of the palm grip is to have larger diameter grips installed on the clubs. The Big-Grip Golf Company (1-800-800-6116, Nunnelly, TN 37137) has such a grip that is very effective. Also, if you buy many grips (about 15) they will give you an excellent 20 page manual on the palm grip and single-axis/plane swing.

The best grip is a grip that lets the individual square the face of the club correctly and not interfere with the swing action. Many will disagree with this statement but many statements are based on perceptions or perceptions of feelings, which may feel different than the laws of physics.

In 1964, Alan Walker's master's thesis at Springfield College, *The Relationship of Distance and Accuracy to Three Golf Grips*, studied the three grips: the overlapping (Vardon Grip), the interlocking grip, and the baseball or ten-finger grip. His experiment found that no grip was statistically superior to the other in terms of accuracy or distance. Further research also makes the same claims of no difference in the grips. Thirty years later we are beginning to realize this fact. Moe Norman and many others have proved it.

Harry Vardon and His Bent Elbow

Study of Harry Vardon's swing shows Vardon with a well-bent left arm at the top of his backswing and straight arm at impact. His swing goes from the standard two-lever system, like a flail, to a three-lever system. If the downswing is executed from the bent left arm position, the arm and club become closer to the whip example. Energy flows out of the body into the clubhead like the whip that is heavier at the handle and goes too smaller at the tip. Vardon's energy goes from the heavier upper arm and shoulder to the lower smaller/lighter forearm and to the lighter club. Surprisingly, Theodore P. Jorgensen, a physics researcher studying Vardon's swing, found extra swing length arc when using the Vardon swing. His computer calculations found that a bent elbow of 100 degrees at the top of the backswing gave him a 50% increase in clubhead speed over the straight left arm. The researcher therefor recommends that one should experiment with this procedure. The bent left elbow philosophy is heretical and could result in excommunication. But, maybe… just maybe…

Jack Kuykendall, founder of Natural Golf and now Lever Power Golf, teaches the bent left arm at the top of the swing.

Jensen, Shultz and Bangerter, in their book *Applied Kinesiology and Biomechanics*, also give value to the bent left arm at the top of the backswing. They claim that extra force can be generated if the left elbow were flexed in the backswing and extended at contact.

Ralph Mann, in *Biomechanics Of Human Movement*, was cited from his analysis of the top 52 professional golfers as saying that the pro's flex their left arm more than 30 degrees at the top of the backswing. Not quite 100 degrees, but it may be a start.

The Set-Up

It is also interesting to note that Mann claims the set-up is 100% of an effective swing. Although this is not clearly stated, it does lend value to the belief that a good swing cannot be executed from a bad set-up.

Tom Stickney II and Peter Morrice in their *Golf Magazine* article "The Keys to Consistency," December 1999, used high-tech measuring equipment to make the following claim: "With more than 500 students tested to date, I think I've identified the number one reason why golfers are inconsistent: their set-up changes from one swing to the next. You simply cannot expect to hit the ball the same way every time when you set up to it differently every time."

Relax

Be careful with this term. What is really meant is to use less tension or to relax the non-working muscles. Swinging a golf club is violent. Don't fool yourself. From a photograph or a picture, look at the face, neck and arms of an excellent golfer at impact, and you will see tension and muscles bulging. What is needed is *Controlled Tension*. Controlled tension is when the agonist and antagonist muscles work in harmony. Muscles can only pull or contract—they cannot push. For movement, muscles work in pairs. One muscle pulls/contracts and the opposite muscle must relax for efficiency of movement. If the opposite muscle does not relax, then its tension will have a counter effect on the working muscle. For example, hold an arm straight out from the body with the palm up. Tense the whole arm. If someone is to push up on the back of the hand, the biceps under tension will actually help to lift the arm and assist in the pushing action. This makes the arm easy to push up. Now relax the biceps and contract the triceps only. The arm is now harder to

move as the biceps do not assist the pushing up action.

As a muscle tenses, the antagonist must relax. This is the key to coordination, as the antagonist muscle must be relaxed while the working muscle/agonist muscle needs tension to work. The hands must grip the club firmly. Maybe not so much on the backswing, but certainly on the downswing. The golf swing has about 2,000 lbs., or one ton, of force at impact—a speed of 100 mph, up to four horsepower, and over 30 lbs. of muscle—and you want to use a loose or relaxed grip? Good golfers may be relaxed during the backswing, but at impact they are under tension. You can readily notice this in the photos.

The laws of physics say a firm grip. Golf teachings say a relaxed grip. What we are dealing with is perception. Perceptions are not always accurate. The good golfers perceive themselves to be relaxed but they are holding the club firmer than they may believe. This feeling is a result of correct muscle control, as only the needed muscles are working while the undesired muscles are relaxed. There are no muscles fighting each other.

A muscle has to be under tension or stretch to respond quickly and efficiently. Such a muscle has tonus. A relaxed muscle has to tense up before it can go into action. This is why the upper body coils to create power. The coil stretches the left side muscles to give a strong muscular contraction for the downswing and power. Loose muscles mean weak power. Tension is not the problem. The problem is a relaxing or tensing of the correct muscles only. This is what coordination is all about.

Loose Grip

A firm grip is needed for energy to transfer from the body to the golf club. According to the laws of science, any "give" in the implement (golf club) at impact reduces the propulsive force on the object (golf ball) being hit. Although it is preached to hold the club lightly, it is never done. A loose grip lets the club vibrate from contact with the ball. These vibrations absorb energy from impact, energy that should be going into the ball and not the club. Studies at the University of Massachusetts, with professional golfers, found that a "tight and rigid grip of the striker" increased the effective mass of the striker as more of the golfer's body becomes involved with impact. They also found that at impact with the golf ball, men could move the clubhead an average of 24 mph faster than women and that the men could achieve a higher mass on the ball at impact. This research may help to answer the question of why the modern golfers are hitting the ball farther than golfers of years ago. The modern golfer is using a firm, a very firm grip.

Mindy Blake, in *The Golf Swing of the Future*, offers an interesting thesis on the firm grip. Mindy claims that the critical factor in determining distance is not clubhead speed but pressure on the ball. The golf club is not a free moving object but an extension of the body. If the golf club were freewheeling, and not attached to the body, the club with its little mass would have little effect on the golf ball. The golf club attached to the large mass of the body is able to transfer so much more energy to the club. Would you rather be hit with a tennis ball going 30 mph or a train at 30 mph?

Mindy Blake says that when the muscles are stretched and used in reflex, time is needed for the muscles to react properly. By swinging slowly, muscular power has time to develop to its maximum. Forcing or rushing the swing does not create power. When you hammer a nail, the swing is slow, you do not try to swing the hammer head with speed. You swing with pressure—a slow, smooth and even pressure at impact. Try to hit a tennis ball with a loose grip?

Pressure through the ball, like hitting the nail or the tennis ball, keeps the ball on the club face longer. This means less energy is absorbed by the club through vibrations of the shaft. Naturally, this means more distance. Women and older people often achieve poor ball flight and distance because their hands are not strong enough to keep the pressure up through the ball at contact. Hitting through the ball helps to achieve pressure on the ball.

At impact, according to Cochran and Stobbs, in their book *The Search For The Perfect Swing*, the golf swing uses 30 pounds of muscle to create up to four horsepower, a force of 2,000 pounds and a swing speed of up to 100 mph. With figures like these, it is hard to imagine using anything but a firm grip.

Choking up on the Club

Some golfers choke up on the golf club so that they can move and control the club more efficiently. In scientific terms, the moment of inertia is decreased because of the shorter axis of rotation. This gives the golfer better control despite a possible slower clubhead speed because of the shorter radius. It's a trade off of longer radius for speed or shorter radius for control.

The length of the lever—the shaft of the club is the lever length—affects the rotary speed and force of the swing. A shorter lever can be swung faster but the force is less. The longer lever is swung slower but the force is greater. This is why some teachers teach the golfer to slow down the swing as the club increases in length from the short irons to the driver. Psychologically, the golfer has difficulty doing this because as he swings from the shorter irons to the driver the golfer's emphasis, often unconsciously, is on distance, and so the feeling is to swing harder.

The Sweet Spot (Center of Percussion)

When you miss the sweet spot, the club vibrates and you often feel a stinging effect in your hands. The sting is energy being spent on useless vibration of the shaft. This is wasted energy, as all the energy is not going into the ball where it is needed for an advantageous ball flight. Hitting the sweet spot puts all available energy into the ball and not the club. This is why it is so important to hit the sweet spot consistently—for accuracy and distance.

Missing the sweet spot on the club face also causes the club face to rotate. We all know how this negatively influences accuracy and distance. Force through the center of percussion keeps the face in line with the target and with no distortion to the shot. This principle also applies to the golf ball. The straight shot requires force through the center of gravity. Actually, due to the loft on the golf club, the force cannot be directed straight through the ball's center of gravity. The force must be directly below the center of gravity and not to the side for the straight shot. Force directed to the side of the center of gravity causes the ball to spin away from the desired direction of travel. These sweet spot factors also prevail in putting, as Dave Peltz, the putting guru, has so often told us, that missing the sweet spot is perhaps the biggest problem for accuracy in putting.

Speed of the Ball

Mass of the clubhead and speed of the clubhead influence the speed of the ball. The greater the mass, the greater the ball speed. The greater the clubhead speed, the greater the ball speed. The only problem with this is that the greater the mass, the harder it is to get the mass moving (overcoming inertia). The golf club becomes a trade-off between clubhead mass and speed. The golfer must swing the highest mass possible without sacrificing swing speed. Probably the best way to determine this is through trial and error.

The Single-Axis or Single-Plane Swing

The single-plane swing is the big revolution in golf. The big advantage of the single-plane is in the simplicity of execution. In the traditional golf swing the arms hang down fairly straight from the shoulders. This means that the arms are hanging down at one angle and the golf club is extended out from the body at another angle. This causes the arms to swing on one plane and the club to swing on another plane. Timing becomes crucial with the traditional swing as the two planes require excellent timing of the swing so that the club face is square at contact. Swinging on two

planes makes the swing difficult, timing difficult, and achieving a square club face for impact difficult.

Perhaps the most dominant aspect of the single-plane swing is in the grip. The right hand especially becomes a palm grip.

The Palm Grip

Unlike the conventional golf system, the single-axis/planeswing uses a right palm grip and not a finger grip. The palm grip lets the club line up with the trailing arm (right arm for most golfers), so that the golfer can swing on one plane. In the stance position, the golf club and the right arm are in a straight line or plane when observed from behind the golfer and down the target line. In the conventional system, the club will line up or point below the right arm to give a two-axis swing rather than the one-axis system. This means that the single-axis swing eliminates the rotary body action needed in the convention/traditional swing. Both swings work and follow the laws of physics. The single-plane golf swing system is simpler.

Early golfers in the Scottish links used an all-fingers grip, with the club handle lying across all finger joints at the palms. This put the hand at almost a 90-degree angle to the club. Vardon came along and changed this. Vardon's grip was not only famous for overlapping the little finger but also in giving the grip more of a 45-degree angle with the shaft. This way the grip angled from fingers to palm. This 45-degree angle gave a more consistent upright swing plane much closer to the desired single plane. The single-plane evolution of the grip is now to the palm grip that places the right arm and club in a straight line for a consistent single swing plane. The right hand and forearm is now at almost at a 0-degree angle to the club shaft to give the straight line from arm to clubhead. An easy way to check for the palm grip is to check to see if the club shaft is in line with the back or trailing forearm (right forearm for right-handed golfers)

The Wide Stance

The single-plane swing theories use the wider stance. This is not new, as many golfers are now going to a wider stance. Greg Norman is one example. The legs stabilize the golf swing as a means of countering Newton's third law of action/reaction (swinging forward gives momentum backward, as exemplified by many inefficient golfers). The wider stance helps to prevent the hips from rotating excessively. The wider stance also restricts the hip movement on the backswing to give a larger differential between the hip and shoulder rotation. This differential was shown by Jim McLean, in his '"X-factor" to give more power and more distance to the golf swings with the larger differentials.

It is interesting to note that with the wide stance hip, movement is restricted. Further hip restriction is accomplished by moving the left knee over the left big toe when the clubhead is in the impact area. By moving the left knee over the left big toe, the hips slide forward with little or no rotation. This is a very notable feature of the Moe Norman swing.

Right Arm/Wrist Power

Jack Kuykendall, the inventor of Natural Golf, claims 76% of the golf swing's power comes from the unhinging of the right wrist around the forearm. Lateral body motion creates 1.5% of the golf swings power. Rotary body motion contributes 4.5% power, and arm motion gives the final 18%. This means 94% of clubhead speed comes from the dominant arm or right arm action. All these percentages are still within the parameters of centripetal force. Body rotary action cannot help in giving power to the golf swing, because the arms and the body are rotating on two different planes. The hips are rotating level to the ground while the arms are angled to the ground. There is no carryover of power from one to the other.

Cochran and Stobbs, in *The Search For the Perfect Swing*, believe that the important levers are those acting at the shoulder and wrist joints. They feel that the difference between the skilled and the unskilled golfers may be in the ability to generate power through these levers. This appears to be in line with the single-plane swing. Cochran and Stobbs also stress simplicity of the swing.

T. J. Tomasi also stresses the importance of the right arm for power in his *Golf Illustrated* magazine article. Tomasi says, "Recent biomechanical research shows that expert golfers exert very little force on the club handle with their lower right arm and hand until just before impact. At this point the force applied to the club by the right forearm and hand becomes eight times as great as it was during the start of the downswing, indicating that a blast of energy has been released." This was also stated by Dave Williams, earlier in the chapter, with his study of Bobby Jones's swing, where the clubhead's speed at shoulder level was 34 feet per second (gravity) to 165 feet per second at impact.

Some think the swing's power is in the legs. The legs and abdominal act as stabilizers for the swing's action. As a result, they are put under great stress. This stress gives the feeling of using the legs for power. The legs, although they may not be directly involved with the power of the swing, are certainly involved in stabilizing the tremendous power of the arms. The body must be stabilized or balance will be lost. Remember, all skills must maintain balance. Performance and execution are dependant on balance.

The Swing Arc

Jack Kuykendall, the founder of Natural Golf who now has his own company, explains the swing arc scientifically in the video *Golf Reform is at Hand*. His interpretation for the late hit reaction is to swing the hands down to the ball in as much a straight line as possible. The center of the arc from such a shallow arc will be way outside the left shoulder. This results in a longer radius and hence more speed. If the arm is swung down to the ball with full extension of the left arm, then the center of the arc is in the left shoulder area for a shorter radius. It appears under this interpretation that golfers who bend the left arm at the top of the downswing are better able to move the hands fairly straight to the ball for the larger swing arc. This goes back to the Harry Vardon swing discussed earlier.

Kuykendall goes on to state that the increase in speed toward the contact area is a result of the shortened radius effect. A figure skater when spinning with the arms extended to the sides will spin fairly slowly. As the arms move into the body, the spin picks up speed and when the arms hug the body, the body is in maximum spin. The scientific explanation is that a shorter radius can spin faster. On the downswing, if we move the hands fairly straight to the ball, the swing arc's center is way outside the left shoulder. As the clubhead approaches the ball, the left arm becomes fully straight and now the center of the swing arc has shifted to the golfers left shoulder to give a shorter radius. In simple science, shortening of the radius from a longer radius will increase the speed of the spinning object. The swing radius is now shortened, and so the acceleration of the clubhead increases dramatically from the larger swing arc. The swing now has speed.

Jack Kuykendall's new swing theory is also revolutionary and even easier to learn and execute. He now teaches the golf swing with no wrist break and with the bent left elbow. His new swing is easy to learn, highly accurate and consistent. With no wrist break, power is still achieved

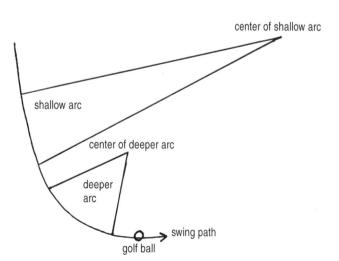

Fig. 1-5. (see text for details)

through the leverage of the arms. Information on this approach can be found at his web site Kuykendall's *Golf Science Magazine*. This approach to the golf swing is highly recommended. Jack Kuykendall is one of the few instructors who are changing the game for the better as well as making it easier.

The Single-Axis or Single-Plane Theories

The main teaching theories for single-plane golf are Natural Golf, Scigolf or the Ideal Mechanical Advantage (IMA) , Lever Power Golf, Heard's Super Swing, and Big-Grip Golf. Contact addresses are listed alphabetically in the Bibliography.

Basically, they all teach a similar theory with some variations. The basic theory comes from Jack Kuykendall when he founded Natural Golf. The following are some of the basics.

1. The palm right hand grip.

2. Club shaft in line with the back or trailing forearm.

3. Head over right or back knee and stays there until after impact.

4. Weight shift is after impact. Some start with the weight on front leg like in Big-Grip Golf, some start with the weight on the back leg like in Heard's Super Swing, and some start with the weight even between both feet from the start of the swing to impact. It appears that the weight remains in these starting positions for impact and then moves forward in the follow through.

5. Hands are usually higher at address because of the palm grip and shaft in line with the back forearm.

6. Lower body is still with minimal rotation. Rotation is in the shoulders.

7. The right arm is lower than the left arm during the swing, especially at impact. Jerry Heard's Super Swing Video shows and explains this through the similarity of the baseball swing. Baseball batters swing with the right arm, or trailing arm, lower than the front arm prior to and at impact.

8. Both feet are flat on the ground at impact. After impact, the follow-through may pull the right or back heel up, but this is after impact, so the body can do anything is wants once the ball is gon—definitely not before the ball is gone.

9. The right arm extends to the target after impact.

10. The front arm is a rod and the back arm is the piston.

11. Jack Kuykendall, with Lever Power Golf, maintains a no-left-wrist break to the swing. This emphasizes the "rod" and "piston" effect. The hands swing back to the right shoulder by letting the left or front arm bend. By the left arm bending at the elbow a longer lever (from clubhead to elbow, not from clubhead and wrists) is created. By the wrists not breaking, the ball's flight is extremely accurate. In this method, the arms roll. In the Super Swing, the hands do not roll, as the clubface always faces the direction of travel of the swing.

2 The Physics of Golf Equipment

In this chapter, we'll take a look at the equipment used in the game, with particular emphasis on the physical effects of particular changes and new materials that have become available in recent years.

Club Face Inserts

Club face inserts, although not new, seem to be most prominent in recent years. New rules allow inserts into irons, and some popularity has been gained, although not as much as some manufactures had hoped. Woods, made of wood, had inserts made of epoxy, cycolac and other synthetics. No noticeable difference was established with any of these inserts. Some may claim a difference in feel, but that is about all. Despite all the marketing claims on the new inserts, ranging from titanium to ceramic materials, distance still has made no significant gains.

Putters

The big change in putters has been the softer insert of balata, polymer, various plastics, etc. The list continually increases. Aluminum, copper, nickel, and even titanium are now having their turn. Remember it is the softness of the insert and not the material that is important. The softness is designed to make a non-balata ball feel like a balata ball being putted. Many claim that the softer balata ball is better for putting feel, but not necessarily most advantageous for distance in getting to the green. Since the rules do not permit changing balls on the green, the golfer can use a harder distance ball to get on the green and then use a soft insert putter on the green for the feel of a balata ball. The softer insert allows the ball to stay on the putter face longer, although it is only in the range of milliseconds. This longer-on-the-face aspect is supposed to give the putt more control.

The soft insert putter can give a perimeter weighting effect to the putter as the insert is many times lighter that the material of the putter clubhead. With the light insert in the center of the face of the putter, the weight is shifted to the toe and heel of the putter and the perimeter.

The rebound qualities, called the coefficient of restitution, of the insert can be adjusted to various degrees by the softness of the insert material. A wise golfer will experiment and try various companies and models to find what works. It will also be a good idea to find the ball that best matches the qualities of the insert.

Wedges

Next to the putter, wedges have made a strong impact with the trend to inserts. The claims are the same as for the putters as marketing focuses on feel. All wedge manufactures claim more backspin with there wedge, but the hype increases with the insert wedge. After all, that is why they put the insert in their wedge, to give you more backspin—so they claim.

It may well be that the insert does not create backspin, but the material of the club face may well influence the ball's spin. The USGA has ruled that the roughness of the face must be180 microinches or less—equivalent to a sandblasted finish— and the insert face must not influence the flight of the ball. Such influence would make the club illegal.

Several companies are using a bronze alloy with embedded tungsten carbide particles to give a roughness of under 180 microinches. The tungsten carbide is not supposed to wear out and will maintain its roughness over time.

Other companies use similar techniques and materials to achieve the same results. Some companies do not stress the spin aspect but focus on the feel of the wedge.

Which wedge fits you? Trial and error. Try the various clubs and decide for yourself.

Irons and Woods

Inserts are slowly making a trend in the irons and a little more impact in the woods. Titanium is very expensive, so the golf club can be made cheaper by using a titanium insert in a regular metal wood or iron. Since it is the titanium that contacts the ball, it may well give the feel of a titanium club. It does make sense, as it can keep the expense down.

But is expense a factor? The all-titanium clubheads are expensive, but they are selling.

As mentioned under clubheads, titanium and other extra hard materials do not make the ball go farther. The USGA does not use titanium or other materials in their testing, as they claim there is no advantage. There is a point where the extra hardness of the material does not create more distance or compression to the ball. The real advantage of the lighter and harder materials is that the clubhead can be made larger for the more forgiving aspects and yet maintain its lightness.

Swing Weight

Swing weights for a golf club have an interesting history. Some swear by them, whiled others see no value. The scale used to measure the swing weight is an arbitrary, or relative-value scale. No scientific evidence seems to prevail in how the scale was established. Swing weight and total weight are two different aspects. The total weight is, just as it says, the total weight of the club. The swing weight is the distribution of that total weight.

Determining swing weight

The diagram shows how the swing weight is measured. As you will notice, the real weight of the club is measured from B to C. The heavier the lower region of the club relative to the total

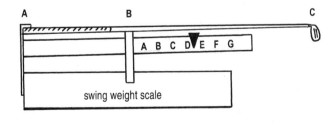

Fig. 2--1. Use of the swing weight scale.

weight, the heavier the swing weight. The scales range from A to E ,with A as lightest and E as the heaviest. Each letter then is scaled from 0 to 9. The average swing weights for women are in the C range and for men in the D range. D2 or D3 seem to be the most common. It is interesting to note, and yet puzzling, that some manufactures use a 12-inch distance from the end of the grip (point A) to the fulcrum (point B), while and others use a 14-inch distance from A to B. It does not sound scientific. When the scales were invented, the 12-inch distance was just arbitrarily set. Some went to 14 inches for various reasons, but not with scientific reasoning.

It is possible to have a heavy club with a light swing weight if more weight is placed in the upper shaft area. Keep in mind that swing weight is the distribution of weight. You could have a golf club weighing 20 pounds but with a B5 swing weight if the upper shaft is weighted accordingly. Or you could have a 10-oz. club with a swing weight well past the E range if most of the weight is applied to the head.

As you can see from the examples, to keep things sensible, the total weight of the club must correspond to the swing weight. The value of the swing weight is to have a reasonable total weight for the individual and then a swing weight for that individual that will be consistent from club to club. This procedure can help balance the set of clubs to the individual. You must also be aware that if you extend the shaft of your club, you also alter the swing weight by making it heavier.

Scientifically, the reasoning seems weak, but for relative purposes in balancing a set of clubs, it may be satisfactory as it may give a consistent and similar feel. The consistent feel to each club goes with the teachings that the golfer learns one swing and uses it for all clubs. If all the clubs have a consistent feel and swing weight then the results should be better. Seems to make sense but in the late 90s most golfers were switching clubs and not using matched sets. The driver and fairway woods are often different among the pros. The irons and wedges are often mixed in style, weight, length, etc. The theory of one swing for all clubs has been argued for years. Perhaps the answer is simply that it is a personal thing: whatever is right for the individual.

Featherlight and Very Light Golf Clubs

In the mid 80s, it was claimed that the featherlight or very light golf clubs were scientifically more advantageous. The claim was based on the fact that the lighter club could be swung faster. Scientifically this was true, but the other part of the equation was that the clubhead became so light that the head had too little mass and as a result impact was reduced. The lightness caused the club to vibrate too much at impact, causing the transfer of energy from the club to the ball to be lessened as the energy was vibrating up the shaft and being wasted. It was also found that the lighter head affected feel. The head was so light, it was hard to feel the position of the club during the swing. This means that the lighter head will go off path much easier than a heavier head. Carpenters use a heavier hammerhead to keep the swing to the nail on plane and to give the hammer head more mass for impact. Maybe the manufacturers should have checked with the carpenters before misinterpreting the laws of physics.

Modality Synchronization

This is a very new method of matching the shaft to the clubhead. Some feel that this process is better than swing weights for matching a set of clubs. The process is done by vibrating the shaft to read the node lines that show on the face of the club. The node lines represent the axis of rotation of the club. The object of the node lines is to get these lines to intersect at the sweet spot, or as close as possible.

Why is this important? It's all at impact. At impact, the energy from the club transfers to the ball and is not wasted through ineffective vibrations that flow backwards toward the hands. Eliminate the backward vibration flow and more energy is transferred to the ball for more distance and control.

It appears that this method is gaining popularity on the tour, and it could be the next move to shaft fitting. It does seem reasonable to assume that when two components are joined together, there should be some system to ensure compatibility and fit, especially in golf clubs, where there is so much stress on the club.

Shafts

Shafts have gone through a wide range of materials. Wood, steel, fiberglass, aluminum, graphite, titanium, Kevlar, etc. have all had their turn at being the magic stick. The search is still going on.

Wood shafts

Wood shafts have been replaced almost permanently, except in some putters. Some golfers like the feel of wood. The wood shaft in a putter does not go through the violent forces and torques of the full swing, so if it feels good then it is probably good. Wood-shafted putters also look good— the classic golf club. Some golfers claim that the wood is inconsistent with the weather. No research has verified this, but if the golfer loses confidence in the club, then it is as good as a bad club.

Steel shafts

Steel initially had difficulty breaking into the market. Golfers did not like the feel of the club, despite the consistency of flex, torque, and feel. As happens even today, a major tournament was won with steel and the market blossomed for steel. Steel was, and still is, marvelously consistent in flex. Also, steel has extremely little, if any, torque. This was a tremendous advantage when making a set of golf clubs consistent in swing characteristics. The claim "matched set" was now much easier to make. With the wood shafts, a club maker had great difficulty making the set of clubs into a matched set. In fact, steel is so consistent, that the modern day pros still prefer steel, particularly in the irons where accuracy is essential.

Steel has gone through several changes over the years. Various types have been used. Stainless steel and lightweight steel is the latest trend. The lighter shaft means that the weight saved on the shaft can be added to the clubhead without altering the overall weight. The lightweight steel was first popular with women, then seniors, and now everyone is in on the act. Steel has gone "hi-tech," with new types to come out in the near future. Many of the newer shafts do not have the steps as in the older style. The more expensive the shaft, the more steps or step-downs in the shaft. The steps used to be spaced consistently on the shaft. Later developments arranged the steps into various patterns to give different flex points or kickpoints.

Kickpoint, bend point, or flexpoint

The kickpoint is the point on the shaft where the greatest amount of flex occurs. A low kickpoint gives a more flexible feel, with a higher ball trajectory. The higher kickpoint gives just the opposite: a stiffer feel and a lower trajectory, sometimes called the pro-trajectory. It is recommended that the lower kickpoint is advantageous to the higher handicap players, while the high kickpoint is best for the better golfers. Again, the trial and error process prevails. Try both. A study by A. Chou and O. C. Roberts, in *Science and Golf II*, found that

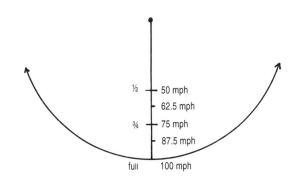

Fig. 2-2. The pendulum and speeds along its length.

the various kickpoint locations on the shaft had little consistency in achieving the desired trajectory of the ball.

The shaft bends backwards as the clubhead approaches the ball and then recovers to its original straightness and bends forward at impact. This has led to the concept that the shaft bends and recovers by kicking forward into the ball for more clubhead speed and hence more ball distance. It is interesting to note a study by G. P. Horwood, also in the *Science and Golf II*, that the concept of the shaft kicking into the ball at impact is spurious. It is the timing of the swing through centrifugal force and inertia, that determines the recovery of the shaft.

This bending forward of the shaft at impact will increase the loft of the club face to give a higher trajectory. This means that the more flexible the shaft the higher the ball's trajectory. A flex point toward the tip of the shaft seems to give the higher trajectory by increasing the dynamic loft of the face. As the flex point move up the shaft to the grip, the ball's trajectory becomes lower.

Another interesting comment by Horwood is that it might seem obvious that longer shafts should also achieve greater clubhead speed. However, his simple mechanical analysis shows this is largely illusionary and that ball contact is more difficult. Horwood's claims seem to go against the standard belief that the longer the club the more clubhead speed that can be generated.

In Fig. 2.2, a swinging pendulum swings at various speeds. The end of the pendulum that is the center of the swing arc is at zero speed. The farther from the center of the pendulum, the faster the swing moves. Halfway down the pendulum, the speed is half of what the swinging end of the pendulum is. If we extend the pendulum and are capable of swinging the pendulum at the same speed, then the swinging end will go faster than its original position. The more we extend the pendulum, the more difficult it is to maintain the original speed and make accurate contact with the ball.

Isotropic and anisotropic

Steel is more consistent than graphite because of construction and material. A steel shaft is isotropic meaning that the strength of steel is consistent when stressed in any direction—vertically, horizontally, and diagonally. Graphite is anisotropic, and stress in various directions is not consistent. Graphite is made of fibers and epoxy with some other substances, such as boron or Kevlar, added for strength. Since the fibers are arranged in various patterns, and the various materials in graphite have different characteristics, it is easy to see why the graphite is anisotropic and not as consistent as steel or aluminum.

Everyone has tried to replace steel with a lot of hype and advertizing, but steel is still alive and strong.

Fiberglass and aluminum

Fiberglass and aluminum left the scene about as fast as they had come in, but they may well have been the start of the quest for a lighter shaft. Fiberglass had to be supported with a steel rod inside the fiberglass tube. Naturally this did not make sense, as it was just a steel shaft in a fiberglass house. The quest for the lighter shaft is explained after this section.

Aluminum now seems to be making a comeback—slowly. Other materials have been added to aluminum to improve the quality of the alloy. Aluminum arrows are the most precise and consistent of arrows. Easton, a big aluminum arrow manufacturer, makes the new aluminum golf shaft, and it may well be the most precise and consistent shaft on the market. The aluminum shaft is also very light—lighter than steel. Aluminum also has the dampening qualities of graphite without sacrificing the consistency of steel. Some golfers like it on their wedges—the accuracy clubs. The new aluminum is considered by some club makers as the best shaft for consistency of straightness, flex, and torque (if any). Since no big name pros are using aluminum, the public has a hard time accepting this material.

$E = mv^2$

The search for the lighter shaft is based on this equation, where E = energy; m = mass; and v = velocity.

$E = mv^2$ means Energy equals Mass times Velocity squared. If you increase mass or velocity, you also increase energy. Increase energy and you can increase the impact on the ball, which in turn increases the distance the ball will fly. With aluminum and fiberglass kicking off the search for lightweight material, manufactures studied lightweight steel, carbon-graphite, stainless steel, ceramic, titanium and many other materials.

If you increase mass, you can increase distance and if you increase velocity, you can increase distance so much more. An increase in velocity is raised to the second power on the energy factor. This means increasing clubhead speed is a more powerful factor in distance than increasing the mass. For more distance, it is best to increase velocity, so let's make the clubs lighter to increase the speed of the swing. As learned elsewhere, you can make the clubhead so light that you increase the speed of the clubhead, but the clubhead has insufficient mass for distance at impact. By using a lighter shaft, you take the weight saved on the weight of the shaft and put it in the clubhead. This keeps the total weight of the club the same. This reasoning should result in greater clubhead speed and greater mass for more distance.

The weight distribution must be checked, as too much mass or weight to the clubhead may make the club slower to swing, and hence the slower swing speed counters the increased mas, resulting in less distance and control.

Graphite

Graphite is the latest rage. These shafts are light, so more weight can be added to the clubhead area. They feel good at contact, if you like the dampening qualities of the vibration from impact with the ball. Despite all the hype on graphite, there seem to be some problems. Graphite has more torque— twisting of the shaft—then steel or aluminum. This can hinder accuracy, although some claim that the torque effect can help create more energy at impact. This seems to be true, but torque requires timing for consistency. In recent years, graphite shafts have made tremendous improvements to give better consistency to ball striking.

Torque

Torque in the graphite shaft is rated by numbers. The higher the number, the greater the torque. A low-torque shaft will be in the 2.0 to 2.5 range while the higher torque will be in the 5.0 plus range. This number represents the number of degrees the shaft twists, or torques, during the downswing or the power phase of the swing.

Tip of shaft

Graphite also has a problem at the tip end of the shaft area. Impact creates a violent force in the hosel area. This is the area where graphite falters. Some companies have corrected this by fortifying the tip so that it is like steel. This makes the graphite heavier and closer to the feel of steel and yet the golfer has the advantage of the dampening, or shock absorbing, qualities of graphite.

Inconsistencies

Graphite is made with fibers and epoxy substances, rolled and molded to the shape of the shaft. Each manufacturer has their own way of making the shaft. Some use more or less fibers, more or less layers and different materials such as boron added to the construction. Very often, these materials are used to strengthen the graphite. Inexpensive shafts will have swellings and valleys, although small, in various parts of the shafts. This inconsistency can lead to inconsistent flex.

There is no doubt that graphite has advantages, but they are not as consistent as steel and aluminum. Another problem with graphite is the lack of consistency with the stiff (S), regular (R), ladies (L), senior (A) flex of the various shafts. Each manufacture has their own definition of stiff and regular. A regular with one company may be a stiff with another company. Perhaps one of the reasons for this may be that each company has their own way of measuring flex. There is no industry standard.

Some golfers have claimed there is even a difference in flex in the same category as some regulars are stiff and some are senior flex. Here again, it is trial and error to find the one that works for you. Do not expect the flex of steel to be the same in graphite. Ironically, some claim that graphite is the modern equivalent of the wood shaft, with a similar soft feel, flex, and torque as wood.

Titanium

Titanium has tried to crack the shaft market, but seems to be more popular in clubheads and not shafts. Titanium is expensive, but expense seems to be a minor problem to most golfers. Titanium is strong and consistent, with minimal torque, if any, and some shock dampening qualities. The weight of the shaft is a little heavier than graphite but lighter than steel. Titanium is a quality shaft.

Length of shaft

The new material and lighter shafts have made it possible to create longer shafts. Longer shafts add distance. The farther from the center of a spinning object, the higher the speed. Longer shaft—higher clubhead speed. Scientifically, this is true, but how long can you go with the shaft and still maintain clubhead control? The larger clubhead, so common today, makes ball contact easier with the longer shaft. Again, experimentation and practice will determine the shaft length you can handle.

Although the shorter shaft and heavier head (greater mass) has not gained popularity, there may be a trend coming this way. The shorter shaft is easier to control, and the heavier head gives more mass behind the ball to make up for the clubhead speed of longer shafts.

Clubhead speed still seems to dominate distance, but the shorter shaft logic does seem to have merit. The shorter shaft is not only easier to control, but some may even find it easier to get clubhead speed increased.

Shaft butt

There seems to be a trend toward the bigger shaft butt to assist in control of the club for better ball flight and accuracy. More and more companies are adding this deviation to their models. More on this in the section subtitled "New Trends."

Shape of the shaft

The shape of golf club shafts has always been in a consistent taper with the grip end thicker than the clubhead end. This is now changing with the bubble shaft and the new fat shaft. The bubble style has quickly become very popular, as it seems to provide very long and accurate shots. The bubble adds stability to the middle of the shaft, so the golfer can swing faster without swinging harder. Taylor Made claims that the bubble driver swings centrifugally around its own center of gravity... to maximize centrifugal force.

The fat shafts are much thicker at the tip end. This reduces the taper of the shaft to minimal proportions. The manufacturers claim that the thicker shaft has less torque and is therefore more accurate.

New Trends

New materials are continually being devised and used. Many are still in the experimental stages. The strategies behind the new materials are still the same: Make the shaft lighter, less torque, more accuracy, and more distance. Various companies have different methods of achieving these factors.

The shape of the shaft is changing. The bubble near the grip is now fairly common, but new trends have bubbles, swells, or bulges in various locations of the shaft. The main claims are accuracy due to decreased torque and more distance by the whip or kick points. Some shafts now have more than one kick point. Shafts with two and three kick, or flex, points are being developed. At the grip end, the shafts are now being made much larger. These are the big-butt shafts, and the claim is again for less torque and more accuracy. A more recent development is the fat shaft, where the tip of the shaft (the end near the clubhead) is much larger than normal. Again, less torque. This trend started with putters and now has gone to the irons and woods.

Aluminum and nickel shafts are being developed. These show promise of dampening qualities for feel and yet have the consistency of steel. Thermoplastic shafts are very new, but these are still basically graphite shafts with nylon and thermoplastic resins instead of epoxy. The alloy Duranium has properties that are similar to those of titanium and may show promise.

Club fitting

There are some standard trends for club fittings. Keep in mind that these are not specific or exact, but they may give you an idea of what to try and where to begin. Trial and error still prevails as everyone does not fit the same trend.

1. The stronger the golfer:

   the heavier the shaft; the lower the torque.

2. Clubhead speed:

   the more swing speed, the stiffer the shaft;

   the less swing speed, the lighter the shaft.

3. Swing speed tempo:

   the faster the tempo, the stiffer the shaft, the less the torque and higher the flex or kick point;

   the slower the tempo, the lighter the shaft, the higher the torque and the lower the flex or kick point.

4. Shot dispersion:

   the more off line the lower the torque;

   the lower the trajectory the lower the flex or kick point.

Remember, these factors are paper tigers that may not hold up in the real world of golf for your swing. Trial and error again. No matter how hard we try to predict what to use, the final analysis comes down to trial and error.

Golf Balls

In the last few years, golf balls have become so advanced and technical that most golfers have lost track of what is happening. Every company has their own construction procedures and materials to enhance ball flight and to create distance. Some claims are valid, some are not. Think back over the years; but for simplicity's, sake lets start around 1980. Every year since, the manufacturers have claimed that their new ball will go 10 to 20 yards farther. It we take the yearly increase of 10 yards for every year, the ball should now be flying 200 yards farther than 20 years ago. I guess this means the average drive should now be 400 plus yards. Anyway, let's look past the hype and study the golf ball.

Hard and softer golf balls

The golf ball has now been altered to achieve various results. The laws of physics and chemistry have been applied to the construction of the golf ball to give extra distance and feel to the ball. Basically, the hardness or softness of the cover will affect spin. The soft cover, like balata or other similar synthetic material, holds the face of the club better than the harder ball surface. This means that the soft-cover ball will have more spin. The harder surface golf ball, with surlyn being the most popular cover type, will jump off the face quicker and even slide up the face a little, especially on the high lofted clubs. The harder-surface ball will also spin less during its flight.

It is fairly well accepted that the two-piece ball and the three-piece ball are now quite close in standards and functions.

Spin

Golf balls are created with more or less spin. More spin holds the green better but usually means less distance. Less spin gives more distance to the ball's flight but less backspin to hold the green. The spin is good if it is all backspin because it will hold the green better. If contact creates side spin, disaster can occur, as the ball will spin more to create a stronger slice, or hook. As a rule, the better control golfers will use the higher spin ball for better backspin to hold the green and to give the softer feel for putting. The higher handicap or less ball control golfer would be better off using the distance or harder ball for less spin, especially the unwanted side spin, to better control the ball. The lower spin ball is considered better under windy conditions as wind accentuates the spin effect on the ball. This is particularly evident when going into the wind.

Multi-layered golf balls

Multi-layered balls are the new trend. These balls have more than one cover—two, three and more. The reasoning is for feel and distance. A hard layer for distance, and a soft layer for feel and spin. The combinations of feel and distance are many, as various degrees of thickness and materials give the desired result of distance or spin.

Size

The size of the golf ball also alters the spin rate. The trend by some companies to a larger ball called the magna or mid-size is to lessen the spin rate of the golf ball for better accuracy. Too much spin is dangerous to many golfers. As in the laws of physics, the smaller ball spins with more revolutions. The larger ball may not be quite as long in distance but is considered more accurate. Decide which is more important to you. Some claim that the larger ball rolls better on putting greens as the larger ball is less affected by imperfections of the green.

In the *Science And Golf II: Proceedings of the World Scientific Congress Of Golf*, M. J. Sullivan and T. Melvin reported on their testing on golf ball size. They found that the new 1.72-inch golf ball meets the USGA and the R&A rules and specifications. The 1.72-inch ball does not lose carry distance or sideways deviation when compared to the 1.68-inch (regular) golf ball. They found that the larger ball reduces spin, which in turn reduces hooking and slicing. The larger ball, with a hard cover and softer core, will give a higher launch angle to help increase distance.

The larger ball also helps in the dimple pattern by being able to use larger dimples. Wider dimples help reduce drag for greater carry distance.

Weight

Some balls are made lighter for the slower swing speed golfer. The lighter ball is supposed to lessen the ball's resistance to flight as well as to gravity. This is supposed to add distance to slower swing speeds. In case you are wondering, a golf ball may be larger than 1.68 inches and lighter than 1.62 ounces, so these factors are legal.

Putting

When putting, the harder ball and the softer ball regulate distance differently. The harder ball will go farther than the softer ball when putted with the same force. For this reason, it is often advisable to stick to the same ball to develop a feel for distance. Switching between a balata cover to a surlyn cover ball can lead to inconsistency in distance judgement, especially on fast greens.

Dave Pelz, in his book *Putt Like The Pros*, found the following facts: A putting impact force used to putt a wound balata 90 compression ball 30 feet will give the following distances with other balls:

❑ a wound surlyn 90 compression ball will go 14 inches farther;

❑ a wound surlyn 100 compression ball will go 31 inches farther;

❑ a 2-piece solid surlyn cover, no compression will go 34 inches farther.

Roll of the Ball

In putting, the roll of the ball is greatly affected by where on the face of the putter contact is made. Contact off the sweet spot is crucial. The sweet spot is the center of percussion—the point of no rotation, turning or wobble. Miss the sweet spot, the putter face vibrates and accuracy is destroyed. Miss the sweet spot, and the ball rolls off line, breaks more and has less energy. Pelz's research claims that if you make a perfectly executed 8-foot putt, but miss the sweet spot by one-quarter of an inch, the ball will miss the hole 95% of the time. This is for putting but similar results occur for all clubs.

The force of impact affects the roll of the ball. In putting, the ball starts to roll where the putter face is aimed, and not in the direction of the stroke. The putting stroke is such a low-impact stroke that no friction is created on contact with the ball. With no friction, the ball rebounds off the putter face in the direction the face is aimed.

This makes putting a little easier, as only the face of the putter face must be square to the target. The golfer does not have to worry about the direction of the stroke. This takes pressure off the putt. Just line up the face and stroke smoothly.

Keep in mind that this only applies to putting, and perhaps easy chips. As impact becomes more forceful, the friction on the ball and the club face increases. As friction increases, the swing path becomes more and more important.

The Ball's Center

The center of the ball can also affect spin. The softer-core ball can also give more spin, as the core absorbs more impact energy to give more spin. The harder-core ball will also go in reverse by giving less spin but more distance. Research shows that the harder the ball, the farther it will fly. The coefficient of restitution (the rebound qualities) proves this. If you want more distance, than hit a harder ball. What is happening now is that the soft-core ball is covered by a harder cover to reduce spin, and the hard core-ball gets a soft cover for more spin.

Compression

The hardness of the two-piece golf ball is determined by the chemical mixture of the core. In the wound ball, the hardness is determined by how tight the elastic band is wound around the center. The hardness of a ball is rated by the compression factor—how much the ball compresses at impact. Recommended compression factors are 80 for women and seniors, 90 for most men, and 100 for hard swingers. As stated earlier, the harder the ball, the farther it will go, so this would mean that everyone should use the 100 compression. This may be true, but the harder ball gives some golfers a bad feel at impact. Some claim the 100 is too hard to control. This is why most golfers use the 90 or less, for a softer impact and better control when putting. Some golfers use the 100 only on very hot days, so that full compression is possible.

Compression is slowly fading from the scene. The newer two-piece balls are rarely classified with compression. Some manufacturers still stamp the compression on their wound ball, called the three-piece bal. What is good for you? Trial and error. Get a ball that works for you. Stick with that ball to learn and feel control, touch, and other characteristics.

Durability

Durability of the cover is simple: The harder the cover, the more durable the ball is to cutting and other markings. The new covers are extremely valuable today for the lasting qualities of the ball. The old golf balls cut and bruised easily. They did not last long. Even today, the new softer wound balls do not hold their shape as well as the harder 2-piece distance balls. Soft covers bruise and cut easily. A bruise can alter the smoothness of the ball to give a swelling effect. This cover imperfection can cause major problems for all clubs, but in particular the putter.

USGA

Golf balls are regulated and controlled by the USGA, the United States Golf Association. They have several criteria that a golf ball must not exceed. Exceed the criteria, and the ball is illegal. A golf ball must not exceed 280 yards in carry and roll when hit with the artificial swing machine at a clubhead speed of 109 mph. Launch angle and spin rate are closely monitored.

Table 2-1. Effect of dimple depth on distance

Depth of Dimple Pattern (inch)	Carry (feet)	Total Length of Drive (feet)
0.002	117	146
0.004	187	212
0.006	212	232
0.008	223	238
0.010	238	261
0.012	225	240

The diameter of a golf ball is regulated, with a minimum requirement of 1.68 inches to achieve a desired drag effect. The maximum weight of 1.62 ounces and initial velocity standards control the kinetic energy of the ball. The overall distance requirement helps keep golf courses from becoming obsolete and making a travesty of the game by turning the regulation golf course into a pitch and putt course. Manufacturers have always been making golf balls to the standards prescribed by the USGA. The balls have been equally close to the standards for over 25 years. Since the standards have not changed, it is unlikely that the modern ball is going much, if any, farther than the old ball of many, many years ago. As mentioned earlier, every year the balls are advertised as 10 to 20 yards farther. Skeptical? S. Aoyama in *Science and Golf II: Proceedings of the World Scientific Congress Of Golf*, claims that among the longer hitters, driving distance has only increased by about 10 yards since 1970. This is supported by the USGA Research and Test Center.

Dimples

Dimples may well be the most important aspect of a golf ball. The flight of the golf ball is pure physics—from the coefficient of restitution to the air dynamics of flight. A well-hit smooth golf ball may fly only 150 yards. Add dimples, and 200 yards is easily obtained. Use the correct dimple pattern, and you are well beyond the 200 yard mark. The best pattern for dimples is difficult to determine, as the various patterns achieve various results. It is a matter of what works for you. It appears that there are more than 150 dimple patterns. That would be a lot of testing to find the best pattern for you. A little knowledge can help narrow the field to your requirements.

New testing equipment has found that by altering one dimple, the ball's flight could be affected in trajectory and distance up to 5 yards.

Golf balls have to be designed with symmetry. A golf ball could be designed with no dimples at each pole of the ball. When teed with the dimples facing the fairway, that ball would fly straight. Naturally, such a ball is illegal.

Dr. Dave Williams, in *The Science of the Golf Swing*, charts the effect of dimples on the ball's flight. He found that when the dimple depth is beyond 0.1 inches the length of the drive decreases.

Aerodynamics

The size and shape of the dimple affects the flight pattern of the ball. Dimples are shallow and deep, large and small, round and square, and lately in a tear-drop shape. The square dimple has not found much popularity and is fading from the scene. The idea is to take these dimple characteristics in various combinations and achieve different results. High trajectory, mid trajectory, and low trajectory is determined by the dimple characteristics. Put these dimple characteristics in combinations with the hard and soft core and the hard and soft cover, and you have almost unlimited combinations. The size and depth of the dimple is so precise that a golf ball improperly painted can alter the depth of

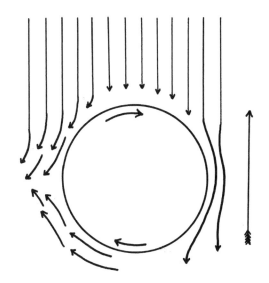

A= air resistance
B= spin of ball
C= spin of ball moves air quickly out of this area to give lower pressure
D= spin of ball moves more air into this area to create higher pressure
E= direction of travel
Higher pressure forces ball to move to lower pressure area to create the curving flight pattern

Fig. 2-2. Aerodynamics of the golf ball.

the dimple to cause problems. In fact, an uneven paint job, with too much paint in one spot, can alter the balance of the ball to give an undesired flight pattern.

Grips

Not much to say about grips. It is a question of your feel. If you like it, use it. No matter what the technology, style, or hype, it is your feel that determines the grip.

Cleaning

Leather grips are fading from the scene. The leather gets slippery quickly and they do not hold up over time as well as the non-leather grips or the composition grips. When new, the leather grips do have a nice feel, and that is the reason many players still prefer leather.

The non-leather grips should be kept clean by washing in soapy water and scrubbing with a stiff brush. If the grips become a little too dry and still a little slippery after washing you may take some sandpaper, usually a more coarse variety, and sand the grips to bring out the fresh or new rubber or composition.

Size

An interesting feature that makes sense but is not as popular as it should be is the non-taper grip. The reason for the taper may lie back with the hickory shafts that were tapered from the butt to the tip. The grip at the time was a leather strip wrapped around the butt end of the shaft. Naturally, the grip shape would be tapered. Now, if you look at your two hands, you will notice that each hand is the same size, so why not have your golf grip with the same size at each end? Seems logical. Many golfers, once they try the same size grip, like the feel of the grip. Some claim it is easier to control the club, as both hands feel the same size shaft.

There is a theory that if the grip is too thin, the golf ball's flight will hook, and if the grip is too thick, the ball's flight will slice. If this theory is true, then what will happen with the conventional tapered grip? Will the thick end of the grip slice and the thin end hook?

Some putter grips now employ the same thickness from one end to the other. Thicknesses are even going larger and thicker. Many golfer claim a better feel to the putt with the larger or thicker grip with the same size at both ends. If it works with the putter, then perhaps it works with the other clubs.

Natural rubber is still very common, although the synthetic compounds and thermoplastic elastomers are taking over the grip market. Cord has been the major addition to the grips. Some like the feel, some don't. The cord seems to firm up the grip and possibly absorb moisture from the hands. Absorbing moisture may be more a marketing claim than actual fact. Good grips provide a tacky feel and adhere to the hands very well. In fact, one wonders why a glove is needed to help grip the club. Some grips are even designed for rainy weather.

Clubheads

Clubheads in recent years have undergone distinct changes, particularly in size. With the advent of lighter shafts, the extra weight was put into the clubhead for increased mass. With the new stronger and lighter materials, such as ceramic and titanium, the clubheads can be made larger without being necessarily heavier.

Center of Gravity

The center of gravity, often referred to as C_g, is the spot on the club face that gives the most solid hit and feel. It is the spot that resists twisting when contact is made with the ball. The C_g can easily be found by holding the club face in one hand and bouncing a ball off the face of the club with the other hand. Listen to the sound of the bounce, and you will readily find the sweet spot. This procedure is particularly good for determining the sweet spot, or C_g, on a putter. The C_g can also be found by tapping a pencil on the face of the club with one hand while the other hand holds the club on the shaft. You will easily see the sweet spot as the pencil tap will have a solid feel and sound on the C_g.

The weighting of the clubhead determines where the C_g will be located. Moving the weight to the heel and the toe, enlarges the sweet spot. In reality the sweet spot cannot be made larger as a spot is a spot. It just makes a larger area that resists twisting on ball contact. Putting the weight to the sole of the club, lowers the C_g to help get the ball up in the air at contact. This is why trouble clubs, like the woods with railers on the sole, add extra weight to the sole to get the ball up quicker when coming out of trouble like tall grass, rough, and other problems.

Clubface

The larger face of the club gives the golfer a larger margin of error on impact. Impact off the sweet spot is less affected by the mishit. All impacts off the center of gravity, or sweet spot, are better. It is just that we do not hit the exact sweet spot every time. The farther from the sweet spot to the toe or heel, the less energy is imparted to the golf ball, and hence a less effective shot results. By making the club face larger, the off-center hits are less affected. This is why the larger-face golf club is called a more forgiving club.

The larger face or clubhead is more evident in the woods. This is natural as the woods are more for distance. Also, the woods are longer than the other clubs, and hence a lager face makes it easier to hit the ball. Since it is easier to hit the ball, the club shaft can be made longer to help create a greater clubhead speed. This is psychological and physical to varying degrees.

Irons have gone to the larger head and face. Some irons became so large that they faded quickly from the market. Titanium was so light and strong that the face could be made quite large, however, too large for popularity. The big problem with the irons is that the titanium heads are so light that the balance of the club is affected unless weight is added to the titanium. Why pay the extra for titanium when it is not really needed? The titanium heads are sometimes so large that the look seems to affect the golfer by looking like a toy club.

Supersize wood heads

As the size of the clubhead increases, the center of gravity moves away from the shaft and face of the club. This means adjustment to the roll and bulge of the club face by making the arc of the face more pronounced (smaller radius). The moment of inertia increases with size.

Bulge and roll

Wood club faces have bulge and roll. Bulge is the face curve from toe to heel (horizontal). Roll is the vertical curve from the sole to the top of the club. Increasing the bulge and roll of a club face can impart more energy to the ball, as the face of the club transfers its energy to a smaller surface to help increase distance. This is the same principle as the footprint. More energy or force, or pressure is imparted to the ground by the heel of the foot than when the foot is flat on the ground. When the foot is flat on the ground, the pressure is distributed over a wider area. Walk on a beach and the heel print will go deeper into the sand than the flat foot or toe area. The trade-off to this is that contact to a smaller area may impede or hamper control. The key to roll and bulge is how far you can go and still keep contact under control.

Experiments by T. Olsavsky, published in his presentations to *The Science of Golf II: Proceedings of the World Scientific Congress of Golf*, found that the supersize driver performed better than the smaller clubheads. The increase in the moment of inertia plays a part in this advantage. Olsavsky also confirmed that the larger face is better for off-center hits because they can have full-face contact with the ball at extreme locations and there is also less energy loss at impact. The less energy loss means more energy is going into the ball instead of back up the shaft in the form of vibrations.

Distance and consistency was found to be much better with the supersize driver. Confidence and ease of hitting seemed to increase as the clubhead increased in size. Olsavsky claims that the supersize heads performed better than the mid-size and standard-size clubheads.

Equipment Summary

Science and research have been having a field day. And yet, with our expanded base of knowledge and the so-called advantages of our equipment, course maintenance, and teaching, we still have not improved much. A study by F. W. Thomas, from *The Science and Golf II*, confirms this point, summarized as follows:

1. Driving distance for the longest hitters from 1968 has increased 12 yards.

2. No improvement in greens in regulation or accuracy since 1968.

3. Putting has improved by one stroke since 1968. Since scoring has also only improved by one stroke, it seems to be that putting improvement has improved the score.

4. Regression of scoring indicates that the average winning score is improving by one stroke per round per 21 years; fifth place at one stroke per round at 17.5 years and the 25th place at one stroke per round per 14 .5 years. This indicates that the fields are getting stronger over time.

These statistics are based on the PGA tour. Although the numbers may be different for the amateurs, the trends are about the same. In fact, some claims are made that the average handicap is the same as 25 years ago.

Does this tell us that we cannot buy a golf game? A wise man once said, aye, laddie, spend the money on lessons and practice, not on new clubs.

Part II
Using the Senses for Learning

3

Evolution of the Golf Swing

The evolution of the golf swing is basically going from a roundhouse swing of excessive body rotation to a more vertical swing with less body movement and more arm action for more a consistent swing.

Yesterday's Swing:

The body

The old swing of yesterday had a very strong body rotation. In fact, Mindy Blake claims that the left arm rotated around the body to a 76-degree angle from the line of flight. Moving the shoulder over 90 degrees of rotation creates this angle. The hips rotate 70 degrees. Of course, these measurements are not exactly accurate to all the golfers of this era, but it does give us a general idea. It is also noticeable that the hips and the shoulders rotate almost the same number of degrees, so that the whole body is considered to rotate away from the ball. The club face is open at the top of the swing and the left wrist is concave.

The legs also move with the hips as the left knee kicks inward considerably toward the right knee, independently of the arms. Almost all golfers at this stage lifted the left heel off the ground and in some cases the lift was quite high. This is not surprising, as the excessive body rotation almost pulled the left heel up. With the golfer's club at the top of the swing, the body is well coiled, but the upper body muscles are not stretched and are loose because the hips are also rotated as much as the shoulders. For the downswing and the uncoiling of the body, the muscles must pull the body around to the ball. For muscles to react, they must be in a state of tonus, or slightly stretched for quick reaction. Unfortunately, this coil did not stretch the muscles, because the hips and shoulder are almost together in the coil. To start the downswing, the golfer slammed the left heel down to tighten the muscles to pull the body around to the ball for the swing. This is what is meant when it was said that the downswing starts at the feet and then works its way up to the hands.

Grip

The grip was usually strong, with three or four knuckles showing on the left hand. The strong grip made it easier to close the open club face from the top of the swing to impact.

The stance

With the strong grip and lots of body rotation, the golfer stood to the ball with a closed stance for the driver and long clubs and progressed to a more open stance as the shorter clubs were used. The stance also altered the ball position. With the driver, the ball was played well forward and then moved back toward the right foot as the shorter clubs were used. As we can see the stance was very inconsistent and varied with each shot. This stance gave a pronounced inside takeaway to the backswing because of the excessive body rotation.

Weight transfer

This swing had a strong weight transfer. Weight went on the right leg on the backswing and the body even shifted back. On the downswing, the body moved forward and the weight shifted onto the left leg. The body rotation was around the right leg for the backswing, and for the downswing the body weight moved forward onto the left leg. Lots of timing factors here.

At impact, the right heel is well off the ground and the hips are well forward into the body rotation. With this excessive rotation the body sway to the target is extreme.

Early Modern Swing

The body

The more modern swing has less body rotation, as the hips now rotate 45 degrees, with the angle of the left arm to the direction of travel also about 45 degrees. Although the left arm angle to the direction of flight is 45 degrees, the shoulders have rotated about 90 degrees to give this angle. As you will notice, the left arm is now moving more in line with the flight of the ball. This means the swing has become more vertical. This swing has put the club face more square at the top, with the left wrist now flatter and even flat with some golfers.

This compact swing requires more coordination between the arms and the legs. The hips are now providing resistance to the upper-body rotation. This resistance means that the muscles are stretched and are being set up for the downswing. This early modern swing has the left foot flat on the ground to give limited hip movement, and in turn resistance to the upper body, so that the muscles are stretched to the limit for a powerful downswing. This swing has fewer moving parts, and as a result it is more compact and more consistent.

Grip

The grip is now moving to a weaker grip, with one or two knuckles of the left hand showing. This is possible because the club face is now placed in a more closed position at the top of the swing. This means less hand rotation is needed to achieve club face squareness at impact.

The stance

The stance is becoming more consistent as the body is more square for all shots with maybe some openness to the short irons. The ball position is also more consistent, as most golfers are playing the ball just off the left heel for all shots. This stance affects the takeaway, as the takeaway is now straight back with little or no hip rotation as the shoulders are rotating. The buzz word for this was the one-piece takeaway.

Weight transfer

The weight transfer still exists, but it is less pronounced. The weight may shift, but the body usually does not slide backward or forward as much as with the old swing.

At impact, the body is closer to square to the ball. The shoulders are square but the hips are a little ahead of the shoulders. In most swings, the body is more perpendicular, with minimal body sway to the target.

The Late Modern Swing

The body

If this trend continues—and all indications seem to point this way—the swing will become more in line with the flight of the ball. Recent teachings support this hypothesis. The line of the left arm to the direction of the ball flight is closing to the range of 15 degrees or less. The hips are almost nil in rotation, as the range of hip rotation is down to a 10-degree range. This shows how the upper body moves the swing, while the legs are strong supporters or stabilizers to the swing. If you believe in the old adage that the fewer moving parts, the less can go wrong, this late modern swing is the answer.

Grip

The grip is now moving to an even weaker position, with one or no knuckles showing. This weaker grip does not mean less power to the swing. It is just that the club face is even more closed at the top. Less hand rotation is used to achieve square contact with the ball. With the swing in a more upright or vertical plane, the hands do not have to rotate as much to achieve squareness at contact. The body rotates less, and the hands rotate less. Some of the late modern teachings even have the hands swinging with no rotation at all. This makes timing and accuracy much easier.

The stance

The stance is very similar to the early modern swing.

Weight transfer

Weight transfer is lessened even more, as some are now teaching to keep the weight evenly balanced until after impact, when the follow-through pulls the body weight onto the left leg. Some golfers are bracing the right leg to achieve minimal weight shift back but no body sway back.

At impact, many modern teachers are now teaching to have both feet flat on the ground and the body square to the ball at impact.

4
The Role of Vision and Nonvision in Learning the Golf Swing and Putt

Typing skills are learned by not looking at the keys. The skill is developed through touch, or feel; hence the name touch-typing. A typist cannot recall where on the keyboard a certain key is located. Ask a good typist where a certain key (e.g. K) is located, and chances are that the typist will move his/her fingers in a typing manner to locate where the K-key is.

Feeling Versus Thinking

The key is remembered through a feel, or touch, process and not a cognitive (thinking) process. If a typist was to learn typing through the visual process of looking for the keys or even memorizing the key's locations, the learning situation would be very slow and inaccurate. This is why many typing teachers often blindfold their students and/or have them look at words to type or even look at the teacher so that they do not look at their keyboards. Typing is taught most effectively through touch/feel or kinesthetic sense. If this is true, then perhaps sport skills such as the golf swing and the golf putt should also be learned and taught through the touch/feel, or kinesthetic, sense.

The terms kinesthetic and proprioceptive refer to the same sense of providing information of one's body position in space (Singer, 1975). Mead (1958) claims that a great proportion of a young child's learning is by the kinesthetic sense. It is this sense that provides information on one's body movement and then subconsciously integrates the information with other cues to enable the youngster to move smoothly and accurately on everyday activities. This sense is often referred to as "feel" or "a feeling for the movement" and is usually stressed by coaches and instructors in skill learning. To the learner this feel or awareness of muscle action and body position is vital to learning a new skill.

Three Stages of Learning

Fitts (1964) and Fitts and Posner (1967) claim that learning a motor skill involves three stages: cognition, fixation, and automation. During cognition, the learner is developing an understanding and a feel for the skill. The second phase, fixation, is the longest and most demanding, as it consists of practice and error correction. Unfortunately, according to Fitts, some learners never get past this stage. For the skilled, the fixation stage develops into the automatic stage, in which the skill is performed fluidly and effectively. In the automatic stage, no conscious thought is required, as the skill is now performed instinctively and reflexively. In this model, the learner goes from a learned helplessness to dependence on other sources and on to the final stage of an independent and self-controlling action.

Kinesthetic Learning

Some research has claimed that kinesthesis is used most effectively in the early stages of learning a skill. This seems natural as the typist learns to type right from the start without looking at the keys. By not looking at the keys, or by being blindfolded, the absence of vision causes one to use kinesthetic sense or "feel" for learning.

In 1931, Coleman R. Griffith, a university professor, may have been the first to study the use of kinesthetic sense as a learning method. His subjects were divided into two groups. The control group learned to drive a golf ball while using vision, while the experimental group learned by the same method to drive a golf ball while blindfolded. During the initial stages of learning, the experimental group was well behind the pace set by the vision group. After about 150 to 200 drives, the blindfolded group was about comparable to the vision group in performance. After each subject had hit 200 drives, both groups performed with vision, and the experimental group continued to show a faster rate of learning and better performance well above the vision group.

Many years later, in 1983, James Suttie did an extensive biomechanical analysis of the golf swing for each of his beginning golfers. He taught half the group the full golf swing by using the conventional methods, while the other half was taught through kinesthetic techniques. He then filmed his subjects again after the learning period. He also measured the body joints and swing segments in relation to the ball and the club. From his filming and measurements, Suttie was able to find that the kinesthetic method of learning was superior to the conventional method.

Right Brain/Left Brain

Two doctors, Wiren and Coop, in their book *The New Golf Mind*, discuss the actions of the two-sided brain in golf. As is well established in the research, the left brain is for analysis, reasoning, and mathematical factors. The right side is for the emotional, feeling, and creative aspects. They call the left hemisphere the "analyzer" as it analyses such things as club selection, playing conditions, alignment, etc. The right side is referred to as the "integrator" as it is involved in the feel, touch, tempo, visualization, etc. The golfer's kinesthetic/body awareness sense is in the right hemisphere. They claim most of the problems that occur in golf is the result of confusion between the two hemispheres and/or one side overriding the other at the wrong time. For example, the golfer is analyzing when he should be integrating (feel) or integrating when he should be analyzing.

The book also tells about a golf pro giving a lesson to a deaf person. The pro's demonstrations, and written and diagramed efforts all failed until the pro put his hands on the deaf pupil and manipulated him and the club into the various key positions. This type of instruction is referred to as body rehearsal or body awareness, as it emphasizes the kinesthetic sense. Wiren and Coup claim that the golf swing can be cued kinesthetically through the use of aids. A putting track devise is an aid to help keep the putter square during the stroke. A swing aid is a ball on a string that is swung like a golf club to help acquire the feel of centrifugal force during the swing.

Clubhead Focus

Morley (1976), a physician and a psychiatric consultant, gives an excellent account of using the mind to teach the muscles for the golf swing:

> The golf swing involves hitting through, rather than at or to, the ball...the mind can concentrate only on one thing at a time — the golfer must mentally become fully involved with the clubhead. This means for all intents and purposes that he must only be aware of, not fixed by, the ball.

Morley continues with his importance of the kinesthetic sense in learning the golf swing.

> The practice swing of the average duffer illustrates the importance of thinking clubhead rather than ball. Without a ball his swing is as free and fluid as any you may see on a golf course, because his mind is not on the ball. But when the ball in introduced, it is a different proposition. The mind has a tendency to short-circuit immediately to the ball, and this will always happen unless other feelings are produced to counteract it. When the mind switches to the ball, it carries the muscles along with it, and hitting through is replaced by hitting at.
>
> In this respect, I suggest that one of the most important exercises to develop consciousness of the clubhead is to swing the clubhead without a ball in sight: to first develop a swing and then superimpose it upon a ball. As a special exercise, I would even recommend swinging the clubhead wearing a blindfold. This exercise, better than anything I know, forces the mind to become aware of the musculature moves that comprise the golf swing.
>
> Minds are easily distracted. When the golfer prepares to swing a club with his eyes open, the primary focal point of his attention is the ball. Then, when he starts to swing, his muscles cause his mind to "see" the motion of the club. Immediately, he is in an ambivalent situation. Part of him wants to watch the ball, while another part can't help noticing, and becoming partially involved in, the movement of the clubhead. Ambivalence in human experience always leads to conflict, which causes lack of concentration. This leads to confusion, which is then passed on to the musculature system. Result: the swing loses rhythm and symmetry.
>
> The golfer who routinely allows his mind to focus fully on the feel of the clubhead and the muscles that sling it by swinging with his eyes closed is establishing a muscle awareness that will remain after he has actually opened his eyes and is actually swinging through a real golf ball. The same stimuli that diverted his attention before he programmed the muscular pattern will still be there, but the pattern will eventually become so deeply impressed into his system that his mind can ignore the diversion.

Gallwey (1979) took his inner tennis to the game of golf and found results similar to Morley. Gallwey found that the primary focus is not on the ball but on the clubhead. Since he could not follow the clubhead with his eyes, he decided to concentrate on the feel of the clubhead moving during his swing. At a practice range, he concentrated on this feel of "clubhead awareness." His initial attempts were uneventful, as he had little sense of his clubhead location during the swing. However, when he closed his eyes and did not worry about whether he hit the ball or not, he found an "awareness of feel" which helped him improve his golf swing.

Gallwey also talks of teaching Al Geiberger, the famous PGA touring pro, putting through his "awareness game" of putting by looking at the hole and then closing the eyes, putting the ball, and stating where the ball went before opening the eyes. He claims that "the sense of feeling is far more important than the sense of sight... To a great extent, excellence in golf is a function of how aware you are of the sensations of your body during the setup and swing… To control your body, you have to feel it. To control movement effectively you have to feel it vividly." Throughout his book, Gallwey stresses that awareness of the body, often referred to as feel, is best learned with the eyes closed.

Visual and Kinesthetic Imagery

Imagery, or mental practice, is how people represent and process information mentally or symbolically. There are two styles of imagery, visual imagery, in which the individual sees the image in his mind, and kinesthetic imagery, when the individual feels the image without actually performing it.

Jones (1965) claims that imagery, particularly kinesthetic imagery, is necessary during the initial stages of learning. How this imagery works is still a mystery. Back in 1930, Jacobson stated that imagery works because the imagery process activates the actual muscles to be used in the execution of the skill. This activation is minimal, but it does help develop a "feel" for the movement required. It was not until 1986, when a study by Harris and Robinson using EMG readings found support for Jacobson's statement.

Skill execution requires attention, or concentration, by the performer. Very little is known of how or what takes place during this concentration phase. Hatfield, Landers, and Ray (1984) summed it up best in their study of right and left brain activity of rifle marksmen. They stated that "individuals may differ in their functional thinking styles while on the firing line, but they all tend to be quite consistent in using that style for nearly all shots."

Nieporte and Sauers (1968) did a survey with golf professionals on the PGA playing tour. On question number 15, the researchers asked: "Do you use any mental tricks to help you putt properly, such as visualizing an imaginary line along which your ball must travel." The replies were quite varied, as the pros showed no consistency as to their focus of attention. The focus of some

golfers was on contact with the ball. Others chose to focus on the target. The rest chose the path of the ball to the target. Similar varied results showed on question number 14, "Do you use any mental tricks to help you drive properly."

A study by Walford (1986) showed that the blindfolded putters seemed to place their focus of attention on the ball for contact. This appeared logical, as subjects unsure of their putting skill would be highly concerned with just hitting the ball. Better putters, who are much more confident of their putting stroke, would be able to focus attention on direction and/or the target as well as contact. Another interesting finding was that some subjects actually scored higher while blindfolded during the learning phase than they scored on the post-test with vision. Perhaps the reason for scoring better when blindfolded is that these subjects eliminated many distractions of trying to sink the putt. Since they could not see the hole, they relaxed and felt no pressure to sink the putt. By not seeing the hole or the ball, they had a built-in rationalization process of being temporarily blind. After all, you could not be expected to sink the putt if you cannot see what you are doing. As a result, these subjects were able to putt with a relaxed attitude.

In the experiment, an interesting aspect prevails: 51% of the blindfolded putt golfers and 40% of the blindfolded pitch golfers scored higher while blindfolded than they scored on their post test using vision. The interesting aspect of this is that many of the golfers did better blindfolded while relying on their kinesthetic feel than when they take the blindfold off and use their vision. Through observation and score comparisons, it seems that some of the golfers became hampered while using vision as their swing became more jerky and inefficient in comparison to their blindfold swing. Although we have no evidence, a logical assumption is that once vision is used, the golfer tries to hit at the ball instead of swinging the clubhead through the ball as would be done under the blindfold treatment.

Some subjects seem to let vision override their sense of feel (Rock and Harris, 1967). With this being the case, the use of blindfolds on such subjects may help tem acquire and develop their kinesthetic sense. Some learners require more practice time than others to develop their kinesthetic sense for the skill learning. It is this time factor that makes it so difficult for some to have patience with learning.

Teaching or learning golf skills is a trial-and-error process. If a learner is having difficulty with a skill, then the blindfold method is well worth a try. Learning a skill through trial and error is not so unusual, as most learning is trial and error. A learning technique may work with some learners, while others may find it difficult or even confusing. When this happens, an alternative approach to learning must be used. Some techniques, no matter how excellent, may require some alterations for some subjects. Good teachers are able to make these adjustments and alterations in their skill teaching.

5
The Use and Misuse of Imagery, Reflexes, and Learning

When golf, or any athletic skill, is being performed exceptionally well, athletes claim they were in a "zone"—just reacting, not thinking. This "performance zone" brings validity to the concept that good performance requires no thinking. In golf, thinking and visualization is done before the shot, and then the mind goes clear or "empty" during the swing. Execute this pattern of mind control, and you may well go into the "zone". Think during the golf swing and you will never reach the "zone."

Clear Mind

During the actual execution of a golf shot, the golfer should not be thinking of mechanics or how to make the shot. Thinking is done in shot preparation. Analyze your distance, select a club, and then fine-tune your club selection on factors like wind, rain, terrain, etc. When your swing starts, your muscles must be allowed to react with no interference from thinking. Let your mind be clear during the swing. Let the swing happen in a reflex manner.

Cochran and Stobbs, in their book *The Search for the Perfect Swing*, claim that once the swing

moves into the later stages of the backswing, the swing cannot be altered or changed. The swing cannot be changed because the body has been programed to swing the club. Your neurons have been fired and your body responds. Your analysis and club selection has programmed your neurological system for the required body movements for shot execution.

When your body performs a skill without conscious thought, a (learned) reflex is occurring. The clear mind, or the empty mind as they say in Zen, is needed for the reflex to happen correctly. If the clear mind is what the golfer has while in the "zone," then why do teachers teach golfers to have one or more thoughts in their mind during swing execution? One thought is still too many. One thought can still tie-up the body in paralysis by analysis. Back in the early 1900s, Dr. Coleman Griffith, the father of sport psychology, claimed that the better-skilled athletes perform their skills automatically with no thinking. Somehow golf teachers and other sport teachers have forgotten this crucial phase of learning. Similarly, the no-thinking philosophy and flow aspect is confirmed by Garfield and Bennet in their book *Peak Performance: Mental Training Techniques of the World's Greatest Athletes* (1984). They claim that the most important factor in experiencing peak performance is "letting go."

Feedback

Learning occurs from the continued interaction between movement feedback and movement outcome. The learner's mistakes and errors provide feedback to the learner. From feedback, the learner knows what to correct or what adjustments to make. Learning needs feedback. It is the most important variable to learning. The incorrect feeling of the elbow flying out provides feedback for the golfer. Mistakes provide feedback for error correction. Errors tell us what corrections we need to make for improvement. This is why we practice. This is the value of physical practice. We watch the ball's flight for recognition of mistakes. We feel our body movements for mistakes. The ball's flight and our feeling of the swing give us feedback. We see and feel our mistakes. This is referred to as *internal* feedback. When we fail to see or feel our mistakes, we need an excellent observer (a teacher) to analyze our swing. Our teacher now provides the necessary feedback for learning. This is *external* feedback.

Automatic Learned Reflexes

There is a trend among psychologists and teachers that the practice of imagery, or visualization, will improve your golf swing. Both terms are the same skill of visualizing the skill in your mind, giving yourself pictures. Pro golfers claim they use imagery to analyze their shot before they swing the club. Once their swing progresses, their mind goes clear of mechanics and techniques. They are swinging to their learned reflex pattern. They let the swing happen. They let their program execute. Their swing is automatic.

Walking and stair climbing are automatic learned reflexes. No thought—no thinking. Just doing it. Try and think about how you are going to make your body move next time you have to climb stairs; think about each detailed move of all your muscles and your body mechanics as you walk up stairs. Notice the unnaturalness of your moves. You may possibly trip, stutter-step, or go slow. You will not have your natural quick stride. Thinking will slow your body movements and create confusion to your muscle response and movement pattern. It is similar to what we previously discussed with learning to type. Typists do not think about the movement of their fingers: they just types. They look or see the word and type it. A good typist can talk to someone while typing a letter. Amazing. The typist is letting go.

Once your swing becomes automatic, it is very difficult to alter or change your swing pattern. Swing alterations must be practiced for a long time to break an old habit and develop a new alteration into a reflex or automatic pattern. A recent article in *Golf Magazine* claims that the basic swing can probably not be changed or altered. Sometimes a poor or strange reflex pattern is developed through lack of coordination, ability, or knowledge. Restructuring this poor reflex is difficult and time consuming. This is why *Golf Magazine* claims "you're pretty much stuck with what you got." (*Golf Magazine*, February 1995). This may be true. Your learned reflex has been established. The basic part of your swing remains the same, despite the minor alterations you may incorporate. We read of the swing changes many of the pros are making, and yet, when we look at their new swing, it still looks basic to the old swing. Many pros have waited years before new alterations occur consistently and automatically under pressure. Many golfers have abandoned their new alterations and gone back to their old patterns.

Pros and Cons of Imagery

The value of imagery is highly debatable. Golf articles often neglect to quote the research that has shown no value in imagery. In truth, research seems to give no conclusive value of imagery. Some claims are positive and an equal number are negative. Some researchers claim that imagery sends minute impulses from the brain to the required muscles for skill execution. These impulses set up motor pathways for learning skills. Some research claim that this is false. Others claim that imagery can only organize the mind for the task at hand. Imagery cannot improve muscle performance if the skill program is not in the body. In other words, imagery cannot do what the body has not been trained to do.

As we previously stated, physical practice gives feedback for error correction. Mental practice does not give the learner feedback. With imagery, a golfer can visualize an incorrect golf swing and visualize the golf ball fly straight and true. This could be detrimental to learning.

While practicing, visualize a pink elephant, a red house, or an automobile while you swing the golf club. You will usually find the same shot result as you would with the golf swing imagery. Some do better with the pink elephant image, because it prevents analysis of the golf swing. It helps them let go and swing. If imagery is a must, then how can the pink elephant image achieve equal results. Imagery does not give us knowledge of results, a form of feedback. When we physically hit an approach shot to the right of the target, our knowledge of result of the shot tells us that we must adjust our aim, or other factors, to bring the ball flight back on target. With imagery, the imagined results of our shots are always perfect, despite our imagined correct or incorrect swing. With imagery, the golfer can picture his swing incorrectly and still picture the ball flying true and straight to the target. In the mind, the image can always have a good outcome or good feedback.

Whenever imagery is discussed, talk goes to the study where a group mentally practiced throwing basketball free throws with no physical practice. The mental practice group scored as well as a group doing physical practice. This study may have come out this way, but many subsequent studies have failed to verify these results. Physical practice is still essential, vital, and better then mental practice, as more recent research has shown. The mind thinks in pictures, not words. Take a second and think about something. Notice how you see pictures or images. This is called imagery or visualization.

Golf instructors profess how Nicklaus uses imagery for his shot making. Nicklaus visualizes what he wants while preparing for his shot. He thinks, and as a result he sees pictures in the mind. These pictures are interpreted into his analysis of the shot and club selection. He has to use imagery, as his thinking process is imagery in pictures.

Now, what about the hacker? Before his shot, he also thinks. His thinking is also in pictures, as the thinking process can only occur this way. So Nicklaus and the hacker are both thinking, in pictures called imagery. The outcome of their golf shots are different, because Nicklaus has better physical skill execution and so a better shot outcome. Mental preparation through imagery and a clear mind during shot execution makes the shot successful and is often the difference between the poor and good golfer. Unfortunately, the hacker is not able to stop his thinking, imagery, and analysis during execution of the shot. Nicklaus is able to clear his mind for the shot, the hacker does not. For some strange reason, golfers are able to believe that imagery made the shot.

Whether or not you believe in imagery, the fact remains that imagery may help but will not replace physical practice for learning. In fact, how do we distinguish imagery from thinking? Both are in pictures. Both are similar. Is Nicklaus thinking or using imagery? Imagery helps in shot preparation, but analysis imagery should not be used for actual execution of the swing. The subconscious must perform the swing through a learned reflex action.

Learning Skills

And how does the golfer learn the reflex action? Well, it is by the old standby of physical practice. Correct and precise physical practice. Zen has highly developed the art of skill learning into a reflex action. The essence of skill learning is to physically practice the skill and parts of the skill to a high degree of perfection. In time, the high degree of perfection is performed automatically in a reflex manner with no thought required. When this automatic stage is achieved, the golfer has developed a learned reflex.

Zen in the Art of Archery, by Eugen Herrigel, gives an excellent account of how to learn archery. Herrigel's skill of releasing the arrow was practiced, and practiced for years in acquiring the precise release with no conscious thought. Unconscious perfection was stressed until it was achieved. Herrigel had difficulty learning to "let go," with no analysis, no thought, but with an execution of freedom. It is this freedom that lets the reflex pattern of the golf swing happen. It is this freedom that is needed for learning golf. Your golf swing must be physically practiced to refine your skill until you can perform the swing in a correct reflex manner, with no conscious thought. Your body must be trained to perfection, so that your mind can become clear while executing your swing. The requirements of "no thoughts" occurring during skill execution helps put you in the zone.

Execution of the golf swing, with no conscious thought, is not easy to learn. In fact, it is difficult. Typists type with no conscious thought. Notice how a good typist does not think about how the fingers move or where the keys are located. Good typists can even talk while typing. How did the typist learn this skill? The typist used physical practice to learn each finger movement. These moves are practiced and perfected until the moves are automatic or reflexive. The skill becomes a learned reflex. The muscles seem to develop their own memory. In learning to type, the typist is not allowed to look at the keys. Typists learn to feel the location of each key. Looking at the keys encourages thinking. Thinking interferes with muscle memory and the learning of the key's location. Thinking also interferes with the speed of the finger movement. The learning of the keys becomes an unconscious, or no-thought, process. Learning the golf swing is similar to Herrigel learning archery and the typist learning to type. Physical practice is essential.

To properly use imagery, you must use the proper style of imagery at the correct stage of learning. In skill learning, the learner goes through three stages of learning. The first stage is the concept, or basic knowledge, stage. At this stage, the beginner learns the basic requirements, the concepts, and an understanding of the skill. The second stage is the practice stage and is usually a long period of time. At this stage, the skill is perfected and refined. The third stage is the automatic stage, where the skill is performed automatically, as a learned reflex, with no thinking. The first two stages are conscious stages. The third stage is unconscious. Crossing over from the practice stage to the automatic stage is difficult because of the mental factor of letting go of conscious thought and trusting your swing completely. Like Herrigel and the typist, the golfer must let go of conscious thought and muscle control. The reflex occurs. The swing is allowed to happen. It is this trust in your swing that makes the automatic stage so difficult. Unfortunately, many golfers never completely reach the automatic stage. Herrigel and the typist practiced this cross-over stage of skill learning until the skill became automatic and consistent. Golfers must do a similar procedure to become successful. Time and practice are demanding.

The thinking process or imagery for these stages of learning must be as follows: At the concept stage, the first stage, the golfer simply pictures an overall image of the swing, not on parts of the swing, but on the full swing. Moving into the second stage, the golfer visualizes parts of the swing with the overall swing to develop an accurate swing pattern or reflex. Once the automatic stage is accomplished, the golfer uses target imagery by simply visualizing the target, and letting his learned reflex happen. Target imagery should not be used in the first two stages of learning, because the correct reflex pattern has not been established in these stages. In the automatic stage, the golfer does not tie up his swing with thoughts on mechanics and techniques. The mechanics and techniques are already established and will execute if desired. The golfer, while visualizing the target, is programming his body's nervous system for the correct swing. Once the motor program is established, the swing happens.

Notice how imagery is on mechanics for the first two stages of learning, but not on mechanics in the automatic stage. Imagery for the automatic stage is on the target. The mind, while focusing on the target, automatically programs the muscles for force, speed, distance, etc. Then the swing happens. This is the same procedure when tossing a coin to a corner. The coin tosser simply focuses on the target and lets the body execute. No analysis or thoughts on force, trajectory, body movements, etc. Focus on the target and execute. Trust it.

6
Neuro-Linguistic Programming (NLP) and Golf

Modeling is one of the basic structures of neuro-linguistic programming, or NLP. Modeling is where you model yourself after someone. You analyze someone successful and then try to imitate or model their successful characteristics. The intent is to create success instead of failure. After you analyze what is successful, you copy it. This is NLP.

Learning the Skill

Learning is done with images and metaphors. This is how kids learn a skill. Kids look at the skill, put it in their mind, and then execute to the picture or model in the mind. Metaphors are used through examples, similarities, parables, and stories that provide information and similarities to other experiences. Practice perfects the skill. Adults should learn like a kid. Kids keep it simple. Adults make it complex. To learn, study a model of the desired skill, then simply practice it. It may be considered a form of role-playing. Be an actor; play the part.

To learn, know exactly what you want to achieve—set a clear, specific goal. The goal is what you want and not what you don't want. A clear visualized goal becomes the target for the unconscious mind. Visualize every shot to your target (goal) and let your unconscious mind determine your force, direction, trajectory, etc. Do this by looking at your target, visualizing the target while looking at the ball, and swing at the ball with all your trust in your mind and body. As mentioned in earlier chapters, the goal is to advance your mind from conscious control to unconscious, or automatic, control.

Once you learn the skill, you must forget it and trust it to the unconscious for execution. It becomes "a stop-learning process" and turns into "a doing process." "Lock in" to your target with all your senses. Forget everything except the target. Obtain the empty mind, the Zen philosophy. Plan what is needed. Visualize the target. Recall a past successful similar shot and with your imagination.

Relive that past successful experience. See it. Feel it. Then do it. Let it take over your body.

By visualizing the target and shot, you have told the body what to do. These are your instructions. Further input may be detrimental. When you toss something to a wastebasket, you do not think of body mechanics or how hard to toss the object. Locking into the target does all this. The toss becomes successful. A jet fighter pilot locks into his target (the enemy) through the computer screen on his instrument panel and then pulls the trigger. Same as the golf swing. Lock into the target and swing. The body knows what to do.

In Zen philosophy, a skill is to be performed with the empty mind. The empty mind is the ideal state of concentration, as there are no mental, physical, or environmental distractions. The body performs unconsciously to an automatic rhythm. The mind and the body are "in the zone." When golfers get into slumps or poor performance periods, they often say, "I must get out of my own way." Similarly, the conscious mind must also get out of the way of the unconscious mind.

When the mind consciously controls the golf swing, the mind moves too slowly. The conscious mind has no speed. The unconscious mind is fast, really fast, and more than fast enough for skill execution.

NLP is designed to help you control your mind and your feeling. Emotions play a critical part in performance. Emotions can affect your thinking and skill execution for the good or the bad. Good emotions can help confidence. Bad emotions can destroy confidence. The mind must control the body and the emotions. Emotional control can be learned with NLP in the same way as a physical skill.

Anchors or triggers, whatever you prefer to call them, are learned when not playing golf, so that they can be used when playing golf. The basic NLP program is used when playing golf or when a desired emotional state is needed.

Anchors or Triggers

An anchor, or trigger, is something that triggers a certain response. A song may trigger the image of an old girl friend or boy friend. A snake or a mouse may trigger fear. Sand traps and water hazards are triggers of fear to many golfers. Unfortunately, most triggers/anchors are negative. Now if a sand trap can trigger fear then why can't a sand trap trigger confidence? Is it not a matter of perception? Well, it is perception and it can be positive. Pros do not fear the sand traps. They do not fear the sand traps because they have many successful past experiences to draw on. They have a positive perception of the situation. They know in their mind that they can play the shot. The poor players have few, if any, successful experiences in the sand. This means that, when faced with the sand shot, their mind recalls their past unsuccessful experiences. It is these unsuccessful experiences that hamper skill execution, as their body is being negatively tuned. This negative tuning (imagery) is sending the wrong messages to the muscles. With NLP, it is possible for the poor golfer to create successful imagery in the mind to help with his or her confidence (emotions) and skill execution. The basis of this skill is mentioned above in the basic NLP program.

There are visual, auditory (sound), and kinesthetic (feelings) anchors. You can develop a trigger to create a certain response. To develop a relaxation response, you could slap your thigh and then go into a relaxed response. Of course, this must be practiced. Practice slapping your thigh and then relaxing. Practice until the skill becomes natural and easy. Once learned, use it. Slap your thigh to trigger your body and mind into relaxing. Actually you can use any sight, feeling or sound for an anchor. You can create different anchors for different responses. Practice your anchor several times each day for several weeks if necessary. In time, the anchor will respond unconsciously. It will be automatic.

Anchors, or triggers, can be developed to create confidence. The procedure is similar. You must still see, hear, and feel your state of confidence. The image must be vivid and detailed. Anxiety, fear, and other emotions can all be controlled in the same way. The basic NLP program is as follows:

1. Recall the past situation when you were successful in a similar experience. If you do not have a similar experience make one up. When recalling past successful experiences, look up and to the left to help in the remembering process. If you cannot recall a successful experience, then makeup, or construct, one by looking up and to the right. When constructing the process, you must also see and feel this image as if it were real life. These eye movements will usually work for about 95% of the people. If your images are not too clear, then reverse the procedure. Left-handed people usually reverse their eye movements. If you have developed an anchor, or trigger, then you can use it here.

2. Put yourself into the state, or frame of mind and body, you experienced when you performed during the successful experience. This will involve all your senses—sights, sounds, and feelings. Achieve detail.

3. Focus on the above—no distractions, doubts, or uncertainties. The mind is clear, precise, and specific. Do not let worry creep into your thought process. Worry is negative rehearsal or negative imagery.

4. When focused—execute. The execution can be the swing or emotional control like anxiety, fear, confidence, etc.

Many pro golfers have set up anchors through self-talk. Prior to his swing, they tell themselves things like, "stay balanced," "back slow and low," etc. These statements can help you keep a single thought in the mind. The single thought is good, but not as good as the no-thought process, the "empty mind" process. Marlin M. Mackenzie, in his outstanding book *Golf, The Mind Game*, says:

> Strange as it seems, the epitome of concentration is paying attention to absolutely nothing. Some golf pros accidentally stumble onto this when they talk about a "no-brainer." For every golfer at every level, thinking about not thinking is close to impossible.
>
> We'll start by whittling golf thoughts down to one per shot—it isn't so hard to achieve as it might seem. The one thought—what I call a cue, or swing key—is the thing that helps trigger a rhythmic effort. The choice of the right cue is partly based, as you may have guessed, on the form of sensory information easiest for you to process—auditory, visual, or kinesthetic—while you're swinging. It is also based on what will work.

Things to keep in mind:

❐ If you performed the skill once, you can do it again, and again. It becomes repeatable.

❐ Telling yourself that you executed a similar shot successfully in the past, so you should be able to do it again, is usually not sufficient. You must recall the past successful experience and use the mind to see it, feel it, and hear it vividly.

❐ In tournament play or other serious play, do not let yourself do conscious thinking analysis. Become target oriented. Focus on the target. Swing to the target. Let the unconscious prevail.

❐ Be aware that pressure is what we create or place on ourselves. If you can put pressure on yourself, you should be able to take pressure off yourself.

Part III
All About the Golf Swing

7 Mechanics of the Golf Swing

The mechanics of the golf swing are simple and essential to skill learning. This chapter covers the entire complex physical factors involved in the golf swing, while subsequent chapters in this part of the book deal with the techniques involved.

Centrifugal Force, Center, and Radius

Attach a string to a ball. The length of the string will be the radius R. The radius can be shortened or lengthened by holding the string at different positions. The ball is B, and the center of the swing is C. If the ball is swung around in a circle, centrifugal force will keep the ball extended to its maximum length (Fig. 7-1).

If the radius R remains constant and the center C does not move then the ball or flight pattern of B will be consistently repeated along the same path or pattern.

Change the length of R, and the flight pattern of B will correspondingly change (Fig. 7-2).

Change or move the position of C, and the flight pattern of B will also move (Fig. 7-3).

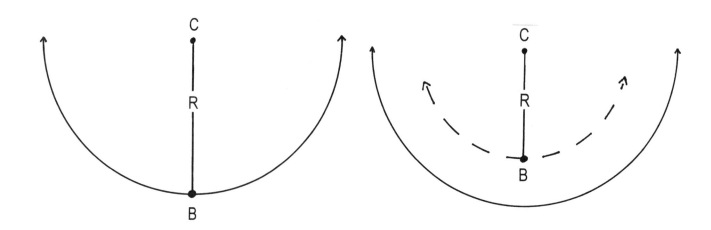

Fig. 7-1. The string analogy.

Fig. 7-2. Shortening the radius.

If X is an object you want to hit, then C and R must be positioned so that B can strike X accurately. If B is swung in its circular pattern, and C and R remain constant throughout the swing, then the object X can be struck squarely and accurately every time (Fig. 7-4).

Changing C and/or R during the swing will alter the swing arc and will result in the object being missed or struck poorly.

If C moves to C1 but R is constant, then the object X is missed or miss-hit (Fig. 7-5).

If C does not move but R is shortened to R1 then X is missed or miss-hit (Fig. 7-6).

The Golf Swing's Centrifugal Force: Center and Radius

The principles previously discussed apply to the golf swing (Fig. 7-7).

The stance, prior to hitting the ball, is to position the body to establish the center for the swing with the correct radius for contact with the golf ball. If the golf swing maintains a consistent center and radius, the golf ball will be accurately contacted (Fig. 7-8).

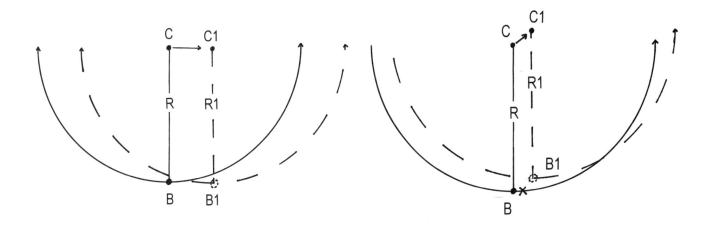

Fig. 7-3. Effect of shifting the center.

Fig. 7-5. Effect of shift of center to different plane.

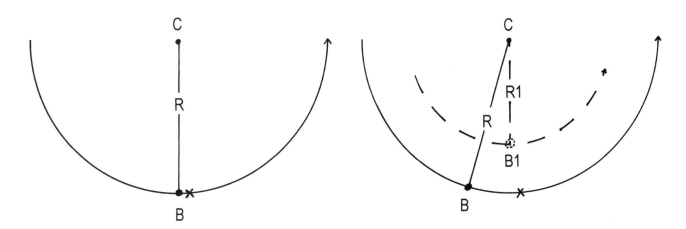

Fig. 7-4 Hitting from fixed location.

Fig. 7-6. Effect of shortened radius.

The 90-Degree Swing Angle

Let's go back and take our string with the ball attached. Hold the end of the string with the elbow pointing down and the hand pointing straight up. Now, slowly swing the ball in a circle and gradually swing the ball to maximum speed. Notice how the ball rises as the speed increases. When the ball reaches maximum speed, it will spin at a 90-degree angle to the center (axis). This is a natural action from the laws of physics in which an object spins fastest then it is moving at a 90-degree angle to its axis.

Applying this law to the golf swing means that the golfer, when swinging with maximum power, should have his arms moving at 90 degrees to the axis. The spinal column is the axis to the swing. When the golfer bends over and extends his arms to the ball for the stance, a 90-degree angle can be created. Some golfers may feel they are reaching more than usual, but this may be a perception from past experiences of holding the hands too close to the body. About a 40-degree body lean will achieve the 90-degree angle.

To feel this angle, take a golf club and grip it with both hands. Stand straight up, so that the spine is perpendicular to the floor or the ground. Extend your arms and the club straight out at 90 degrees to your body and spine. Now freeze your body and arms in this position and bend forward at the hips until the clubhead touches the ground. You are now in the basic position. You may feel comfortable with a few minor adjustments, but keep them minor.

In a *Golf Magazine* article by Tom Stickney II and Peter Morrice, the authors claim their research shows that "as the handicaps go up, the setups get worse—almost always following the same pattern. For instance, amateurs tend to stand too upright at address. The higher the handicap, the taller they stand." This means that the taller they stand, the farther they are to achieving the 90-degree angle for the golf swing.

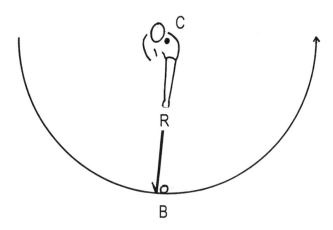

Fig. 7-7. The string analogy applied to the golf stance.

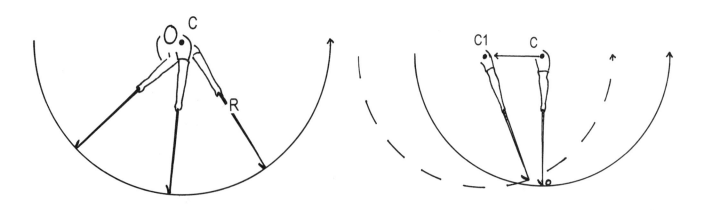

Fig. 7-8. Hitting the ball with the correct stance.

Fig. 7-9. Effect of shifting the center back.

Golf's Swing Problems: Center and Radius Changes

Problems in the golf swing occur when C and R change. Topping the ball, missing the ball, taking a divot before striking the ball are all caused by changing C and/or R. In diagram 7-9, C has shifted back, causing the club head path to change. As a result, the club head may hit the ground prior to the ball, top the ball, or even miss the ball. This action is usually caused by falling backward or pulling away from the shot.

In diagram 7-10, the golfer maintains the C position, however, R the radius of the swing is changed by bending the elbow.

Poor contact is usually the result of changing the swing's center or radius. Such changes are usually caused by:

1. Forcing the back shoulder (right shoulder for the right-handed golfer) to rotate into the downswing too early. This is often referred to as using too much right side or right hand/arm into the swing. This action forces the left shoulder and the corresponding swing's center out of its original position (Fig. 7-11).

2. The body weight not being on the front leg (left leg of right handed golfers) or the body weight falling backwards during the swing.

This is often the result of the golfer's reaction to overpowering the swing. This lack of balance fails to let the weight move onto the front leg for contact with the golf ball. Very often, the right side problem (item 1, above) coincides with this error. This error usually changes both the center and the radius of the swing. For every action there is an opposite and equal reaction. Swing forward or push forward and react by falling backward. Newton's third law.

3. Bending the elbow or the wrist to change the swing's radius. Often during the backswing, the golfer lets the elbow and/or wrist of the radius arm bend. This bending action changes the radius of the swing. If the player is unable to get the arm and/or the wrist straight again for contact with the ball, there is a radius change and a resulting miss-hit. This bending action is usually the result of the player's trying to overextend the backswing for the feeling of more power to the swing. Sometimes this error is referred to a wrapping the club around the neck.

Body Weight Placement

At contact, the body weight should be on the front leg. Some teachings stress shifting the weight back

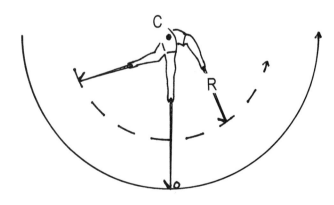

Fig. 7-10. Effect of shortened swing due to bent elbow.

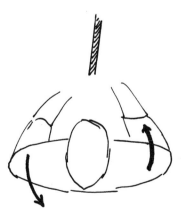

top view of golfer

Fig. 7-11. Effect of too much right side.

on the backswing and then forward on the downswing and follow-through. This weight shift action requires excellent timing and lots of practice. Excellent results have been achieved by not shifting the body weight but by simply putting the weight on the front leg while in the stance and keeping it there for the backswing, downswing, and follow-through. An excellent drill for this feeling of weight being forward on the front leg is detailed in chapter 3 (the stork stand).

Wrist Action

The wrist action in the golf swing is a result of the swinging action of the arms. The wrists must not be used or forced into the swing. Snapping or forcing the wrists to increase club head speed for greater power will actually result in a slowing of club head speed and an inconsistency in the flight of the ball. Snapping the wrists counters the timing effect of the swing. For consistent timing of the swing and accurate contact with the ball, simply swing the arms and hands and let the wrists flow with the swing.

Shoulder Rotation

Shoulder rotation is the key to power in the golf swing. The shoulder rotation moves the arms and helps govern arm speed. The faster the arms swing, the farther the ball goes. The lower body rotates little in comparison with the shoulders. Jim McLean showed this in his study of the X-factor. The greater the difference between the shoulder rotation and the hip rotation, the greater the power to the swing. The greater the difference, the more the muscles of the body are stretched. The more the stretch, the more the power.

Golf professionals practice daily and for many hours. They have good flexibility and are able to achieve excellent rotation while maintaining balance. The average golfer may have to shorten rotation to stay in balance and within his or her flexibility range. If you push beyond your flexibility you will loose balance, consistency, and power. It is important to stay within your limitations.

The Arm Roll

The arm roll is important to power and accuracy. It is not a wrist roll, because a wrist roll has a collapse of the wrists at or near contact. In the arm roll, the back of the front hand (left hand for right-handed golfers) maintains its flat or square position with the front forearm. To acquire the feel of how the arms roll, stand balanced with your feet slightly apart. Bend forward at the waist and let the arms hang fully extended. Clasp the hands together with the fingers interlocking each other and let the thumbs point straight out in front. Keep the head stationary and swing the arms back and forth to shoulder height or above. Notice on the backswing how the thumbs move from pointing straight out in front to pointing straight up into the air. On the downswing, the thumbs return to their original position of straight out in front at the contact position and straight up into the air on the follow-through. The follow-through is just the reverse of the backswing. This drill is not only important in learning to feel the arm roll and the correct wrist action, but it also gives the feel of the complete golf swing.

If the arms roll naturally, the clubface will be square to the ball at contact. When you try extra hard to keep the ball's flight straight to the target, you often steer the club in an attempt to keep the face square to the target. Unfortunately, this steering action rarely puts the face of the club in a square position. This same phenomenon occurs when a baseball pitcher starts to aim, or steer, the ball to the target or the catcher. This steering of the ball causes the pitcher to lose control and become wild. Pitchers often have to be told to just throw the ball and let the body flow. This same recommendation applies to the golfer's swing and flow.

The next stage of development is applying the mechanics to your body muscles for efficient skill execution.

Lever-Powered Golf

Jack Kuykendall developed this system from his knowledge of physics and biomechanics. This is a powerful, and yet easy, method. More can be learned at his web site (see Bibliography)

The Only Necessary Movement

There is only one necessary movement in the golf stroke. The movement of the right hand from just above shoulder high in the backstroke (start of downstroke) to just after impact (release or free rotation of the forearms through impact). The following section describes this only necessary motion (Figs. 7-12 through 7-14).

At the top of the stroke, the right shoulder and hip have rotated approximately 45 degrees. The right elbow will be around 5 to 8 inches away from the body and in line with the shoulder and hip. The right hand is fully flexed (back of the hand bent toward the back of the forearm). The white circle at the belt is the body's Center of Gravity (COG). The COG, at the top of the backstroke, is over the inside of the right leg. The

head is directly over the COG. The width of the stance is such that the insides of the feet are the width of the shoulders. This allows the COG to remain inside the feet and maintain optimum balance. The feet stay flat on the ground. Any movement of the feet reduces support and balance.

❑ Action: all forward motion is controlled by the right arm

❑ Reaction: and supported by the body.

Action:

The right hand moves backward and downward, which causes the clubhead to move backward and downward. The clubhead is well behind the body.

Reaction:

The body has lowered (knees flex and body seeks centering of the COG) and the COG has moved several inches forward to support the arm move-

Fig. 7-12. Top of the stroke

Fig. 7-13. Power turned on by forearm.

Fig. 7-14. Correct position at impact.

ment. The head is still over the right knee and behind the COG (Fig. 7-13)

At this point in the downstroke, the clubhead speed is about 40% of the impact clubhead speed.

Power Turned on by Forearm

This is when the right forearm produces the major power of the swing. The right forearm both rotates and extends the right hand. The correct application of forearm force at the exact correct time is what separates long hitters from short hitters.

It is also at this point that centripetal force or the flail action of a golf swing makes its

contributions to the swing. In a 100 mph swing, it will be around 20 mph or about 20% of the clubhead speed.

Impact

Action

To the maximum of its strength, the right forearm has rotated and extended the right hand.

Reaction

The head is over the right knee. Body center has moved slightly forward to support the action of the rotation and extension of the hand. The body is in optimum balance because both feet are flat on the ground (Fig. 7-14)

Action:

Approximately one foot past impact the right hand has rotated (released). The back of the hand is pointing away from the body. The right arm is extended and is as far away from the body as possible.

Reaction:

The head is still over the right knee—support for the arm. Body center is just slightly forward—support for the arm. Both feet are still flat on the ground—support for the arm.

8 Learning the Swing

If you go to a blackboard or a wall and draw a large circle with your hand, you can do this fairly efficiently. Drawing this circle is easy because you simply follow an imaginary line at your fingertips. The mind pictures a circle and the fingertips follow this circle while the body flows to the movement of the fingertips.

Making the Circle

Now try to draw this same circle whereby you tell your body how to move the hand. Draw the circle by positioning the shoulder so that the arm has a 60-degree bend at the elbow and the wrist has a slight cocking action. The palm and the elbow should be pointing downward. Draw the circle so that the hand is moved to the left by the elbow swinging from the downward-pointing position to pointing to the right. The wrist rotates slightly and the arm gradually extends as the circle pattern moves downward. As the circle moves downward, the wrist uncocks and the arm straightens. The elbow pointing slightly upwards must now rotate inward again as the hand comes to the bottom of the circle. At the bottom of the circle, the arm is fully extended, etc. By now you should have the idea: drawing a circle by this method is jerky and inaccurate. The hand does not move in a smooth pattern. Actually, you will find it difficult or impossible to draw the circle without seeing the circle in your mind.

Trying to draw a circle by analyzing each body movement is analogous to the way the golf swing is usually taught. We teach how to move the body and hope that this will give us our circular pattern or swing arc for striking the golf ball. *We teach from the wrong end.* You should develop the swing path through a picture in your mind and swing the clubhead along this swing path by letting your muscles adjust the club to this swing line. This is how you drew the circle. There are times you must teach the body movements to achieve the swing pattern, but you must not let it become your main emphasis.

If you study the various top professional golfers, you'll see each golfer perform with a different swing action. Despite the different swings, each golf pro is able to achieve excellent results. Quite often, a golfer is identifiable by his characteristic swing. Although the various golfers have different swings, they all have one similar characteristic to their swing. This similar characteristic is how they all meet the ball at contact with the clubface square to the target and the clubface going through the ball straight to the target. The clubface at contact is the same with all good golfers, even though their body mechanics are different. This is like drawing the circle. People drawing the circle, as earlier described, will look different in how their body moves, but all the circles will look similar.

Chevreul's Pendulum

An excellent example of how the mind controls your muscular movement is Chevreul's Pendulum. Chevreul's Pendulum is also used to prove the effectiveness of mental practice for muscular action or skill execution. Make a pendulum by tying a weighted object (ring, binder clip, etc.) to a string or a thread about 12 to 15 inches long. Holding the end of the string between your dominant hand's thumb and forefinger, sit in a chair and rest the dominant arm's elbow on a desk or table top so that the pendulum hangs straight down. Relax the body and visualize the pendulum swinging from side to side. Make no hand or finger movement just hold the string stationary. Make a vivid picture in your mind of the pendulum swinging side to side. In a few seconds, the pendulum will begin to swing as you had visualized, despite the lack of hand or finger movement. Change your focus to visualizing the front to back swing. In a short time the swing will be moving front to back. Practice changing your focus to circle patterns and various side to side angles. The better the visualization the more dramatic the pendulum action. The pendulum swings despite the lack of hand and finger movement.

What is amazing about this pendulum action is that no conscious movement of the hand is made. The hand is held stationary and yet the pendulum moves as if guided by the hand. Actually, the muscles required to move the pendulum were responding to directions from the brain, but at a subconscious level. Chevreul's Pendulum shows us that our muscles respond to our visualizations and it is important to understand that this is the basis of imagery or visualization practice. By visualizing the desired outcome, the muscles

and mind respond to execute this desired outcome even though the muscles do not make a noticeable action. The practice of imagery connects the mind and the body so that when the real situation occurs the mind and body is able to respond correctly and quickly.

The practice of imagery is like building a road from the mind to the muscles. In the beginning stages of skill learning, signals from the brain are confusing and uncertain as to where the road or path is to the muscles. In time, the signals learn the path or road and the road becomes a super highway. The super highway takes the signals from the brain to the muscles at a faster and more efficient path. The building of this mind-to-muscles super highway can be done with mental practice as well as physical practice.

Visualization

Efficient golfers are in the automatic stage of skill execution and do not swing by thinking about body movements or positions. They see the target, visualize how they want the ball to go and swing. The muscles react to the desired results. If a golfer wants a hook shot or a slice shot, he/she usually lets the muscles react to the desired shot. This is much the same as tossing a golf ball. Toss a golf ball about four yards, then toss the ball ten yards. Both tosses were executed efficiently and accurately. You looked at the target and tossed the ball with no thought as to length of backswing, arm or wrist action. Now toss the ball about four yards with a backspin action. Again, it was easy as no thought as to how much to roll the fingers or snap the wrist or length of backswing was needed. *You looked at the target and let your muscles react to the picture in your mind of the ball spinning and flying to the target.* This is what you must do with your golf swing. To achieve maximum golf swing results you must picture the desired outcome and trust your muscles to react as they did in the ball toss example. This trust of the muscles to execute the swing is often quite difficult, however, it is an essential requirement to good golf.

A young boy or girl learning to hit a golf ball learns through the trial and error method. He or she tries the swing, and if it doesn't work, tries again by correcting the errors. The young golfer does not know about wrist break, weight shift, etc. Such aspects are skills he or she develops through the trial and error process. A child not become paralyzed by analysis because youngsters do very little or no analysis. They just change the feel of the skill until performance improves. They simply hit the ball.

If the youngster wants to hit the ball to a target then he or she simply swings to the target. The child visualizes where the ball is to go and then swings to send the ball in the intended direction. The mind is concentrating or "seeing" where the ball is to go. The mind is free of extraneous thoughts and potential muscle commands. The body moves freely. I am sure you have noticed and marveled at how free and natural a child is able to execute and learn new golf skills. As adults we must learn our skills by resorting to childhood simplicity. This chapter outlines a system of learning through feel. The drills are designed to accomplish this. You must feel the swing, and practice each drill until the feel is thoroughly ingrained in your muscles. When the swing is ingrained in the muscles your golf swing can be accomplished through muscle memory.

Scrape-the-Grass Drill Without Golf Ball

Grip, stance, and alignment:

For the scraping the grass (or carpet) drill, use a 7 or 8 iron. Pick a spot on the grass or carpet to serve as an imaginary ball. With the right hand (for right hand golfers) holding the club at the bottom of the grip, place the sole of the club head flat on the ground and line up the face of the club in the direction of the target. With the club "frozen" in this position, the left hand will shake hands with the top of the golf club grip. The right hand will now slide up to also shake hands with the golf grip immediately below the left hand. The palm of the right hand forms a cup and the left

thumb lies in this cup. The two hands should be held close together and if desired the little finger of the bottom hand may override the pointer finger of the top hand, or it may interlock with this finger, or it may simply stay on the shaft of the club. Do whatever is comfortable.

Once the hands are positioned then move the feet to a natural and comfortable position without moving the club's position. Once the body is positioned, point the chin to where the golf ball would be, if the chin is not already pointing to this area. The importance of pointing the chin will be discussed later. Do not let the club move or shift out of position once it is lined up with the target. This technique sets up the grip, stance and alignment in one simple procedure. It must be practiced until it is automatic. The sequence again is as follows:

1. place sole of the club head flat on the ground/surface

2. square the club face to target

3. at the top of the grip, shake hands with the left hand

4. shake hands with the right hand on the grip

5. adjust the feet, and then

6. point the chin at the ball.

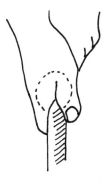

Fig. 8-1. Detail of the grip.

When griping the golf club the thumbs of both hands should ride along besides the pointer finger except near the end of the thumb area (Fig. 8-1).

By adjusting our body to the club, we are achieving direction through a feeling position. We feel and sense our direction. With practice, our muscles will sense direction and our alignment will become increasingly easier and more accurate. The importance of this stance and alignment cannot be overestimated. It is vital in the establishment for the center and the radius of the swing. If the center and the radius are not firmly and accurately established prior to the swing, then great difficulty and inconsistency will result in hitting the ball (Fig. 8-2).

The Basic Swing

Once the grip, stance, alignment, and chin positions are established, you are ready to swing the club. Using about a 20-inch backswing and a 20-inch follow through, swing the club back and forth. Without changing the swing center or the swing radius, let the sole of the club scrape the grass or the carpet forward and backward. Do not think of anything but scraping the grass or the carpet and staying balanced. While swinging the golf club, you must keep the chin pointing to where the golf ball would be. The chin points to this area throughout the basic swing from the top of the backswing to the top of the follow-through (Fig. 8-3).

As you swing the club to this pattern, visualize nothing more than the clubface being square to the target and scrapping the grass through to the target. Develop this picture in your mind as the club swings smoothly back and forth. The more accurate the picture, the more accurate the golf swing will become. If desired, try to visualize the sound of the club face striking the ball. Remember: squareness at contact.

This stage of the swing is vital, as it is the key to your full golf swing. What happens at contact will determine what happens to the ball. The golf swing is two inches in back of the ball and two inches in front of the ball. Accuracy in this four-inch area will result in a well executed golf shot for all clubs and putters.

After a few minutes of practice, tense the body and continue the short swing. Follow a few swings of tension with a few swings of relaxation. The reason for alternating tension and relaxation is to acquire the different feel of swinging under tension and swinging with relaxation. In time, you will be able to readily recognize the tension in your golf swing and be able to adjust to the

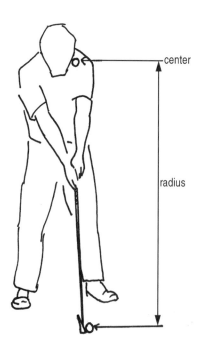

Fig. 8-2. Establishing center and radius of the swing.

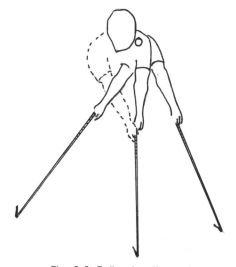

Fig. 8-3. Following the swing.

relaxed swing. The skill of recognizing tension is important during game play.

This short swing drill with visualization is developing the muscles to memorize the pattern of movement. Your muscles must remember the pattern, so that the muscles know what to do when called upon. Your objective should be to be able to visualize the clubface scraping the grass and letting your muscles execute the golf swing. This is like calling up a program in a computer and then clicking the mouse to execute the program. Muscle memory is the program and the mind is the mouse button.

Nonvisual Practice

Practice this drill and the drills to follow with your eyes shut. Closing your eyes will help you develop your feel for balance and the swing. When the eyes are open, you have a tendency to let your eyesight dominate your adjustments and body movements. By closing your eyes, you must use the kinesthetic sense for movement and body awareness.

The beginning stages of closed-eyes learning may feel strange, but a little practice will soon have you swinging correctly. The closed eyes will promote faster learning of the feel of the swing. Sometimes, alternating a visual swing with a closed-eyes swing will give you control of all your senses for efficient learning.

The Full Swing

As you become proficient in your short swing, you will slightly increase the length of your backswing and follow-through. Practice scraping the grass or the carpet with the longer backswing and follow-through. Once proficiency is reached at each stage, gradually increase the swing length again and again until the full swing stage is reached. Again, it is important to keep the chin pointing to the ball area even with the longer backswing and follow-through. A long follow-through will cause the chin to lift a little well after

contact. The chin must be pointing to the ball area immediately after contact so that the hands will swing past the body and be able to achieve maximum club head speed. At each swing length stage, practice the visualization, the tensing and relaxing of the muscles. Also, be sure to practice the full swing with your eyes shut.

Hubbard and Seng (1954), in research with baseball batters, found that the major league batters were more consistent in their stance and moved their head less than college batters. In fact, the major league batters only moved their head one degree. This is why in golf we teach head still to help keep the center of the swing in place and to develop a consistent stance prior to hitting the ball.

The Backswing

As you move into the longer backswing, you must be careful not to bend your radius arm's elbow. Such a mistake will alter the radius of the swing. You must swing back only as far as your straight arm will permit. Longer backswings are achieved by rotating the shoulders and not by bending the elbow. Some golfers let the radius elbow bend near the top of the backswing. This is satisfactory if you get the arm straight for ball contact. Also, it is vital not to let your head sway, as such a sway will alter your swing's center. The swing must remain within the flexibility of your body.

The Weight Shift

As the golf swing increases in length, a weight shift may occur to a natural rhythm of the swing. On the backswing, the weight will shift back, and on the downswing, the weight will shift forward. The head should not shift or sway, because the stationary head helps prevent the body from swaying on the weight shift as well as helping to maintain the center of the swing. Pointing the chin to the ball also helps prevent this sway. If the body is relaxed, then the weight shift is natural. If the body is tense, the correct weight shift may not occur.

The Arm-and-Hand Roll

The arm-and-hand roll is also a natural movement. In the backswing, the arms and hands roll in a manner such that at the top of the backswing, the back of the radius hand (left hand for right-hand golfers) will be pointing ninety degrees (right angle) from the line of flight. As the downswing progresses, the back of the radius hand becomes more in line with the target. At contact, the back of the radius hand is in line with the target. After contact, the hands and arms continue to roll. The arms and hands must roll, so do not attempt to fight this reaction (Fig. 8-4). It is natural.

A good drill to help acquire the feel for the arm roll is to stand a few inches from a wall. Lean forward at the waist and let the head rest against the wall. With both arms hanging, clasp the hands together by interlocking the fingers. Now swing the arms back and forth and notice how easy it is if you let the arms and hands roll with the swinging action. Also, along with the arm roll, you will experience the body movement of the golf swing. As you perform this drill, focus on the "feel" of the overall swing and the important positions of the top of the backswing, contact, and top of the

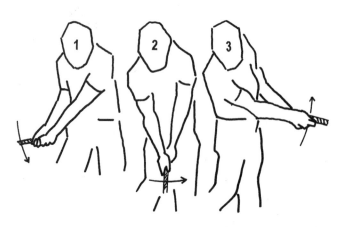

Fig. 8-4. Rolling arms and hands through the swing.

Scrape-the-Grass Drill With a Golf Ball

When you become proficient in the scrape-the-grass drill, you are ready to hit a real golf ball by repeating the previous drills with a golf ball. Visualization, tension, and relaxation practice must also be continued. When using the golf ball, it is important to remember that you are not hitting the golf ball: *You are scraping the grass under the golf ball toward the target.* When hitting the ball, the chin should be pointing at the ball. Contacting the ball is a result of scraping the grass under the ball. The ball is just in the way of the swing. This seems simple, yet it is extremely difficult to strike the ball without thinking or becoming obsessed with the ball. You must focus on scraping the grass and not on hitting the ball.

Be sure to practice this drill with your eyes shut. After a few shots, you will find, and you may even be surprised, that you are hitting the ball far and straight with your eyes shut.

When things are not going right, then go back to the very short swing of scraping the grass with no ball. Gradually work back up to the stage of scraping the grass with a ball.

Ball Placement

Ball placement will vary from individual to individual. Ball placement is determined by the center of the swing. The center of the golf swing establishes where the low part of the swing arc will scrape the grass. It is at this low part of the swing that the ball should be placed. This low part will vary from individual to individual because of the different stances and swings of the golfers. To say that all golfers must play the five irons from the middle of the stance would be incorrect.

Although many teachings say the ball must be played in this and only this position, it is easily refuted by the fact that the pros play the ball in varying positions. Some play all shots off the front heel. Some play all shots two inches off the front heel. Some play the woods off the front heel and progressively vary the ball positions back to the wedge off the middle of the stance. Some progressively vary the ball position from the front foot with the woods to the wedge off the back foot. The ball is placed according to the individual's swing, and this is determined by trial and error.

The placement of the ball is determined by how the golfer moves into the ball for contact. Some golfers slide forward, more than others, by a more pronounced weight shift. It is this distribution of the body weight at contact that determines where the ball is placed. The more the weight is to the left leg at contact, the more the ball is usually placed forward in the stance. For example, golfers who hit their wedge with most of their weight on the right leg at contact will play the ball well back in their stance. You'll have to experiment with each club to determine which method of ball placement works best. This is usually a simple procedure that takes very little time.

Swing Problems and Failures

One of the most common causes for the failure of the golf swing is the changing of the center of the swing at the front shoulder. Go to a driving range and position yourself at the end of the line so that you are looking down the line at front of the golfers. Most golfers are right-handed, so this is quite easy. Notice how all the ineffective golfers change the center of their swing as their front shoulder pulls away from the shot. The failure of the front shoulder to remain over the ball or pointing at the ball at contact is caused by a loss of balance, a falling away from the shot or lack of an arm roll.

The third law of motion—a swinging action forward and a reaction backward—causes falling away from the shot. The harder you swing forward, the greater the reaction to fall backward. If you fail to roll the arms during the swing, the right arm moving forward will push the left arm up and force the left shoulder (right-handed

player) out of position. This failure to roll the arms often causes the backward fall.

Pointing the chin at the ball, and keeping it pointed throughout the swing, will help keep the front shoulder over the ball at contact. The pointed chin will also help prevent body sway, as well as assist the body in moving the weight onto the front leg during contact with the ball.

Another common problem is that golfers fail to let the arms rotate on the backswing. Usually, this causes the front hand (left hand for a right-handed golfer) to be under the club rather than the hand having the thumbs pointing straight up and the back of the hand pointing at right angles to the flight path. This under-the-club hand position gives a weak swing, as well as shortening and constricting the backswing.

The One-Leg Stork Stand Drill

One of the best drills for learning or feeling body rotation is to balance on one leg with the ball positioned at right angles to the front foot. The back leg is bent and only the toe is placed on the ground, just to the side and slightly behind the front foot's heel. By swinging in this position, the body must rotate and not sway. The term weight shift is a little confusing, as many think the weight shifts back by swaying back with the backswing and then shifting or swaying forward with the downswing. Actually, on the weight shift, the weight goes to the back leg, but the body does not sway back.

This one-leg stork stand drill is so amazing in that it only takes a few swings to learn to maintain balance and strike the ball cleanly. Most golfers hit the ball as far and more accurately this way then they do when standing on both legs. This drill will convince you that the arm's swing and the body follows. You do not hit with the body, you hit with the hands swinging and with the body following the action of the hands. Also, it shows that it is the rotation of the body, and not the weight shift, that determines distance and accuracy. Golfers who execute this drill find that their shots go far and straight. Amazingly straight.

The String Drill

The string drill and the stork stand drill are both excellent drills to acquire the feel of the golf swing. The string drill develops the correct take-away and backswing for the golf swing. It emphasizes the arm extension from the top of the backswing to the top of the follow-through.

Tape one end of a string about 20 inches long to the end of the golf grip and tie the other end of the string to a paper clamp. The end tied to the paper clamp is tied so that the string can be adjusted to different lengths if needed (Fig. 8-5). It is also possible to stick a tee into the end of the grip and tie the string to this tee.

Refer to diagram 8-6. Take your stance for the full swing and then clamp the paper clamp to your shirt at the breastbone of the chest. Adjust the string so that the string will be fairly tight or straight while in the address position. When executing the correct golf swing, the distance from the end of the golf club grip to the breast bone of the chest must remains the same from the stance position to the top of the backswing, down and through the contact area and on to the top of the follow-through. In order to achieve this distance factor you must swing with arms extended and with good shoulder rotation. In making the swing for this drill, you must do the following:

1. Swing the arms back so that the string remains straight and in the center between the two arms. To accomplish this, you must swing both arms together and rotate the shoulders. If the shoulders do not rotate, then the radius arm will hit the string.

2. The string must remain straight and between the two arms until about waist-high level when the string begins to move to the radius arm until the top of the backswing.

3. On the downswing, the string remains straight and will almost repeat itself to the pattern it took on the backswing. Both arms continue to swing through the ball with extension to keep the string straight and between the arms to about waist high on the follow-through when the string will move towards the non-radius arm.

Do not become quickly discouraged with this drill as the shots may be erratic. Often, you'll become so focused on the string that you forget to swing the club. You may find it helpful to have a friend watch the string to give you feedback as to what is happening. Be patient: this drill is powerful in swing development, as it not only helps in proper execution but it is also tremendous in developing power to the swing and straightness to the shot.

Putting

The four-inch swing applies to putting. Once again, it does not matter what stance the golfer takes to putt. The putt will be determined by the squareness of the blade to the target. Golfers assume various stances, and sometimes strange contortions with the belief that by standing in such a position the putter will be square at contact and the blade will move accurately to the target. Accuracy is determined by the mind visualizing the squareness and direction while the hands and arms move the putter to the target. This can be easily proven by taking various stances and foot placements and putting the ball to the target

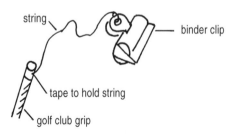

string
binder clip
tape to hold string
golf club grip

Fig. 8-5. The string drill.

through the action of the mind, with the hands moving the club in the direction of the target. Besides, common sense should tell you the putter blade movement will determine the direction of the putt and not the stance. Despite the stance, there are a few basic keys that apply. They are:

1. The eyes should be directly over the ball.

2. When lining the putt prior to contact, the head should rotate, without lifting or dropping, so that the eyes move along the direction of target line.

3. Maintain perfect balance throughout the stroke.

4. Be as comfortable as possible.

5. Do not let the head or the upper body move prior to contact.

Practice is essential to develop a feel for distance. Learning how hard to hit a putt is essential to good golf. Three putting is usually hitting the ball too hard or too soft. A good method to learn the feel of distance is to practice rolling a golf ball to the hole or the target with the hands and the body moving similar to rolling a bowling ball. When

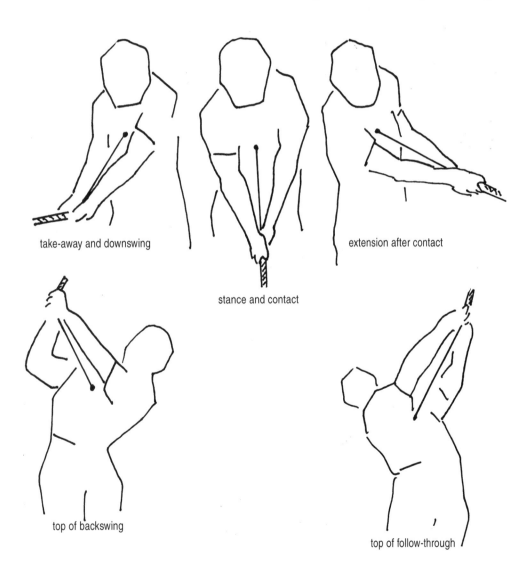

take-away and downswing

stance and contact

extension after contact

top of backswing

top of follow-through

Fig. 8-6. Stages of the golf swing represented by the string drill.

you get the feel of how hard to roll the ball, then practice the golf putt by using the same arm force as you used when rolling the ball. The length of the backswing in rolling the ball with the hand is similar to the length of the backswing in putting the ball with the putter. Rolling the ball with the eyes shut can enhance the skill of developing touch. As mentioned before, having the eyes shut helps increase the feel or kinesthetic sense. Putting with the eyes shut also develops a feel for the skill.

The putting stroke can be either a pendulum or a piston. In either stroke, the left wrist is not to break down, it must stay firm throughout the stroke. The hands and the arms can then move in a pendulum action. In the piston action, the firm left wrist is pushed to the target by the right hand's palm. The right palm is lined flat to the target, then wrapped around the grip, and then pulled back and pushed forward to the target. In either method, the right palm is very important because it has many nerve endings for direction and control.

Subconscious Putting

Putting is also a subconscious action. It is recommended that you look at the hole to register terrain and distance and then let the subconscious react. Stand behind the ball to study the terrain and the distance. This is the analysis stage. As you move into position to stroke the ball, your body goes into the feel mode—you feel the shot. Now look at the hole for two seconds to register a good distance in the mind. Then look at the ball and stroke the ball within 5 to 8 seconds. Wait longer than eight seconds, and you'll lose the feel and distance. Also, repeated looks at the hole often adds confusion and uncertainty as to distance to the hole, because the second and third looks may not agree with the first look. Putters who glance at the hole lose the distance feel quickly so they have to repeat looking at the hole to determine the distance. Give the hole just one good look.

One of the biggest problems in putting is to let the putterhead decelerate at contact. One method

of help to cure this problem is to look at a spot a few inches in front of the ball and stroke the putter past and through the ball to the spot.

When putting, the squareness of the putter face is more important than the direction of the stroke. It is possible to swing the putter off line but still make the ball go straight ahead to the target, providing that the face is square to the target. The reason for this is that the stroke is so soft, there is no friction on the putter face. Without friction, the ball goes where the face is aligned.

When the first putt goes long, the next putt is usually short. The reverse of this also happens. The problem here is that one putt is used to reference the next putt. When the first putt is long, the golfer's mind says "don't hit the ball so hard," so the next putt is hit easier and goes short. This is what happens when you let your conscious mind override your subconscious. You are analyzing when you should be feeling the shot subconsciously. When you go long, short, or whatever, on the first putt, you should start your routine again without the reference of the last putt. If the first putt is long because you were surprised by a fast green, then the green speed goes into your pre-putt analysis and then you still execute to the subconscious.

Lining up the Putt

An interesting aspect of lining up putts is to take a tape measure about 10 or 12 feet long and then standing in line with a distance object line up the tape to the distance object while you are facing the distant object. When the tape is lined up, you should be able to stand behind the tape, look down the line of the tape in a straight line to the distant object. Now go to the side of the tape and take a putting posture. Rotate your head and look down the tape to the distant object and see if the tape is still in line to the object. With most people the tape will line up a little to the left. As you can see, this is not too encouraging to line up putts. Get the feel for this aspect and you may be able to make adjustments to your line up of putts.

SP Golf Company has come out with the Bald Eagle golf ball, which has six symmetrically placed smooth or "bald" spots among the dimples. When the logo is lined up to the hole or putting target, the putter face will contact the bald spot for accurate contact. Sometimes the edges or rims of a dimple catch the putter face and the ball deviates from its intended direction. Dave Pelz, in his book the *Dave Pelz's Putting Bible*, also states this problem of inconsistency to putting contact. The Bald Eagle golf ball comes in three styles: the Tour Balata (three-piece), Tour Spin (two-piece with a soft cover) and the Distance (two-piece).

Some balls are difficult to line up by using the logo; in that case, draw a thin line with a permanent marker. This can be helpful as the ball's line is placed in line with the target and then the putter is aligned square to the line and then stroked.

The advantages of this line became very evident when the authors did the following experiment: Take a measuring tape, a rope about 15 to 20 feet long, and line it up to a distant object by standing behind the tape facing the object. When it is accurately aligned, move to the side of the tape as if putting and look down the line at the tape and where it is pointing to. Most people will find that the tape now looks aligned to the left of the hole, some to the right and very few are straight in line. The reason for this alteration is that when lining up the tape, you are using binocular vision as the eyes are level to the ground. In the putting position, the eyes are vertical and parallel to the line. This putting position often gives a miss-read.

Putting Distance

Putting distance can be helped by using backswing length to determine distance. The short game chapter gives an explanation as to how speed is determined by the backswing length. Go to a flat spot on a green and experiment. Take a yard stick or a measuring tape, and practice the different length backswings. Place tees in the green every two yards or so and then see what

kind of distance you get with the different backswing lengths. The authors have found that the best way is to use paces as a measurement, as it is so easy to pace the distance. The authors have found one inch backswing for every pace of distance. One pace is about 2½ feet. Rhythm and pace of swing will vary with individuals, so each individual may have different distances for every inch of backswing. The easy way to measure your back swing is to measure the face of your putter. Most are four inches. Some are five or six inches. If you need an eight-inch backswing, then it is two four-inch putter faces. Then if you want, place your back foot in line with this eight-inch mark and then use the back foot as a reference mark for your backswing length.

Chipping

Chipping is rolling the ball to the hole when the ball is very close to the green. This shot is executed exactly like a putt, with the same amount of force as if a putt is being performed. This shot is played with a putter, 3, 4, 5, 6, or 7 iron, so that the ball will fly low and land with little or no backspin and roll like a putt. Balls on the fringe can be stroked with a putter and rolled to the pin. Some golfers like to use a 3, 4, or 5 iron from this position for a low flight with good roll. When the ball is off the fringe and a little farther from the edge of the green, a 5, 6, or 7 iron is used to fly the ball over the grass to land on the green and roll to the cup much like a putt

As for putting, practice tossing the ball to the pin with the hand to get the feel of distance. Again, practice with the eyes shut. Some golfers and even pros, are using 3, 4,and 5 woods to chip. The wood gets under the ball as the flat sole slides along the ground and not into the ground. Some golfers like to use a higher lofted club to chip, but remember, with such a soft shot, the ball may take backspin or it may not take backspin. This uncertainty of backspin makes it difficult to control distance, as the ball may go short or long, depending on the action of the backspin.

Pitching

The pitch shot is striking the ball with a lofted club, 8, 9, or wedge, so that the ball flies high to the green with backspin for little rolling action. The shot is performed the same way as the full-swing shot, except that the length of the backswing will determine the distance of the shot. The length of the backswing to determine distance is important in preventing the golfer from taking a long backswing and then slowing down the swing in the contact area. It is this slowing-down action that gives inconsistency to the shot and miss-hitting of the ball.

Once again, it is essential that you *scrape the grass under the ball to the target* to achieve accuracy in putting, chipping and pitching. This fact cannot be overemphasized.

The Fade, Slice, Draw, and Hook

Fading and drawing the ball is easy once your swing becomes fairly consistent. To fade the ball (a slight slice), take your stance, but open the club face a little and then swing the club in your regular pattern. To hit a draw (a slight hook), take your stance but close the club face a little and proceed with your normal swing. By opening or closing the club face, the golf ball is struck so that a spinning action is imparted to the golf ball. The more the club face is opened or closed, the greater the spin action on the ball. With increased spin action ,the fade becomes a slice and the draw becomes a hook.

Learning the Skills

Your natural objective is to learn golf skills. You can learn the golf skills, but it will take some effort on your part. Practice is important. The skills must be practiced not only physically, but also mentally. Learning golf skills, or any skill for that matter, requires a mind-set. The mind must work with the body to ingrain the skill into the body, so

that the skill can be executed spontaneously, accurately, and effortlessly.

When learning a motor skill, an individual goes through three stages. The first stage is the concept stage. During this stage, you try to get a concept or an understanding for the skill. A gross pattern of the skill is studied. When the overall concept of the skill is understood, you move into the second stage of practice and error correction. The skill is practiced and the errors of execution are corrected until the skill is correctly executed. Once the skill is accurately performed, you go into the third stage whereby the skill is performed automatically. In the automatic stage of learning you perform the golf swing automatically with no conscious thought of mechanics or how to hit the ball. The golf swing has become pre-programmed into the body.

In the concept stage of learning, you focus on the overall pattern of the golf swing. Detail is not important until the second stage. The target and direction are not important, as you are focusing on only the overall swing pattern.

As an understanding of the swing and basis of the game develops, you move into the second stage of practice and error correction. While still working on the whole swing, you will break the swing down into parts and practice the parts for error correction. If the right elbow flies too high then you should focus on the correct elbow movement and with repeated practice, you will try to acquire the feel for the correct movement. Once you feel that correct elbow movement is achieved, the elbow movement is put into the whole overall swing. In this stage of learning, it is important to mentally focus on the body movement (e.g. flying elbow) until it can be performed correctly through conscious thought. Conscious thought is when you about the body movements.

As skill improves consciously, you must make a critical adjustment. You must now move into the automatic stage by focusing on the target and not the body movements, or mechanics. The body is in "muscle memory" that was built into the muscles through the practice stage. The skill was practiced until the muscles learned the move or the feel of the skill. In the automatic stage, the feel of the skill now executes the swing, as the muscles have no reliance on the mind or conscious thoughts for input. Expert golfers, like the pro tour players, swing with no thought of body mechanics. These golfers look at the target and let the muscles react towards the target objective.

It is important to remember that, while in the automatic stage, you must trust his muscles to respond correctly. The muscles will respond correctly if you practiced and trained the muscles correctly. The big problem, and it happens even at the pro level, is that as pressure mounts and you want to try extra hard, the mind starts to think about body movements in the attempt to make sure the golf swing is performed correctly. It is this very attempt at thinking of body mechanics that takes the body out of the automatic mode and sends confused signals to the muscles. When the body is in automatic mode and the mind starts thinking about how to execute the swing, a performance breakdown occurs. The breakdown is a result of the mind sending signals to the muscles on how to do the swing when the muscles are already pre-programmed on how to do it. These additional signals sent to pre-programmed muscles confuse the muscle in its interpretation of the signals. Confused muscles mean a confused golf swing. The doubting mind has never hit a good shot.

Another reason for the performance breakdown is that when you are in the automatic mode and start to think about body positions and how to swing the club, the mind has changed focus from the target to body position. It must be remembered that when in the automatic mode, you must focus on the target and not on the body.

While you are taking golf lessons, develop a complete understanding of what the instructor is telling you. Then practice the skill and practice parts of the skill until you feel proficiency for the skill. Focus on your body movements. As proficiency develops, change your focus to the target and execute the skill automatically. If you are unsuccessful in automatic execution, go back to focusing on correct body movement to reprogram your muscle memory. As your muscle memory get stronger, retry your automatic swing. This

procedure may have to be repeated several times and over a period of time. The time span will vary from individual to individual.

Correct practice is important. Your instructor can help you with this phase. Your instructor can do the mechanical with you and get you into the correct basics. Your instructor can give you the drills and knowledge of the game. Unfortunately, your instructor cannot give you feel and focus. This you must do through your own mental practice. Practice what your instructor tells you, but be sure to acquire a feel for your movements. Develop you focus and mind control to your stage of learning.

Perhaps the most difficult part of learning golf is to take your learning from the practice range and apply it while playing on a golf course. Your instructor can help you learn the skills, but on the course you are on your own. When on the golf course, you must play in the automatic mode with a target focus. As explained earlier, do not go into a body focus. You play in the automatic mode and you focus on the target. If this is unsuccessful, then it is back to the practice range to work on re-building and strengthening your muscle memory.

On the golf course, you will meet many distractions that will force you into focus problems. The first tee with strangers and friends watching you, may well be the toughest shot all day. Water hazards, trying too hard, trees, opponents, etc. are all distractions to your automatic mode. Coping with these distractions takes time, practice, and lots of frustrations. Don't give up: it does get better.

Keep it Simple

Research based on modern technology, including high-speed photography and video taping, has produced a wealth of technical information on skill technique and skill execution. This information is valuable; however, we must not over-use this information and fall into the over-coaching syndrome. We must glean this technical information and learn it in a simple, organized and logical manner. Many coaches, teachers, and instructors are so technique-oriented that they prevent the athlete from developing a natural feel for the skill. Some coaches confuse the athlete's mind with too many technical facts. This stimulus overload of information confuses the mind and prevents a strong focus of attention.

While putting, a golfer may have a distance problem. Such a golfer may be concentrating so hard on body movements, that the objective of sinking the ball becomes secondary. Over-coaching causes the putter to focus on body movements rather than on the objective of sinking the ball. I am not advocating the elimination of correct body techniques. Correct execution is desirable, but it must not lay the seed of confusion in the mind of the golfer. You have to acquire your own feel for the skill. Feel cannot be taught, but an instructor can help a student learn how to acquire feel. Maybe if Miller Barber had a coach or teacher who felt there was only one way to hit a golf ball, then Miller Barber may never have acquired the touch and skill he has despite his unusual golf swing.

Learn Like a Kid

When learning a skill, kids are on a trial and error process. They try, and if it doesn't work they try again. Very little coaching is involved or needed. The kid attacks skill learning with wild abandon and enjoyment. They "fool around" with different ways to perform a skill like throwing or hitting a ball. They experiment. As they fool around and experiment, they learn a feel for the skill—a feel of control, balance, and body manipulations that fits each individual's musculature and bone structure. A child does not become paralyzed by analysis. If he or she wants the ball to go to the target, then they simply swing to the target. The child simply visualizes where the ball is to go and then swings to put the ball at the target. The child's mind simply sees where the ball is to go, and the body responds freely and naturally.

Adults, when learning skills, become victims of paralysis by analysis. They think there is only

one way to perform a skill, and they try so hard to emulate this presumed correct skill movement that they do not let their natural movements and feelings come into play. As a result, when attempting a skill, the adult's body moves in a jerky and uncertain manner that lacks flowing movement. Adults emulating a skill often focus on body movements. Trying to focus on too many movements cloud the mind and creates mind confusion. The confused mind sends confused and uncertain impulses to the muscles, and it is only natural that the muscles will respond in a confused and uncertain manner.

As adults, we must learn our skills like a kid. We must focus on feel. The mind must be clear with a simple single focus. Often, adults become so serious that they forget to have fun and enjoy the learning process. Fun and enjoyment help you cope with the frustrations of learning. Be a kid: have fun, experiment, and freewheel your movements.

Let the season be fun. Play the game quickly. Don't out-think or over-analyze yourself. Step up to the ball with a clear mind, and swing the club. Enjoy the game, so you can control the game. Have fun.

Be Natural

Brad Faxon had an illustrious career as an amateur golfer. He was labeled for professional stardom. After qualifying for the pro tour, his success was not imminent. With the hard times, he took the route of so many struggling pros by placing blame on his swing. Practicing new techniques and mechanics was not enough to bring him to stardom. Finally, after years of frustration, his game began to improve.

Faxon's playing improvement was the result of a mental attitude change. He revealed this on CBS television (April 22, 1989) during the Greater Greensboro Open. Brad made two statements that apply to athletes and coaches of all sports. He attributed his recent success on the pro tour to the fact that he made the decision, "I just got to go back to being natural." With this decision, his practice and playing began to focus on results and objectives, not on body mechanics. His body was now allowed to move naturally to his feelings and rhythm.

When the interviewer asked Brad if he had any advice for future young golfers, Brad replied, "Trust yourself—it's simple but it works." This statement is vital to any golfer come tournament time. You must learn to trust your body once you have achieved proficiency in your skills. Trusting your body to perform a skill is much more difficult than you may think. So many times, you will focus on your fears instead of the target or results. Trusting your body is a mental process that in time can be accomplished through regular mental practice.

In golf, a swing alteration will affect the timing of the swing as well as the your rhythm and tempo. When making a skill alteration, you must be sure the alteration will fit your rhythm. Some golfers have taken years to adjust to swing changes. Some have never recovered. What would happen if the golfer had taken this time to work on their natural swing. Gary Player stated that he has seen so many successful variations and oddities to the golf swing, that he no longer knows what's a good swing. Remember, sometimes changes must be made—just be sure they are really needed.

Playing Outside Your Own Rhythm

Sandy Lyle won the 1988 Masters golf tournament. At the Masters in 1989, he failed to make the cut. Physically, he was in good health and ready for the tournament. Certainly, his game didn't deteriorate that much over a year. Obviously, his problem was mental, and he even stated this in his television interview on Sunday, April 9 (CBS).

What was intriguing about the interview was how he stated his problem. He claimed he was "playing outside his own rhythm." A simple statement that so well covers the problem of pressing or trying too hard. Sandy Lyle tried so hard to repeat his last year success, that he over-extended himself. He forced his shots. He over-analyzed. He thought too much at the wrong time. His expectations may well have been out of line. This problem is common among golfers. In fact, the golfers on the pro tour now call this problem, "getting out of your own way."

A golfer has his own rhythm. It is his pace for the game. It is his way of doing things. It is this rhythm, or tempo, that maintains skill proficiency. A loss of rhythm is a loss on skill proficiency. When warming up for a tournament or a match, you should focus on your rhythm, tempo, and pace. It is too late to learn how to hit the ball; yet, this is what many golfers do before the event. The warm-up is for establishing the focus on rhythm and tempo. Feel the pace. Flow with the game. *Play within your own rhythm.*

9
The Twin Pendulum

The golf swing is often compared to a swinging pendulum. Ernest Jones started this trend in his book *Swing the Clubhead*. The philosophy has merit, even though it may be an oversimplification. Jones claims that the clubhead should be swung like a pendulum. We all know what a pendulum is and how it swings, so we just swing the clubhead like a pendulum. This action is a single pendulum.

The Pendulum Analogy

It is our belief that the Ernest Jones Pendulum is not a single pendulum but a double, or twin, pendulum. The golf swing is a twin pendulum because of the two arms and two shoulders giving the pendulum two centers. The left arm (for right hand golfers) and the golf club form a single pendulum if you do not put the right hand on the golf club. Unfortunately, this one-arm swing lacks power. With both hands on the club, you now have maximum potential power, but you have lost the single pendulum effect. You now have what we call the twin pendulum, in which the left arm is a single pendulum during the backswing and downswing, and the right arm is a single pendulum at impact and the follow-through.

As the swing moves down to the ball, the right arm, which is bent on the downswing, begins to straighten with the left arm to impact. At impact, both arms are straight. After impact, the left arm begins to collapse and the right arm straightens to

become the new pendulum arm. As you can see, the right and left shoulders give the golf swing two centers to the pendulum.

The following diagrams and demonstrations will explain this twin pendulum swing effect. The diagrams are understandable, but if you make your own pendulum, the visual effect is more dramatic and will make an indelible impression on your mind.

The Single Pendulum

Take a string about 2 or 3 feet long, and attach a weight to the end. A small nail tapped into a golf ball makes an easy attachment for the string. Hold the string about 18 inches above the weight. Mark the mid-point of the string with a black mark. Color the top half of the string red and the bottom half blue. The black mark represents the hands, while the red string represents the left arm and the blue string represents the golf club shaft. The weight at the end of the string represents the clubhead.

Hold the top end of the string and swing the weight in a pendulum fashion. You now have the pendulum swing (Fig. 9-1). Notice the smoothness and timing of the string and the weight. It is automatic. Notice how the string leads the weight to the bottom of the swing arc. At the bottom of the swing, the weight catches up with the string to form a straight line. As the weight swings past the bottom of the arc, the weight continues to speed past the blue string and the slower red string. Notice how the red string, or left arm, swings slower than the blue string and the weight. This is necessary for proper timing.

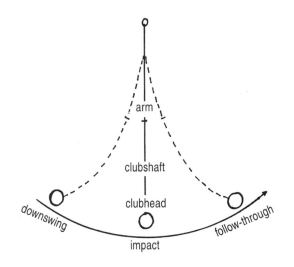

Fig. 9-1, The pendulum swing.

It is this timing that lets the weight or clubhead catch up to the arm and shaft at impact. When the weight catches up to the red string, or left arm, the weight, or clubhead, continues its speeding action past the shaft and the left arm. You will readily notice how the red string and the black mark move less distance and slower than the clubhead. This is a natural law of physics. Not letting the clubhead catch up to the hands and the left arm is a common problem.

Too often, golfers force for power and distance, and steer the club for accuracy. The golfer forces the arms and hands past the impact zone at a speed too fast for the clubhead to catch up to the hands. This action gives the you the feeling of power, but unfortunately the power is staying in the your body and is not being transferred into the clubhead. Let the swing happen. Let the energy transfer out of the body to the club by letting the motion take care of itself. Let the pendulum swing—do not force the pendulum.

Now place a finger at the black mark, the hands area, and try to speed up the swing by moving the finger faster than the swing of the pendulum. Notice how, if you move the finger too fast, the weight, or clubhead, does not catch up to the finger at the bottom of the swing. This same action happens during the golf swing when you move your hands too fast through the impact area (Fig. 9-2).

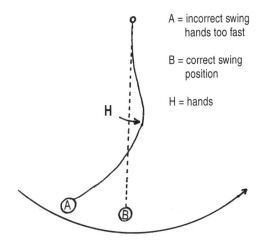

Fig. 9-2.
Moving the hands too fast through the impact area.

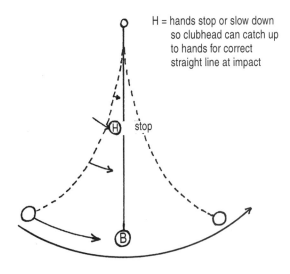

Fig. 9-3. The correct golf swing.

This time, stop the finger at the bottom of the swing, so the ball can catch up to the finger and string, and you will notice how the ball swings faster to the bottom of the swing area, so that the string is straight at the impact area. This is the correct golf swing (Fig. 9-3). The hands must stop or slow down at the impact area for the clubhead to catch up. Move the hands too fast through the impact area, and the clubhead does not catch up to the hands. This causes a lack of clubhead speed and in turn a lack of distance and direction. Also,

since the clubhead is late coming into the impact area, the shot will usually be a slice or a push.

Early release

Notice how you can stop the finger early in the downswing, and the ball will still pick up speed to the impact area (Fig. 9-4). This means an early release is OK. Some teachers are now advocating the early release. Leadbetter (*Golf Digest*, October 1996, p. 40), as well as Peter Croker, in his *Path to Better Golf*, have even made this claim.

The Twin Pendulum

This single pendulum is all good and understandable, but the golf club is held by two hands with the arms separated by a chest and shoulders. Take your string and add another piece of string, colored green, the same length as the red, and attach it to the black mark area. Attach the red string to the end of a stick or a coat hanger and the green string to the other end of the stick. The stick represents the shoulders, the red string is the left arm, and the green string is the right arm. We now have the triangle of the arms and shoulders so often mentioned in the set-up to the ball (Fig. 9-5).

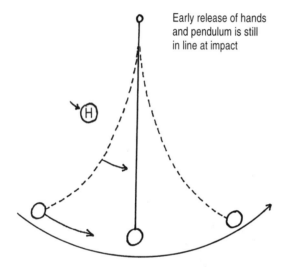

Early release of hands and pendulum is still in line at impact

Fig. 9-4. Early release.

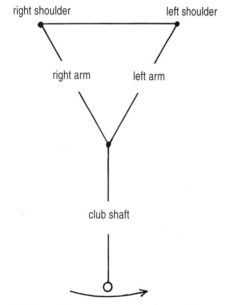

Fig. 9-5. Pendulum representation of the arm and shoulder triangle.

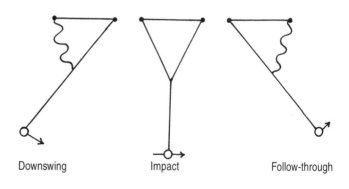

Downswing   Impact   Follow-through

Fig. 9-6. Swing of the pendulum before, during, and after impact.

84

Hold the stick level, and swing the weight. Notice how in the backswing, the red string (left arm) is straight, while the green string (right arm) folds. In the downswing, the red (left arm) is still straight, while the green string begins to straighten to the bottom of the swing (impact). At the bottom, or impact area, both the red and green strings are straight. After impact, the red folds, as the green straightens toward the target (Fig. 9-6). It is this coordination of the red and green strings that is similar to the left and right arms in the golf swing. The left arm is the pendulum for the backswing and downswing. At impact, the right arm becomes the pendulum and maintains the pendulum action into the follow-through.

This is the arm action of the golf swing. You must not let the body interfere with this arm action or the laws of physics. Let the body follow the action of the arms, and you will have the picture-perfect swing. The golf swing's power comes from the right arm action of straightening the right arm and right wrist for impact. It is essential to straighten the right arm on plane to the target to keep the golf shot straight. Do not let the body rotate too fast for the arm swing, as this will throw the arm swing off plane and away from the target. The lower body remains fairly quiet or fairly restricted in its rotation. Essentially, the lower body provides stability for the upper body and arm action.

It is also interesting to note the direction of the right arm through impact. If the shoulders are square to the ball at impact, as they should be, the right arm will extend to the target for a straight ball flight. The right arm has to go in the direction of the target, because the chest is in the way and prevents the right arm from going left of the target. The square shoulders and chest force the right arm to the target. If the left shoulder pulls to the left, the right arm follows through impact across the ball. Keep the shoulders square to the target, like the twin pendulum, and the left shoulder will stay over the ball, without pulling away from the shot, and the right arm will go through the ball to the target.

With this swing, you do not need a wrist break. Take this swing with a minor wrist break, and the ball will fly amazingly straight. This can be highly advantageous to the short game of about 120 yards into the green. You may desire more wrist break for the longer shots, but the less wrist break, the straighter the shot. When using the no-wrist break, take care to swing the club correctly with no extra force by the body. With the no-wrist break, you'll feel like there is inadequate power and try to add the extra power. Such feelings will destroy the swing. Take the swing. It may feel powerless, but it is not. The power is there—do not let yourself be deceived.

Execute this twin pendulum arm action, and the timing and rhythm of your swing will improve. Some students simply visualize the string action for their arms as they swing the club. When learning, it may be best to start off swinging slowly. Feel the force of the swing. Let it happen; do not rush it. You will be amazed: this is all there is to the golf swing.

10
Science of the Short Game

The science of a swinging pendulum will explain how you can achieve accurate distance for your shots to the green. A pendulum swinging from position 9 to 3 will take the same time as when the pendulum swings from 7 to 5 (Fig. 10-1). The reason for this is that the longer the swing action, the faster the pendulum swings. Therefore, the farther from the 6 o'clock position the pendulum moves, the faster the pendulum will swing.

Swing Speed and Distance

This means that if the golf club is swung like a pendulum to various lengths we will achieve various swing speeds to the golf club. Various swing speeds mean various distances.

With a little practice a golfer can swing similar to the pendulum. Just practice swinging the club with no golf balls to different club lengths similar to the hands of a clock. Practice the 7 to 5 o'clock swing, then the 8 to 4 o'clock swing, then the 9 to 3 o'clock swing and the 10 to 2 o'clock swing (Fig. 10-1). Timing and pace will soon develop. Remember that each swing is to be executed within the same time frame. As this feel is acquired, the golfer can then do the same drills but with hitting golf balls. Mark an area every 10 yards up to 100 yards and measure your distances for all your wedges. Practice until a consistent distance is achieved with each swing length. Once the

distance is consistent, mark the swing clock position and distance on a piece of tape and tape it to

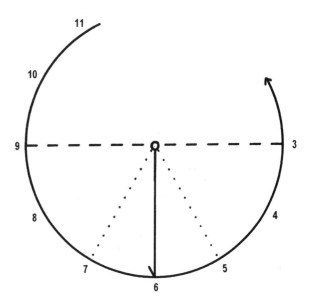

Fig. 10-1. Pendulum swing speed and distance

the club shaft just below the grip. If you carry a booklet in your pocket for all your club distances and course markings, then keep a record there also.

Perhaps the most difficult phase of learning the timing for these swings is that when the swing gets shorter there is a tendency to rush the swing action. The swing action cannot be forced. If the swing is forced then the golfer is fighting the laws of science. All skills are based on the laws of science so maintain the pendulum action.

Table 10-1 is a sample chart of distances and swing lengths. Remember, this is only a sample. You must determine your own distances.

The Killer Bee "Stinger" Golf Club Method

The Killer Bee system with their three wedges of 61, 55, and 49 degrees uses a different technique but it is still based on the science of the pendulum. In a swinging pendulum the farther you move from the center of the swing the faster the end of the pendulum will swing.

Table 10-1. Distance by Swing Length

Yards	PW	Sand	Lob
100	10:00	–	–
90	(:30	10:30	–
80	9:00	9:45	–
70	8:30	9:00	10:00
60	8:00	8:45	9:30
50	–	8:00	9:00
40	–	–	8:30
30	–	–	7:45
20	–	–	–
10	–	–	–

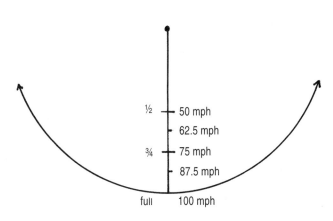

Fig. 10-2. Speed relationship along the pendulum.

Table 10-2. Killer Bee Distance by Swing Length

49 distance		80 yards		90 yards		100 yrds		110 yrds		120 yrds	
		full	½	full	½	full	½	full	½	full	½
49	1	80	60	90	68	100	75	110	83	120	90
	2	70	53	80	60	90	68	100	75	110	83
	3	60	45	70	53	80	60	90	68	100	75
55	1	65	49	75	56	85	64	95	71	105	79
	2	57	43	67	50	77	58	87	65	97	73
	3	49	37	59	44	69	52	79	59	89	67
61	1	45	34	55	41	65	49	75	56	85	64
	2	39	29	49	37	59	44	69	52	79	59
	3	33	25	43	32	53	40	63	47	73	55

Notice in the diagram that if the end of the pendulum swings at 100 mph then the half way point will swing at 50 mph or half the speed (Fig. 10.2). This means that the longer the shaft, the faster the clubhead speed. Killer bee then marked the grips on their wedges with a yellow line about 2 inches and 4 inches down the grip. The number 1 position is the end of the grip, the number 2 position is 2 inches down, and the number 3 position is 4 inches down. As you grip down on the shaft, the shaft becomes shorter, and thus the end of the shaft swings slower—providing your hand speed remains consistent. This changing of the grip position gives different clubhead speed and in turn different distances. This system uses only two swing length positions: the full swing and the half swing.

Table 10-2 gives the distances for the full swing and the half swing at the 1, 2 ,and 3 grip positions. Determine your distance with the full swing for the 49-degree wedge. If you hit your 49-degree wedge 90 yards, then follow the chart for the remainder of your distances. If you want 70 yards, then grip the club at the number three position and take a full swing. The rest is on the chart.

Chipping

In chipping, the ball flies low and rolls to the pin. Chipping can be done with one club or many clubs. The emphasis is to get the ball on the green as quickly as possible and roll it to the hole. The

Table 10-3. Fly/roll ratio for chipping

Club	Fly/roll ratio	Club	Fly/roll ratio
4	1:7	PW	1:1
5	1:6	Sand	1:1^2/3
6	1:5	Lob	1½
7	1:4		
8	1:3		
9	1:2		

following chart is a sample of the fly/roll ratio for the various clubs. For example, the fly/roll ratio for the seven iron is 1:4. This means that the ball will fly one part and roll four parts to the hole. These ratios are only a sample of base figures, as each golfer will have his own distances. The environment will alter the numbers. The speed of the green, dew or moisture, slope, etc. all require adjustment to the base numbers. Adjustments are easier and more accurate if you have a base number to adjust from, and not just an arbitrary number.

Ball position must be consistent for chipping each club, as playing the ball too far forward or backward in your stance will alter the loft of the club and hence affect the distance. To find your distance, place a tee on the green 10 yards from where you are going to chip. Then place tees every 10 yards down the green. Fly the ball to the first tee at 10 yards and then notice the distance of the roll.

Putting

Science also works for putting on the same theory as pitching the ball to the green. Develop a consistent swing in timing and pace for the putt. Now putt the golf balls, and you may notice how for every inch of backswing, the ball will go one foot. Phil Rodgers has claimed this; however, some have found one inch of backswing is closer to two feet in roll. Some claim one inch goes about one pace or an easy walking stride. It really does not matter what your individual distance is, just as long as it is consistent for you.

Practice by laying a yardstick or a measuring tape alongside the golf ball to get the feel of backswing length. Also measure the length of your putter head, usually 4 to 6 inches, so that, when playing, you can use the putter head to see how far your backswing must go. Just don't get too mechanical and so focused on swing length that you lose your feel for the swing. The backswing length is only a guide to help.

Sand Shots

The new method of sand shots is an open stance, lay the club face back or well open and take a divot about the size of a dollar bill. The sand divot is always the same size. Distance is determined by the club being used. Refinement to distance can be added by swing length. Here again the science is similar to the pitching section. Under the old method, distance was determined by the how far behind the ball to start the divot, how much sand to take and how fast the swing is made. Also, in the old method the same club, the sand wedge, was used for all sand shots.

To find your distances just use the methods previously discussed. Hit several balls with each of your wedges and short irons, and determine your average distances. Remember, when playing, the distances are to the pin and not the green.

Table 10-4. Sand trap distances

Distance	Club
8–15 yards	Lob wedge
12–15 yards	Sand wedge
18–20 yards	Pitching wedge
25–30 yards	9 iron
30–40 yards	8 iron

Short and Simple Method

A simpler method can be used, although it does not have the same accuracy as the above methods. However, with some practice it can be very accurate to various distances by just taking a slightly longer backswing and/or choking down on the club.

Table 10-5. Blank chart for distances

yrds			yrds	pw	sw	lob	chip/roll ratio			
			95				4=1:5			
195			90				5=1:4			
190			85				6=1:4			
185			80				7=1:3			
180			75				8=1:3			
175			70				9=1:2			
170			65				pw=1:1			
165			60				sw=1:2/3			
160			55				lob=1:1/2			
155			50				KB		full	½
150			45				49	1	90	68
145			40					2	80	60
140			35					3	70	53
135			30				55	1	75	56
130			25					2	67	50
125			20					3	59	44
120			sand		chip ratio		61	1	55	41
115			8-10yds=61		5-30 yds			2	49	37
110			12-15y=55		49=1:1			3	43	32
105			18-20y=49		55=1:2/3					
100			25+ = pw		61=1:1/2					

Learn your full swing distances with the various golf clubs, and then take off 25 percent for a half swing and 10 percent for choking down 2 inches on the club's grip. For instance, a full swing of 90 yards with a pitching wedge will give a half swing distance of 68 yards. Choke down 2 inches on the half swing, and the distance will go to 61 yards. Choke down 2 inches on the full swing, and the distance will be 81 yards. As you can see, we have covered distances of 90 yards, 80 yards (81 yards), 70 yards (68 yards), and 60 yards (61 yards) with the one club. Other wedges will give different distances, and a little practice will determine the distances.

These percentages will also work for the other longer clubs. Choke down on the 7 iron, and you can take off about 10 percent of your distance. This strategy works well for short and long pin placements, where you may want to just take off a little distance on your approach shot.

Distance/Club Chart

The accompanying chart Table 10-5 is a sample of a page from a golfer's booklet kept in a pocket during play. The booklet can also contain the yardage markers and distances for each hole. Fold the sheet, and it will fit into a 7½ by 4 inch cover. This is a convenient size to fit into the back pocket.

The blank spaces are for you to put in your club for that distance or the clock positions. There are two columns for 195% 100yds to record any changes that may occur in your distance. This chart also has the Killer Bee "Stinger" distances for the 49-degree full swing distance of 90 yards. The chart also has the distances for 90 yards and less using the clock positions. Some golfers may prefer to use their wedge degree numbers (49, 55, and 61) instead of pitching wedge, sand, and lob. This sample will give you an idea of how you may like to set up your own chart.

Part IV

The Mental Aspects of the Game

From the Practice Range to the Golf Course

Taking your golf swing from the practice tee to the golf course can be a very difficult process. Golfers are often mentally destroyed when they hit the ball fairly well on the practice range but fail to execute simple shots on the golf course. Many golfers practice, and practice, and hit excellent shot after shot on the practice range—but when playing the golf course, the excellent shots do not always come to their rescue. Playing good golf is accomplished by proper thinking, and not necessarily through extra practice. Physical practice is important, and swing flaws must be corrected on the practice area, but once corrected, it is the thinking process that will determine the effectiveness of the golf swing on the golf course.

Mind Confusion

Golf practice ranges are wide open spaces. When you hit balls on the practice range, you are not worried about problems to the right or the left and having to keep the ball in a certain area. When using practice range balls, you are not worried about losing a golf ball. You have a bucket of balls, and if you miss-hit one, so what, you can always hit another golf ball. On the practice range, there is no delay between shots, as hitting ball after ball establishes a rhythm that carries over to the next shot and helps make the next shot easier.

Your mind is clear on the practice range, and your golf swing is free and easy, with no problematic thoughts to interfere with your swing action.

Unfortunately, this atmosphere changes when you play the golf course. Problem thoughts of people watching you, rough to the right, and water to the left, the narrow fairway, etc., are all potential fears that cloud and confuse the mind. Your mind can become so cluttered with thoughts, that you fail to focus on the golf swing. You *think* and *analyze*, and you try to steer the club to the ball, hoping for the perfect swing. You fail to let your body execute the smooth, free swing that you used on the practice area.

You know how to swing the golf club, as you have proven this on the practice tee. The reason you failed to swing properly when playing the golf course is simply that your thinking changed from the clear mind on the practice range to a confused mind on the golf course.

Do Not Try to Hit the Ball

Another reason golfers fail to hit the ball correctly is that they are trying *to hit the ball* instead of swinging to *scrape the grass under the ball*. Have you ever noticed how many golfers take a beautiful practice swing, and then look like a gorilla when they go to hit the ball? Most golfers could lower their handicap simply by hitting the golf ball with their practice swing. When taking the practice swing, their mind is clear and free, because there is no thought of hitting the ball into the rough, the water, or even missing the ball. The mind is not confused with thoughts of execution. Unfortunately, as you step up to hit the ball after the practice swing, the mind becomes hyperactive with thoughts of execution, thoughts of trouble to the right and the left, and thoughts of "don't embarrass yourself by missing or miss-hitting the ball." These thoughts are negative images in the mind. As previously described your body muscles react to images, or pictures in the mind. So, if you have a negative picture, the muscles will execute to the negative picture.

When stepping up to the ball, you need only think *"scrape the grass"* one inch behind the ball and two inches in front of the ball. If you can get

your mind to visualize scraping the grass on each shot, you will be amazed at the end result. Simply executing the "scrape the grass drill" could eliminate this action of trying to hit the ball. Perhaps the best way to hit a golf ball is to sneak up on it and hit it with a practice swing.

How to Practice

The practice tee is for learning, and the golf course is for execution. On the practice tee, work on your flaws. For example, if you are having a problem with keeping the radius arm straight, then practice swinging with the conscious thought of correction until you are reasonably proficient. Next, swing without thinking, and hope for the proper straight radius arm. If you fail to achieve the proper effect, then make conscious thought again for several swings. Again, try the swing with no thought of mechanics. This procedure is repeated until you put the correct maneuver into your muscle memory. As previously discussed, practice some shots with your eyes closed to feel your correct movements and your corrections to the swing.

Mental Strategies

The following chapters detail many mental strategies that can be used to help the learning process for the practice tee and for playing the golf course. These mental strategies are effective; however, they become more effective with practice. Fortunately, they are simple, and the rewards are well worth the effort.

12

Golf Strategy: The Percentage Game

Better golfers are able to think better. Better golfers use better judgment and strategy when playing. The thinking process sets up strategy. Proper thinking makes you *play within your capabilities: your percentage game*. Playing your percentage game is simply playing the shot that has the best percentage of favorable results for your ability. An example of the percentage game is to play to the center of the green. This is the safest route. If you are on the green, it is usually a two-putt situation. Go for the pin near the fringe, and it may well be a three- or four-stroke situation if you miss the green. Get on the green and putt, it is the percentage play.

Positive Thinking

Golfers are told to *think positively* and eliminate negative thoughts. It is not just that simple. Negative thoughts will prevail until the physical problem is eliminated. You cannot think positive in a sand trap if you know your skill level is insufficient to hit the ball out. Physical practice is necessary in building confidence for the positive thought process. *Physical* golf and *mental* golf go together.

Consistency

Consistency is a must. As a golfer you must develop consistency to your game. Consistency to the ball's flight will help strategy. If you don't know whether your ball will slice or hook, you'll have difficulty in planning strategy and executing the required shot. Such uncertainty causes mental confusion. Mental confusion, as we all know, will influence the golf swing. If your golf ball is consistently fading then play for the fade so that there will be a consistent flight pattern to your shots. The obsession of trying to always hit the ball straight every time causes many golfers to lose their consistent flight pattern. Develop a consistent flight pattern of straight, fade, or draw—so that you know where the ball will end up and not how it gets there. Read "Don't hit the ball straight" for more on consistent flight patterns.

Be careful when experimenting on the golf course. If the ball is fading, then play the fade. Pro golfers do it. They will play the slice or fade, if it prevails during a round of golf, by allowing for it. If necessary they will go to the practice tee after the round to correct the error. Consistency to your golf game will also help your positive attitude, as well as helping to eliminate mental confusion.

Equipment

Although a golf club's lie, length, weight, and grip size can influence the results of a golf shot, you must not overestimate their effects. If the clubs are a problem, then get new or different ones. If you are thoroughly convinced the clubs are to blame, then this psychological factor will influence your play. A lack of confidence in your club will make the club far more ineffective than it actually is. But remember, you cannot buy the swing. New and different clubs will not make up for swing faults. Save the big money for lessons—not a new driver. Three hundred dollars spent on lessons instead of a new driver is so much more productive.

Do Your Own Thinking

Experiment and learn to use the *right club for you*, not what someone else uses. Do not let your ego influence your club selection. Many golfers succumb to their ego when trying to outdrive or outhit another golfer. Know your distances and flight patterns for all your clubs. Your strategy depends on this knowledge. It is extremely important to always watch the flight of the ball for all shots. By doing this observation, you will learn the distance and flight pattern for each club. Such knowledge will help in decision making and is vital to playing your game.

Club Selection

To estimate distances to the hole, some players will pace off the fairway's distance by using landmarks along the fairway. For example, "it is 120 yards from the large tree to the center of the green." Other golfers simply feel it is a certain distance. Once the distance is determined, you can decide which club will place the ball there. Some players indirectly determine distance through club selection by imagining shots of increasing distances to the green. For example, a 9 iron will drop the ball at the tree. An 8 iron will drop the ball in the trap in front of the green. A 7 iron will drop the ball on the fringe to the green. A 6 iron will drop the ball in the center of the green. A 6 iron is the club for the distance. Another method of judging distance is to learn the 10 yard distance and then just determine how many 10 yard distances to the pin. Actually it is good practice to learn to judge distances. Look, estimate, and then pace it off. Try this technique when walking. Pick a spot ahead, estimate the distance, and then count the paces as you continue walking to the spot.

If you cannot decide between two clubs, then it probably will not matter which club to use, as there is only about 10 yards difference between clubs. One club will put the ball 5 yards in front and the other club will put the ball 5 yards behind the pin. Whatever, select one club and be positive about your selection, so that the element of doubt is eliminated. Doubt will destroy your shot.

Off the Tee

"Off the tee," play for position. Distance is helpful but not the main criterion, as a well-placed shot off the tee is often best for the approach to the green. Remember, the tee shot is for setting up the approach shot. A well-placed tee shot is often closer to the green than a longer drive to the side of the fairway. The tee shot is not an ego builder to outdrive the others or to see how close to the green you can get. Pin location and hazards knowledge can help plan your drive placement, so that you can approach the green with your best percentage shot. Pin locations can often be observed from your car while driving by the golf course to the parking lot, or by looking over at the other greens while playing another fairway, etc.

Notice where the trouble is on a fairway, and then tee up the ball on the same side as the trouble and hit away from the trouble. Most golfers tee up away from the trouble and then end up hitting into the problem. The *center line system* of teeing off is to visualize the fairway with an imaginary line running down the middle of the fairway. Determine which side the trouble is on, and then tee-off on the trouble side and hit across the center line. Do not play down the middle of the fairway. Play from one side to the other.

Another method along similar lines is to aim across the fairway to a spot about 270 yards along the rough. When aligned to this spot, open or close the face of the club slightly to direct the ball to the aimed spot. The ball will start to the aimed spot, but the open or closed club face will fade or draw the ball back into the fairway. If the ball does not fade or draw, then it will go straight, but not into the rough as your aiming mark is too far away. Hitting the straight ball is the hardest shot in golf, so slightly open or close the club face to play the controlled fade or draw.

Many golfers go to the middle of the tee area and try to hit the ball straight down the middle. If the fairway is 50 yards wide, you have only 25 yards on each side of the centerline to land the ball if the ball is not hit straight down the middle. If you do not know whether your attempted straight ball will slice or hook, you only have 25 yards of landing area for your drive. The smart golfer will play for a fade by aiming across the fairway; this way, if the ball goes straight, it will still be on the fairway, but near the far edge. If the ball fades like expected, then the ball has 50 yards of fairway to fall into. The same strategy prevails for the draw.

Club selection

Many golfers are now realizing that the driver does not have to be used off the tee. The 2, 3, 4 and 5 woods are often the better club. The loss of distance, if any, is small, and the ball control is so much greater. It is this ball control with the 3 wood that makes the average distance with the 3 wood greater than the average drive with the driver. Although the driver is capable of hitting the ball farther, most golfers do not hit the ball consistently straight and far with the driver. The variance in distance and directions are so much greater with the driver, that if an average is taken of all drives, many golfers would find their average drive not as good as the average 3 wood drive. We talk of false assumptions, and this applies here. If you make the occasional big drive, do not make the false assumption that all your drives will be big drives. Determine your average drive distance, as this is your percentage shot. The big drive is your low percentage shot.

The wind is often a factor in club selection for the drive. With a backwind, the 3 wood may be the best club. A front wind may be best with a 1 or 2 iron. Allow for the side wind pushing your ball. Assess the wind, but do not let it psych you out. A well-hit ball is often less effected by the wind than you may think. Books and experts tell you to hit the ball low into the wind. This is good advice if you are very good at hitting low balls with your driver. If you are not, then disaster may be in the works. Wind or no wind, play your percentage shot, and just allow for the effects of the wind.

Long Fairway Shots

Play for position. Long fairway shots usually fly in a low trajectory and land with little backspin for plenty of roll. It takes a very well hit long shot to land with little roll. Unless you can consistently hit your long shots with little roll, you must play and allow for this roll. Do not make false assumptions that your long shots will bite. If you cannot reach the green with your second shot, then play for position, to make the third shot as easy as possible. It is especially important to realize that if you cannot reach the green, then do not try to over-power the shot with the intention of being as close to the green as possible. Hit your percentage shot toward the green for position, even if it means a third shot being a few yards longer. If you are capable of reaching the green with a long shot, be sure to allow for the roll action, as most greens are difficult to play if you go over the green. If the green has traps and hazards, play for a safe position, so that the next shot will be as easy as possible. Often, this means to play short of the green.

The Approach Shot

In the following sections, we'll discuss the club selection technique for the approach shot.

The long irons

Basically go for the center of the green, and not the pin. Be safe. Be intelligent. Do not let your ego make you play dangerously or stupidly. A ten-foot putt is a ten-foot putt, no matter what the direction of the putt, unless it is a dangerous downhill putt.

The approach shot using the long irons is extremely difficult, except for the best golfers. Modern sets of golf clubs are now replacing the 2 and 3 irons with the 5 and 6 woods, as most golfers are able to hit these woods higher and with less roll than the long irons. The long irons require precise timing and execution. The woods are well lofted and heavier to get the ball up and to give the ball distance. The 5 wood is almost the same as the two iron for distance, but it has the advantage of a higher trajectory for dropping the ball to the green. Some golfers do not use the 5 and 6 woods because they consider such clubs to be women's clubs. Again, do not let vanity interfere with your percentage game.

The middle irons

The middle irons are your all-round clubs. They are used for off the tee, for approach shot to the green, for chip shots, and even out of traps and the rough. These clubs give distance and accuracy. In fact, many golfers would score better if they played with only the middle irons and a putter. Using these clubs, you can keep the ball in play and yet achieve distance. Many golfers hit their 5 irons 150 to 160 yards and their drives 210 or 230 yards. This is a difference of only about 50–60 yards. It is this extra 50 yards that cause the scoring problems. For example, a hole of 480 yards is a par 5, and the green can be reached with three 5 iron shots of 160 each. With two putts, you have your par. Unfortunately, many golfers try to over-power the drive off the tee for extra distance (going for the birdie), only to find trouble. Remember, a good drive is only about 50 to 60 yards more than the 5 iron, so play your safest shot.

When using an iron off the tee, *use a tee*, but tee the ball low. Take the advantage of making a good lie by using a tee. The golf pros use tees when the rules permit.

The middle iron clubs are used to go for the green, so selection is for the green, but with a safety factor for the margin of error. If a 7 iron may put you on the green, but a trap is in front of the green, then maybe a 6 iron is the club to be sure to clear the trap. If the trap is in back of the green, then the 8 iron may be the club. Remember, your distance is based on your average hit—not on your perfect hit. Do not make false assumptions. Unless you hit the ball perfectly on your approach shot to the green, the ball will always go short of your expectations. Only the better golfers hit the ball consistently to the same distance; so, unless you hit the ball consistently accurate, give yourself a margin of error by taking enough club or even less club.

The short irons

Play the safest route to the center of the green, unless you have plenty of green to work with when

97

playing to the pin. If a sand trap or hazard is in line with the pin, then play for the side of the pin and away from trouble. A ten-foot putt is a ten-foot putt from any direction.

When playing to sloping greens, try to leave an uphill putt to the hole. Uphill putts are easier to judge distance, as they can be stroked firmer. Downhill putts are hard to stop near the hole, as they require a very delicate touch.

The biggest problem with the short iron approach shot is that most golfers hit the shot too easy and usually land short of their objective. More time should be spent on practicing the short irons, especially the less than full swing shots. Many golfers make the false assumption that the short irons are easy, so they practice these clubs less than they should. In fact, the short irons are difficult clubs, so practice accordingly.

The cut shot

The cut shot should be learned and practiced, as it will save many strokes. It is a normal pitch shot with the face of the club opened or laid back excessively. The stance is also very open. The swing is directed to the left of the target and not at the target. Although the swing is left of the target, the ball will fly to the target as the clubface is square to the target. This shot requires lots of practice to acquire the correct alignment and distance, but it does give a soft, floating shot to the green with little roll. This shot is excellent for over traps, water, and other hazards. It works best with the 9 iron, wedge and the sand wedge. You should use the sand wedge more for fairway shots and cut shots, as it will give excellent backspin.

The rough or trap approach shots

In the rough or a sand trap, the middle irons will give distance to the shot. Do not try to overextend this shot. For fairway trap shots, the ball must be picked clean with the full swing. If the ball is sitting up and the lip of the trap does not interfere

with the ball's trajectory, a four or five wood is often a good club to use if a long-distance shot is required. The flat sole of the wood will not dig into the sand as it bounces on the sand and picks the ball clean. From traps near the greens, the chip shot can be used if the ball can be picked clean. If the trap does not have a high bank to go over, then the ball may be putted if the target line is fairly smooth. Knowing the flight characteristics of the ball's trajectory will be of great help in club selection for trouble shots.

The cut shot is an excellent explosion shot from the sand. Just make sure that the clubface is laid back and well open, almost flat. Using a sand wedge and a backswing of the hands going waist high, experiment to find how far the ball will fly and roll. Determine your average distance. Using the same swing, experiment with your other wedges and the 9, 8, 7 irons, and determine the distance these ball will fly and roll for each club. Record your results, and then when playing, you will know what club to use for a certain distance explosion shot to the pin.

The chip shot

The chip shot is valuable and should be used whenever possible near the green. The 5, 6 and 7 irons are usually the best clubs to use. The stroke is just like a putt. Some actually use a putting grip for such a shot. Do not make the mistake of using the wedge or 9 iron when you are very close to the green. The wedge or 9 iron will impart too much backspin to the ball, which gives an unpredictable roll to the ball. This excessive backspin on soft short shots to the pin tends to give an inconsistent roll to the ball because it is so difficult to determine how much the backspin will counter the forward roll of the ball.

The Greens

In the following sections, we'll discuss the different factor that influence the condition of the green.

The grain

Grass grows and lays or bends to the effects of nature's terrain, drainage, and sunshine. The direction of bend is referred to as grain, and it is this grain that will affect the path of the ball. If the grain lays to the left, the ball will drift to the left, even if the terrain is flat. The heavier and coarser the grain or grass, the more the effect the grass has on the ball. Putting with the grain gives a faster roll to the ball, and putting against the grain will slow up the roll of the ball. On long putts, the effect of the grain will be more pronounced, especially near the cup where the ball slows down.

It is illegal to use a club, putter, or parts of the body to brush the green to determine the direction of the grain. The grass on the fringe area of the green is usually bent in the same direction as the green, and it is legal to brush or feel the grass in this area to help determine the characteristics of the green. In most cases, eyesight will be sufficient to study the grain. Often, when the grass appears shiny, the grain is with you, and if the grass appears dull, the grain is against you. Sometimes, looking at the hole to determine the growth of the grass around the edge of the hole is helpful. By all means, do not overreact to the grain by allowing too much for the grain effect.

Reading the Greens

Greens usually are of one of two types of grasses: *Bermuda* and *Bent*. The Bermuda grass is bristly and sticks up, while bent grass bends over and lays much flatter. There are many varieties to both these types of grasses. Bermuda grass is usually more to the southern areas, while the bent goes to the more northern regions. Bermuda grass is harder to read. It also affects the ball more than bent grass.

When approaching the green, look over the general terrain of the green, and then study the area of the putt. By studying the general lay of the land around the green, you can be forewarned of any contours or slopes that may not be noticeable once you reach the green. Approach the ball from behind, so as to get a good study of the line. Mark the ball and clean it. Place the ball back down if it does not interfere with anyone's line. Walk the line, and check for ball marks or scuffs. Study the area around the pin for wear, slope, etc. If desired, take a look at the line of the putt from behind the hole to the ball. Now proceed to putt. Remember to do all your analyzing before putting the ball. Once you step up to the ball, start your recall for the feel of the stroke.

Many golfers line the putt from behind the ball, behind the hole, and from the side. Some pace off the length of the putt to subconsciously acquire how much power for the distance will be required to stroke the putt. A quicker method to pacing the full putt is to pace halfway, and then double the count. This is just as good and it is faster. Once again, be careful not to overanalyze the situation.

Always putt a little past the hole, so that the ball has a chance of going in, and if it misses the hole, the path of the ball going past the hole is often a good line on the return putt back. If the putt is a downhill putt be extra soft, so as to get the ball to die at the hole. This is one time that it is usually best not to be bold, as the return putt may be long or dangerous. On downhill putts, some golfers contact the ball on the toe area of the putter blade. By doing this, the ball has a slower roll, because the toe area of the putter is dead, unlike the sweet spot area, and the ball is not able to jump off the putter blade.

The plumb-bob method

Another method for reading the contours of the green is the plumb-bob technique. Standing behind the ball, draw an imaginary straight line from the hole to the ball and past the ball. Straddle this line, behind the ball, with the feet equal distance on both side of the line. Lock the knees, so that the body will form a straight posture perpendicular to the slope of the land. With the thumb and forefinger at arm's length, hold the putter high on the grip. Looking with the dominant eye only, the lower part of the shaft should split the ball. Now look up the shaft to see on which side of the shaft the hole is. If the hole is to the left of the shaft, then the break is to the left, with the amount of break determined by how far from the shaft the hole appears. With practice, this plumb-bob method is accurate, as well as extremely valuable in reading greens.

General rules

A general rule to follow on green reading is that greens tend to break to water and away from mountains. At times, a green will appear to break in one direction, when in actuality the ball breaks in the opposite direction. Whenever a putt breaks opposite to your reading of the green, check for the water/mountain characteristic. The plumb-bob method often allows you to notice this phenomenon, or deception. Also, wet greens putt slower and break less than dry greens. Breaks react more, as the ball slows down near the target. It is usually good practice to have the pin attended on long putts, as the body of the person attending the pin helps to judge depth and distance.

Some teachings recommend various stances for straight or breaking putts and different putters for fast and slow greens. You can almost forgot about these ideas, as they are just more variables to cause confusion and require adjustments. Do not try to counter slope and grain by trying to spin the ball with an open or closed clubface. As to using heavy putters for slow greens and light putters for fast greens, the answer is do what you want, although it is usually best to simply get used to one putter and just hit the ball harder or easier on the heavy and fast greens.

Scrambling

Scrambling is the *art of thinking*. Good golfers scramble. Even good golfers will hit bad shots or find themselves in trouble situations. Scrambling requires concentration to analyze the situation and then execute the shot. Do not play for the "once in a lifetime shot." Play the percentage shot.

Good scramblers do not overestimate their abilities. Good scramblers control their emotions, as they remain calm, knowing that one good shot can often make up for the bad shot.

Countering trouble is best achieved by a positive attitude. Golfers often psych themselves into failing by a negative or a feel-sorry-for-themselves attitude. There is nothing you can do to change the situation, the ball has to be played so play it: *quit rationalizing: quit crying*. When playing trouble shots, emphasize good contact as contact is essential to getting the ball out of trouble. Directions, distance, and flight pattern are all secondary to making good contact. Keep the head down and swing through the ball. Do not make a quick head lift to see the ball.

The uneven lie

The main criteria for shots from uneven lies is to simply maintain balance and take the normal swing tempo with perhaps a shorter backswing to help in balance. Once again, keep the head still.

A ball hit from an uphill lie will have a higher flight trajectory and often a pull, draw, or hooking action. The stance on the uphill lie causes the clubhead to lay back a little more, so that a 5 iron gives the effect of a 6 or 7. A ball hit from a downhill lie will give a lower flight trajectory, with a push, fade, or slicing action to the ball. The stance for the downhill lie causes the club face to lie forward a little, so that a 5 iron gives the effect of a 3 or 4 iron. A change in clubs and aim is often necessary to counter the effects of uneven lies. For instance, if the ball is in an uphill lie then you may have to use a 4 iron instead of a 5 iron to make up for the higher flight pattern. Also, you may have to aim a little to the right to allow for the pulling or hooking action. For a downhill lie, you may have to use a 6 or 7 iron instead of a 5 iron to make up for the lower flight pattern, and also may have to aim to the left to allow for the pushing or slicing action. Quite often this pushing or pulling action to the ball is the result of slightly losing balance from the uneven lie of the terrain.

On sidehill lies, when the ball is lower than the feet, there is a strong tendency to fade, slice, or push the ball. When the ball is higher than the feet, the tendency is to draw, hook, or pull the ball. To counter the sidehill lie, some golfers will aim to the right or the left to allow for the fade or the draw, while others will open or close the club face to counter the fade or the draw. Experiment with both methods to determine which works best for you. In some cases, you may find that a combination of both is best. Whatever the lie or stance, maintain perfect balance and let the clubhead swing to the target. Do not let the terrain alter your balance. If you can keep perfect balance, the shot will go satisfactory.

The Rough

When playing out of the rough, the first rule is to get out in one stroke. Use a club with sufficient loft to get the ball up and out. Do not let the distance requirements of trying to reach the green influence your club selection. Often, when trying to reach the green, a club with insufficient loft is used and the ball is unable to rise above the trouble. Once in the rough, it usually takes two stroke to get to the green, so plan on a stroke out and a stroke to the green. Be intelligent and use excellent judgement if going for the green from the rough. It may not be worth the risk, as a bad shot from the rough may not only leave you in the rough, but with a more difficult shot out or even an unplayable lie.

Balls coming out of the rough are often fluffed out as the grass between the ball prevents clean contact. This usually results in no backspin to the ball. With heavy grass, it is often a good idea to close the face of the club a little, as the pull of the grass will help pull open the club. The swing out of the rough is usually best with a short backswing to help in the preciseness of the shot.

A golf ball lying in a divot requires mental toughness. No matter how much you may feel it is unfair to be penalized for someone else's divot, the rules require the shot to be played as is. Crying or remorse will not help, so get tough and

hit the ball. Physically, the shot is executed by contact on the downswing to pinch the ball out. In most cases, just play the ball back a little more in the stance.

If the ball is on a bed of pine needles, leaves, or dead grass, the pick shot is needed. Do not rest the club on this area, as it may cause the ball to move and cost you a penalty stroke. If your ball is on tarmac, the road or parking lot, or on hard bare ground, use the pick shot—but with a little more of a sweeping action. The pinch must be precise, because if the club hits too far behind the ball, the club will bounce up and skull or miss-hit the ball. The trouble shots previously mentioned are not as difficult as you may think. A little practice will help your confidence and skill level. Most of these trouble shots are missed simply by fear of the shot.

Since you do not have a left-handed club in your bag, it is often possible to use the back of the four or three iron with the left-handed swing to get a ball back in play. The back of a putter can also be used. If you must get down low, then a swing while kneeling can be helpful. Sometimes the "carom shot" is handy. This shot is simply hitting the ball to rebound off a tree, wall, building, etc. into the desired direction.

Trouble shots should be practiced, so that when the time comes, you will not only be experienced in the trouble shot but you will also be confident.

Sand Trap Shots

The sand shot out of the trap is often the easiest shot in golf, because you don't hit the ball. The club face just scoops the sand under the ball and the ball lifts up. This shot does not have to be as precise as the shot off the grass, where the club head must meet the ball with some accuracy. In the sand blast, the clubhead can be one or two inches behind the ball, and the shot will still be fairly good.

The sand shot is best executed with the simple cut or lob shot. With an open stance, lay the face of the sand wedge way back (open). The club will be swung to the left of the target, but the clubface is aligned to the target. Practice this swing with no ball. Just try to take a smooth, shallow divot about the size of a dollar bill. When the divots are consistent, then try the swing with a golf ball.

Swing at the ball with a consistent swing to find your distance and direction. Alter the stance, swing line, and open clubface if necessary. Once this is determined, record your distance from the average of all the shots. Now repeat the procedure with your other wedges, 9, 8, 7 irons. When you have gone through your short irons, you will notice a consistent distance to each club. When playing the golf course, determine the distance to the pin, and then you will know which club to use. When determining your distances, remember to keep the swings consistent to each club. Also, take the same size divot with each club. Distance is determined by the club, and not by the amount of sand to blast.

If the sand is heavy and the trap is smooth with no lip, then often the best club to use is a *putter*, so that the ball can be rolled or putted out. Allow for more drag on the ball in the sand area. If a putter is not the club to use, then a chip shot may be the play. The ball is just picked clean with a five, six, or seven iron. This shot requires accuracy, as no sand can be contacted before the ball.

When the ball is embedded in the sand—the "fried egg" lie—a pitching wedge or 9 iron may have to be used to dig into the sand to blast the ball out. A sand wedge may have too much bouncing action and may not be able to get under the ball sufficiently. When digging for the ball, it is a good idea to close the face of the club a little, as the force of contact with the sand will open the face. *It is crucial on all sand shots to swing through the ball.*

Uphill lies, downhill lies, and sidehill lies in the sand trap are played the same way as uneven lies on the fairway.

Sand trap shots should be analyzed the same way as any other approach shot. Read the greens and see the best approach to the pin. Some cases may result in an approach shot to the side of the green simply to get out of the trap.

Before taking the sand shot, wiggle your feet into the sand for a good solid base; but do not overdo this action, as it may lower the body too much into the sand. This wiggling action is an excellent means of reading the sand for heaviness or lightness and if the sand is dry on top and wet or heavy underneath. Also, this action may help reveal if there is a good sandy base and not just a little sand on top of the ground soil.

Powdery sand and heavy sand affect the sand shot differently. Wet and heavy sand is easier than dry or powdery sand when picking or putting the ball out of the trap. When blasting, more sand is excavated from powdery sand than from heavy sand. Learn to play the difference.

Water Shots

The best advice for water shots is, except for rare instances, *don't*—unless some of the ball is visible above the water line. A ball in the water is played much like a sand shot. It must be remembered that the water between the clubface and the ball will cause the ball to *squirt off* in any direction. The club face digging into the water also has a tendency not to hold its direction. Sometimes the club face will skip on the water, or dig in deeper than usual near the contact area.

The Weather

Wet weather is a nuisance. An umbrella is handy to keep the yourself and the clubs dry. Golf gloves are good in rainy weather to help give a better grip to the club. New golf gloves are now designed for play in wet weather. A handkerchief wrapped around the golf club grip also helps to get a better grip in the rain. You should keep a towel handy to keep the clubs and balls clean. Golf shots in wet weather may squish off the face at contact from the water on the grass. The best hat for the rain is the bucket style or any wide brim hat, as such a hat will keep the rain from running down the side of the head into the neck area. Baseball caps only keep the rain out of the eyes and do not prevent the dripping down the neck.

When the temperature is high, enjoy it. When it is very hot, drink plenty of fluids. To help keep the hands dry in very hot and sweaty weather, wear wrist bands to stop the sweat from running down the arms to the hands. In cold weather, dress warm with expandable clothes, like sweaters, that will give with your body movement. Windshirts are now popular and do an excellent job of protecting the body. Do not let the heat or cold discourage you. Let the other golfers be psyched out.

Some golfers use a lower compression ball in cold weather and a higher compression ball in hot weather. In cold weather, some golfers put a ball in their pocket to keep it warm, and then switch balls every hole to take advantage of using a warm ball. If in a tournament, be sure the ball exchange is of the same type and brand.

When playing the wind, do not try to hit the ball harder to counter or take advantage of the wind. Play the shot normally but adjust for the effect the wind will have on the flight path of the ball.

The Rules of Golf

Know the rules of golf. For instance, a golfer is not required to stand in water to putt or hit a ball.

This is considered casual water and relief is given with no penalty. Knowing the rules has saved many strokes.

Your Own Par

It is often advisable to devise your own par for each hole and round. This can help you stay within your capabilities and prevent overextending your abilities. Playing for par causes some golfers to tie up. Most golfers are not par players, so they should not plan their strategy to par. Again, for better scoring, it cannot be overemphasized that you must play within your capabilities.

Without improving your physical skills, many golfers could improve their scores by adhering to the following rules:

1. Plan within your abilities.

2. When swinging, focus your attention on a single item (e.g. scrape the grass).

3. Play your percentage shot and game.

4. Keep it simple.

Another old adage that gives you the chance to score well is *keep the ball in play*.

13 Mental Strategies for Golf

Although the use of psychological strategies are helpful, it is important to understand that no psychological technique can be employed that will make an athlete perform better than his physical skill ability. Psychological strategies can only help to bring out the maximum physical skills of an individual. A high level of performance requires a high level of skill. This is a fact that must never be overlooked. Psychology will not make up for a lack of skill. For example, the use of hypnosis, or other psychological strategies, will not be sufficient to make a beginning golfer an overnight sensation, nor can a golfer with high handicap skills be made into a pro-tour golfer just by using mental strategies.

Strategies and Abilities

A few golfers have the mental ability for high level play but simply do not have the physical abilities or skills. Such athletes may already be performing to their maximum potential. There are, however, many golfers who are not achieving their maximum potential because their mental skills are lacking. Most golfers can improve their scores simply by using psychological strategies to create a mental atmosphere that will let their body perform their physical skills to the best of their ability.

Mental strategies may not do wonders the first time out on the golf course. There will be ups and downs and times when one thinks such skills do

not work. The psychological skills outlined in this book do work and are very effective. Like physical skills, mental skills must be practiced. Fortunately, learning and practicing the mental skills are simple, very simple, and actually take very little time. Practice will soon bring beneficial results.

There are two basic situations for using psychological strategies. One of the situations is when actually performing, *The performance phase*: and the other is when not playing but preparing for the game or season: *The preparation phase. The preparation phase* involves setting goals determined from an assessment of your needs and abilities. This is the phase for developing the mental skills of relaxation, imagery and visualization. It is also the time for fine tuning your coping strategies that will help you to cope with anxiety, fear, confidence, etc. The performance phase uses quick recall strategies that can be strengthened through our preparation phase practice. The performance strategies will be discussed first as they can be readily applied to your next golf game.

The Performance Phase

Psychological strategies for use while performing

While reading the following strategies do not believe that these strategies are two simple to be effective, or that you already employ such strategy. If you feel that you already are using such a strategy, then make an honest appraisal as to how effective it is. Psychological strategies applied in a careless manner will be more hazardous than if not applied at all. Carelessly applied mental strategies send incorrect or confused messages to the muscles. Incorrect mental messages will result in incorrect muscular movements. Confused mental messages will give the muscles confusing and uncertain directions. Simple mental strategies are often more effective than complex strategies because the simple strategies are easier to develop and send clear, accurate messages. The following strategies must be practiced and practiced correctly until you are able to respond automatically.

Thought stopping

The effectiveness of this technique lies in its simplicity and ease of application. Most athletes use it. Some athletes are even unaware that they use it. Whenever your mind is not settled or is confused by the thinking or feeling process, simply stop the thinking/feeling process and reorganize your thoughts. Once you step up to hit a golf ball, your mind must forget the thinking and analyzing processes and focus on the feel of the shot. If thought stopping is not used then the mind is confused with facts and feelings.

To swing a golf club, while in a confused state, can be disastrous. Prior to swinging a golf club, you must clear the mind of all analysis relating to distance, wind, stance, club, etc., and focus on your feel of the swing. If the mind is not focused, then stop the thinking process, step back from the ball, reorganize your thoughts, complete your analysis, step up to the ball again, and then focus on the feel of the swing. Baseball players do this at the plate when they are not completely ready for the pitch. Each time you feel that your mind is not set for execution of the swing, then stop your thinking process and start over again. Naturally, this seems simple, however, the effectiveness of this technique lies in the ability to recognize the confused mind set and to be able to stop the thought process and start over again. Good golfers do not execute a golf shot when the mind is confused or partly confused. Lesser ability golfers often feel that they can correct their confusion during the swing. Do not take a chance in hoping the shot can still be made with an unclear mind. Remember—a clear mind, a simple focus and a free moving swing. Thought stopping must be practiced.

Pre-shot thinking routine

As an aid to analyzing a golf shot, one should develop a pre-shot thinking routine. The effectiveness of the pre-shot thinking routine is similar to the effectiveness of the pre-shot physical routine. All good golfers do it. The following is an example of a pre-shot thinking routine. You may altar it to your own needs, however, whatever routine you use, just make sure you execute it consistently.

The order of pre-shot thinking routine:

1. *Distance factors:*

❏ landing area for ball:
terrain of landing (slope);
elevation of landing area, higher or lower
estimate distance

2. *Initial club selection:*

❏ for the ball's flight to landing area

❏ for roll of the ball at landing area

3. *Wind effect:*

❏ change club selection for wind direction

4. *Other effects—change club selection for following factors:*

❏ hitting ball long or short today

❏ atmosphere (rain, hot, cold)

❏ lie of golf ball (uphill, sidehill, downhill, heavy grass, short grass, etc.)

5. *Final club selection:*

❏ review previous four steps if necessary

Use this routine for every shot so that you do not forget a factor that may influence the ball's flight. Once final club selection is determined, do not second-guess your decision. On making the final club selection, clear the mind, feel the shot and execute the shot.

This pre-shot thinking routine is helpful in covering all information needed for the golf shot. It is best to never vary or change the order of the routine, so that no factor is forgotten. Also, by keeping the routine in the same sequence every time it is executed, you will find it easier to remember and process the information. The pre-shot thinking routine is especially helpful when you are under pressure and anxiety may be developing. Anxiety hinders information processing, and the use of a pre-shot thinking routine develops a habit of processing all the information— even while under pressure. An example of inadequate information processing would be a golfer failing to process the wind factor for his golf shot.

Thought-stopping is effective in situations other than the pre-shot routine. Thought-stopping is effective while walking to the ball between shots . While walking to the ball, you should make yourself aware of your somatic, or body,

activity. Such things as a quickened pulse, faster respiration, sweaty palms, and muscular tension may be indications of anxiety, fear, or mind confusion. If your evaluation of these signs leads to the possibility of tension creeping into your swing, then stop your thought process and talk to yourself.

Self-Talk

Self-talk can be effective in lowering anxiety, confusion, and fears. Self-talk should be positive. Negative talk may develop negative and destructive pictures in the mind. If you note your palms sweating more than usual, you may recognize a fear for your next shot from the sand. An example of correct self-talk would be, "easy shot, I practiced this shot all week and I have been very successful. Besides, last time in a pressure situation I blasted out and one putted. I can do it again. Relax. I feel good." The idea of recalling past successful experiences is important in developing the positive attitude. Past successful experiences develop positive successful pictures in the mind. Negative self-talk like, "boy, I'm in trouble now. Last week I took two strokes to get out," reinforces in the mind the inability to execute the sand shot. Negative pictures of failure reinforce the mind. Negative self-talk can also increase pressure and raise your anxiety level.

If interest or motivation is low, then self-talk can be used to stimulate the body and mind to perform better. This type of self-talk is used to help prevent carelessness in thinking and swinging the golf club when motivation is low. You must be careful not to turn stimulating self-talk into pressure self-talk. An example of stimulating self-talk would be, "Stay alert, only four holes left. Concentrate. Stay energetic. I must play my game. I will continue to play aggressively." Pressure self-talk for the same situation would be, "I must concentrate more. Only four holes left. I need three pars. I must get the pars. If I don't, then I am in trouble. I cannot lose the match. I must win."

Self-talk must be within the physical abilities of the talker. Remember that you cannot talk yourself into executing shots beyond your capabilities. To be effective, self-talk must be positive and realistic.

Rational Thinking

Rational thinking often coincides with self-talk. Rational thinking must be realistic, as the thinking must be to the capabilities of the golfer. Many golfers destroy themselves by feeling that every shot they play must be perfect. Most golfers know that every shot cannot be perfect and that they will make errors. Unfortunately, almost every one who believes this will not accept the bad shot when it occurs on the golf course. This bad shot often upsets the golfer so much that future shots and even the round of golf is destroyed.

Good rounds of golf are played despite bad shots. Professionals win tournaments despite bad shots. Every golfer, even the top pros, will hit bad shots. Most people are unaware of the number of bad shots in a round of golf by the top pros. Some claim that as many as 10 bad shots a round are made by the top golfers. The distinguishing feature of good golfers is their ability to make comebacks after the bad shots and not to be discouraged by a bad shot. The good players are mentally tough.

The rational thinking golfer, on making a bad shot, will tell himself something like, "this is one of the bad shots I am allowed to make on this round of golf. I will make this shot up later with a good shot or a good putt. Besides, I allowed myself six bad shots this round, so I have five left." This type of thinking will help reduce anxiety and tension. Compare this to the golfer who thinks, "my god, this is terrible, how could I make such a stupid mistake. Now I have to get a birdie on the next hole. I must get the birdie. I'm a stroke down. I may never make that stroke up." This is not rational thinking; it is irrational thinking and helps create a pressure situation. This type of thinking helps increase anxiety and tension. Chances are that if the birdie does not come on the next hole, than the negative thinking will continue to destroy play.

Rational thinking will help turn defeat and mistakes into learning situations. You must learn from your mistakes, otherwise there is little chance for improvement. Mistakes will occur, so accept this fact and continue to perform without the worry of past mistakes.

Another important aspect of rational thinking is to not make false assumptions. For example, if a golfer once hit his five iron 190 yards, he continues to play under the false assumption that all his five iron shots will go 190 yards. All golf shots will not go your maximum distance. Actually, very few shots go maximum. Plan on a little less, as most of your shots will be a little less than maximum.

Positive Thinking

Positive thinking is most helpful if it is regulated by rational thinking. No matter how positive you are, it is essential to have the skill to live up to those positive thoughts. A golfer may be positive about blasting a ball out of a water hazard even if the ball is one inch below the water. Intelligent golfers know that such a shot is rarely accomplished. The club will slide off line going that deep into the water and the ball may not be exactly in the position it looks, as the water distorts the visual effect of the ball. The smart play, the rational-thought play, and the correct positive thinking play, is to take the stroke penalty and continue to be positive on the next shot. Be cool. Positive thinking is not a cure-all. Positive thinking is intelligent analytical thinking with no foolish reasoning and wishes.

Some golfers confuse positive thinking with wishful thinking. Remember, this is not a fantasy game or a fantasy shot, you are in a real world, requiring correct thinking and execution. Hoping or wishing will not achieve the objective. Positive thinking should be a part of your self-talk and rational thinking skills, but it must be realistic to be effective.

Successful results from positive thinking reinforce a positive attitude. If you are positive about his shots and are able to execute them correctly, you have then reinforced your confidence and knowledge of being able to execute the shot. Your mind is developing good pictures for future recall.

Positive thinking can easily turn into negative reinforcement if positive thoughts are beyond abilities and skill level. Continual adverse effects, despite the positive thoughts, will cause a lack of belief in the positive attitude, as well as a loss of confidence and trust in your golfing ability. This is why it is important to keep positive thinking in line with your abilities. Know your capabilities so that you can apply positive thinking correctly.

Lessening Importance of the Situation

Pressure increases with the importance of the situation. As pressure increases, tension may also build in the body. Some athletes, in order to cope with anxiety and tension, convince themselves that the situation is not as important as they believe. Sometimes this can be effective if properly used. The big problem with this technique is that if you convince yourself that the situation is not important then an informal attitude, a lazy attitude—even a careless attitude—may be created. Such a careless attitude may well develop into careless performance. Feeling that a shot is not important, you may become careless in the execution of the skill and suffer drastic consequences. An example of carelessness would be to forget the head wind on an approach shot and then have the ball fall short into the water hazard.

Another aspect of this type of thinking is that it is sort of lying to yourself. If you are trying to convince yourself that the situation is not important, although you really believe it is important, then you may well develop a confused mind. It is very difficult, if not impossible, to lie to yourself.

Some golfers have compared an important shot to its importance with other values. This is a more realistic approach to lessening the importance of the situation. An example would be, "I will try my best on this shot; if I make it, great; if not, well, it's not the end of the world. My wife still loves me. The sun still shines. So let's see what happens. This may be fun."

Perceptions

Perceptions are the big psychological factors in controlling anxiety and tension. How we perceive the situation may be vital to our anxiety and muscular tension control. Good golfers perceive the situation as within their capabilities. Poor golfers perceive the situation as too much to handle or with uncertainty. Good golfers realize that pressure is what they put on themselves as a result of their perception of the situation. Good golfers are good because they know how to handle pressure. They have been there before, and their past experiences have taught them how to cope.

Different golfers have different perceptions of the same situation. Some golfers have a strong fear of sand traps; some have no fear whatsoever. The other golfers range between these two extremes. Negative perceptions of a situation can be improved by mental and physical practice. Mental strategies will help you perceive the situation as less threatening. Successful physical practice will help develop successful recall. Successful reinforcement and a successful positive attitude come with successful skill execution. As practice develops better skills, negative perceptions slowly disappear, while the positive perceptions increase. Imagery can help you perceive a situation as less threatening, and this will be discussed later in the preparation phase.

Mental Recall

Your perception of a situation is usually based on your past experiences. For this reason, you should develop a backlog of successful experiences in certain situations, so that you can recall these successful experiences from memory. This recalling of successful past experiences will reinforce a positive attitude, confidence, positive self-talk, and a good mental image for coping with the situation.

Confidence

Confidence is not a result of positive or rational thinking, nor is it a result of someone telling you how good you are. Confidence is a result of a thorough knowledge of your abilities for the situation at hand. Confidence can be situation-specific. You may be confident on the green when putting and yet be lacking in confidence in the sand trap. Confidence is gained through successful past experiences. Practice and experience build confidence, a true confidence. False confidence is an exaggerated belief in your abilities. All the confidence in the world will not blast the ball out of the trap and near the pin if such a skill is lacking. Successful skill execution is needed to convince the mind that you are capable of performing the skill. As skill improves, the mind becomes more and more convinced of the body's ability to perform the skill. Confidence improves.

Sometimes a confident golfer will lose confidence after a bad round or after a few bad shots. This is natural, as the mind is receiving negative reinforcement from the bad shots. This negative reinforcement causes you to re-analyze your swing, to worry about your game, to have doubts about your abilities and skill execution. The mind is now confused. If such a problem continues, you may go into a slump of an undetermined length. When this happens, you must recall successful past experiences to re-convince yourself of your abilities. If the problem is in the skill area, then physical practice is needed until the problem is corrected. As successful skill returns, so does confidence. The problem in correcting the slump is getting you to achieve the success you once had. Sometimes this can take time. Baseball batters in slumps lose confidence but come back strong when the big home run or the big play reinforces in their mind their successful ability level. This successful reinforcement triggers the player's confidence and brings him out of the slump.

Anxiety and Tension

While performing, you should check your somatic, or body, activity for signs of irregularity, the warning signs of anxiety. The signs of irregularity are easily checked by monitoring your breathing rate, pulse, sweaty palms, and/or muscular tension. If the breathing rate is a little fast, then you may simply force yourself to breathe slower by concentrating on the slower breath rate. Sometimes a little hyperventilation of several quick deep breaths will slow the breathing and the body activity. Imagery can also be effective by visualizing yourself as a relaxed, calm, and cool golfer in total control, breathing slowly and playing with a relaxed body.

Sometimes you will recognize that your heart is beating faster than normal and/or your palms are so sweaty that you are having a hard time griping the club. Again imagery can help the situation. Sweaty palms and muscular tension are usually good indicators of anxiety. Reduce or eliminate the anxiety, and the sweaty palms may go away.

Coping with anxiety requires imagery and the various mental strategies outlined in this chapter. Employing these techniques is simple enough; however, the problem may be in recognizing the situation. Sometimes you can become so wrapped up in the moment, that you forget to check your body activity. Body awareness must be practiced between shots, so that the carry-over will last into the shot execution.

This section has discussed various mental strategies to help achieve maximum physical skill performance. These strategies can be more effective if used in a systematic pattern, so that it is easier to remember as well as to employ correctly when under pressure. Pressure can create anxiety. Anxiety affects the muscles through muscular tension and the mind through the mind's inability to process information correctly. Anxiety creates muscular tension and mental confusion—the enemy of skill execution.

Routines

While playing on the golf course, the following routine, or a similar routine, of strategies should be used to develop a mental reflex pattern to assure that all information is being processed:

1. On approaching the ball, do all your thinking and analyzing for the required shot.

2. On completing the shot analysis, step up to the ball and focuses on the feel for the shot.

3. If the mind is not set and the feel is lacking, then utilize the thought-stopping technique, talk to yourself with rational thinking, and then refocus your imagery. Once the mind is in order and set, repeat steps 1 and 2.

4. When the mind is set to swing, visualize the clubhead scrapping the grass to the target.

5. After the swing, study the ball's flight and roll to the target.

6. On walking to your next shot, check your body activity for signs of irregularity in breathing, pulse, palms, and tension.

7. If necessary, use thought-stopping, self talk, rational thinking, controlled breathing and imagery to control your body activity.

8. While approaching the ball, the next shot is analyzed and the psychological factors are again utilized as the process is repeated.

This routine will soon become a habit that will get easier and easier, as well as more effective, as practice continues.

The Preparation Phase: Psychological Strategies for Use When Not Performing

The psychological strategies to be discussed here are practiced when you are not playing. These strategies require more time and preparation than the previously discussed strategies. The time spent is well worth it. In simple terms, you are using mental exercises to train the muscles to perform physical skills correctly. Mental practice also helps you cope with the constructs of anxiety, fear, confusion, confidence, etc.

There are numerous mental strategies to help a golfer. Some strategies focus on the development of correct skill execution. Some strategies focus on the control of tension and anxiety. Other strategies focus on various positive factors, such as confidence, self-talk, rational thinking, and positive thinking. Various researchers have developed their own mental strategy programs, and there are many of them on the market with their books and articles. Research has proven that they all work. As to which is best, it would naturally depend on individual and situational needs. It is interesting to note that almost all these mental strategy programs involve the skills of relaxation and imagery. Since most programs are basically similar, this book will outline its own mental strategy program specific to your needs. Our program involves the following phases:

1. goal setting;

2. physical and mental skills assessment;

3. relaxation;

4. imagery; and

5. evaluation.

Goal Setting

Before developing a mental practice program, it is best to assess the situation as to where improvement is needed. This assessment is in the form of goal setting. You must analyze your golf game to determine where mental practice is needed and what goals or objectives will meet this need. It is important to keep the goals realistic. A big problem in goal setting is that most people set goals that are too high. High goals are not to be eliminated, but high goals should be achieved in stages. Start off simple; achieve the goals, and then reset your goals to a higher level. Work your way up the ladder. If you start off too high, you may become discouraged by a lack of success in meeting your objectives.

A technique that the business world developed and that coaches have been using for years is the Management by Objectives program. In this program, you develop a plan of long range and short range goals or objectives. Usually a date is set to achieve a certain objective. Everything is done to meet the objective; however, if the objective is not met, then a reassessment of the technique is done with new dates set. This method is successful and can be applied to your golf improvement program. The following is a plan as to how you can evaluate your golf game and set your goals. Answer the questions with "good," "satisfactory," or "poor."

A. Physical ability evaluation:

1. putting

   reading the greens

   force (how hard to hit ball)

   direction

   from the fringe

2. chipping

   club selection

   force

   direction

   swing mechanics

3. pitching

   alignment

   force

   swing mechanics

   misreading distance

4. short irons (8, 9, PW, SW)

   force

   swing mechanics

5. mid irons (5, 6, 7)

   direction

   club selection/distance

   high flight pattern

   swing mechanics

6. long irons (2, 3, 4)

   proper distance

   contact

   swing mechanics

7. fairway woods

   proper distance

   swing mechanics

8. off the tee

   direction

   swing mechanics

9. sand shots

   near green

   fairway traps

   blast shot

   putting out

   pick the ball out

   fried egg lie

10. rough shots

    no grass lie

    tall grass lie

    off dead leaves/grass

    water

11. uneven lies

uphill

downhill

sidehill

12. weather

cold

rain

heat

Wind

B. Mental ability evaluation

1. swing execution

feel for swing

focus on scrape the grass

focus on single item

clear mind

fear for the shot

2. thought stopping

3. self-talk (positive)

4. rational thinking

5. positive thinking

6. confidence

7. anxiety

8. tension

9. fear of embarrassment

10. fear of hazards (traps, etc.)

11. fear of failure

Another means of evaluation is by score card record keeping while playing golf. The codes in table 13-1 are used to record your physical and mental play for each shot. These codes are very detailed.

Table 13-1. Physical and mental codes

Physical code	Mental code
Hook	CM (Confused mind)
Slice	VI (No visualization)
Pull	AX (Anxiety/tension)
Push	FC (No focus)
Short of green	PJ (Poor judgment)
Long, over green	CN (No concentration)
Side green	CF (No confidence)

In Fig. 13-1, on the first hole on the score card, the golfer sliced his drive off the tee, the result of a confused mind. The second shot was a hook shot, with no visualization, while poor judgement caused the third shot to go over the green. On the green, the golfer three-putted from 20 feet as a result of anxiety. After several rounds of score card record keeping, you can easily determine where the problems are occurring. This can be done by keeping a tally or count for each code.

This score card evaluations will help you plan your goals and objectives. Keep in mind that your

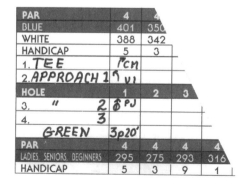

Fig. 13-1. Sample filled-out scorecard.

goals must be realistic and in progression from simple to more difficult. Once your goals are established, begin your physical and mental practice. As previously mentioned in the other chapters, physical practice is needed to help the mental game.

From your evaluation, decide what skills you need to develop. Your physical skill can be helped with mental practice in the form of imagery. Imagery practice is performed while the body is in a relaxed state. Relaxing the body is usually done through imagery and self-talk.

Relaxing the Body

Select a comfortable position in a chair, recliner, bed or flat platform. Close your eyes and prepare your body for the relaxed state. Think relaxation. Picture yourself relaxed. Focus your attention on your breathing. Breath in a relaxed and controlled manner. Keep it even and rhythmical, with equal time on inhalation and exhalation. Sometimes a picture of yourself floating on a cloud may help. With each exhalation, feel yourself getting more relaxed, with tension leaving the body with each breath.

As the body becomes relaxed, feel the body becoming warmer and more comfortable. As the body goes more and more into a relaxed state, focus your attention on specific parts of the body and use self talk to increase your awareness of relaxation to the body part. Start at the toes/feet and gradually focus to all body parts in turn. Talk to yourself, and picture your body relaxing more and more. Tell yourself the leg is getting heavier and heavier, it cannot move, tension is easing away, the leg is lifeless. Develop your own pictures and self-talk that is easy for you. Once the body is in the relaxed state, the mind is receptive for imagery development.

Imagery

Brainwaves occur in two major wave lengths. They are ALPHA, the fully relaxed state and BETA, the more active or fully awake/alert state. Imagery should be practiced in both states.

Imagery is an effective technique, providing you keep it simple, vivid and accurate. As with goal setting, you must work from the simple to the difficult. From your assessments, you can easily determine your order of priorities. Imagery is used to help cope with skill development and mental development.

Imagery for skill development

As an example of skill development through imagery, the correction of a bent/collapsed radius arm and wrist at the top of the backswing will be discussed. Before you go into a relaxed state, you must get an accurate understanding of the correct position of the radius arm and wrist at the top of the backswing. This can be done through studying golf books and photographs or with the help of a golf professional. Once this position is accurately understood, relax the body and develop the picture. Picture yourself taking the club away from the ball. Develop a clear picture/image of the correct arm and wrist position at the top of the swing. Repeat this image several times. Focus on the complete swing, then focus only on the top of the backswing image several times, and then refocus on the complete swing again. Your images progress from the full swing, to stressing the top of the backswing, and then putting it all together again in the full swing. Remember, whenever stressing a part of the golf swing, always put that part of the swing back into the full swing image so that the full swing development occurs.

The same procedure is used to stress other parts of the swing. Sand trap blasts can be mentally practiced the same way by focusing on the overall swing, with emphasis on the club head going through the sand. All physical skill problems can be practiced in this manner.

Imagery for Mental Development

Imagery for mental development is performed in much the same way as for skill development. An example of mental development imagery would be the control of fear/anxiety for the sand trap blast.

Picture yourself walking to the ball in the sand trap. As you approach the ball, you know that it is a difficult shot, but you have been successful in the past, so there is no need to fear this situation. Your breathing and pulse are normal. Your palms are dry and your body is relaxed but alert. You walk confidently to the trap and assess the situation. You pick your sand wedge and step up to the ball. As you walk through the sand, you evaluate the sand as to heaviness and depth of sand. You step up to the ball, dig your feet in a little for a solid base, picture the desired shot, and then you swing. The swing is smooth; the correct amount of sand is taken, and the ball flies out and onto the green. You walk away confidently, as once again you have been reinforced in your ability to correctly play the sand blast.

This procedure can also be used to cope with other types of golf shot fears. Anxiety and tension problems can be attacked with this type of imagery. The golf shot over the water hole is a common fear that can be controlled by imagery. It is important that you do not use a negative statement in your picture or imagery development. Imagery is thinking with pictures, and the mind cannot see a negative picture. If you develop your image with self-talk, such as "don't hit the ball into the water," then the mind sees the ball going into the water and you now have a detrimental, or negative, picture. You know that the body will react to this negative picture by moving the muscles to make you hit the ball into the water. Remember Chevreul's pendulum and how our mind controlled the swing action of the pendulum. The correct approach for the water hole is to picture the ball flying in a desired flight pattern over the water hole, as if the water hole was not there.

Imagery should be practiced when you put your body in a relaxed state. Practice in this alpha state is best for developing the muscle memory in coordination with the mind. Imagery should also be practiced while not in the totally relaxed state but in the beta state. In the beta state, imagery can be practiced for a few short minutes or for seconds, while behind the desk at work, during a television commercial break, or while waiting for a bus. Imagery practice in the totally relaxed alpha state will assist the imagery practice in the beta state. Imagery practice in the beta state is also helpful in developing the use of imagery for playing conditions.

Imagery used while performing is called visualization. Most professionals use visualization of the shot before execution, even though they may not formally practice imagery. Children use a lot of imagery and visualization when they are learning and playing sports. They often dream of their performances in the big time. Many children play imagery or fantasy games against the top golf professionals, or how they are winning the Master's or the US Open tournaments. As adults, we would be so much the better if we incorporated our childhood dreams into our development and learning situations.

Evaluation

It is best if you continually evaluate your learning. The best way to evaluate your learning is to keep records. Such things as how many fairways off the tee are hit, how many one-putt greens or putts to a round. Records can also be kept on the practice range. How many good drives out of fifty attempts? How many pitches to within three club lengths of the pin? These are all examples of what can be done to evaluate your improvement or lack of improvement. Comparing your score cards may reveal improvement. If improvement is not developing, then a recheck of techniques, imagery, etc. must be carried out to find the reason why progress is retarded.

Concentration

Concentration is focusing the mind on an object or procedure. In golf, this means focusing on the golf ball, the flight of the ball, or the golf swing, and not being distracted from this focus. The golfer's complete attention is directed at executing the golf shot. The previously outlined program can also be used to improve one's concentration. Imagery is used to develop the picture in the mind of a relaxed and undistracted golfer. Picture yourself in crucial situations and seeing yourself behaving in a calm manner, analyzing the situation accurately and then executing the swing correctly. Use self-talk to convince yourself of proper behavior and proper focus of attention. Use statements such as "despite the large gallery, I am completely focused on the shot. I only see the ball and its flight pattern. I am relaxed."

Concentration can also be practiced in the beta state. While sitting at a desk, or in a car (but not while driving), focus your attention on an object and see how long you can keep the focus before being distracted. Also practice your imagery for confidence in this state.

Sometimes a lack of concentration is the result of a lack of confidence or confusion in the mind. Very often, golfers are concentrating, but their mind is wandering from focus to focus, causing confusion. Concentration must be focused on a single item or phase of the swing. The effectiveness of concentration is on the single-item focus. Again, imagery can be used to develop this single item focus.

Hypnosis

There is nothing magical about hypnosis. Hypnosis cannot make a golfer perform beyond his or her physical ability or skill level. If tension, anxiety, or fear of the situation is a problem, then hypnosis may be helpful in reducing these emotions so that you can physically perform to your ability. Contrary to the belief of many people, some claim very few (about 30%) people can actually be hypnotized. Many golfers, including some professionals have actually tried hypnosis. Success has been limited to some, and when it was successful it didn't seem to last long, or hold up very well under some pressures. Golf professionals will do anything to win the big money, so if hypnosis was a successful venture, then most of the professionals would be using hypnosis. The tour professionals, when confronted with golfing problems, seek help from sport psychologists and teaching golf professionals. The sport psychologists work on the mental game while the teaching golf professionals work on the physical game. Sport psychologists use various techniques, but hypnosis is rarely used.

Another detrimental effect of hypnosis is the assumption that you are left to the control of another person. People like to control their own situations and can often be uneasy when under the control of someone else.

Self-hypnosis can be helpful to the golfer as this mental strategy is under personal control. It must be realized, however, that self-hypnosis is nothing more than effective concentration, or focus of attention. Self-hypnosis is a form of imagery. If you read the literature on self-hypnosis, you will find the techniques very similar to the relaxation/imagery mental strategies.

Some of the research on hypnosis claims that it is not the hypnotic state, but merely the positive suggestions or positive self-talk used in hypnosis, that is effective.

Meditation

Here again, we find that it is similar to the relaxation/imagery mental strategies. The subject is focusing attention on a single item, usually called a mantra. Relaxation and imagery are key factors in meditation, as they are in other mental strategies. At times, some athletes have praised meditation for relaxing the body. This relaxed state has helped some golfers. If you are only interested in relaxation, then this technique may be of merit. If you have tension problems and require relaxation skills, then meditation may be helpful, but meditation in and of itself has little merit in helping the golf swing.

Reminiscence

This is an interesting mental strategy. Reminiscence is the improvement that occurs while one has been away from an activity. Sometimes a golfer is away from the game for a period of time and then returns to only perform at a higher level than at the time he or she left the game. This is contrary to logic, as it is generally believed you must practice for improvement. The reason for improvement despite being away from the game is the result of imagery practice. Although the imagery practice may not be of a formal nature, you do visualize and think about the game despite the lack of physical practice. Sometimes this period away from the game is an excellent motivator to renew playing interest, especially if burnout or boredom is at hand. This period is also an excellent time to reevaluate your game, your swing, and other problems you may have. It can be a time to establish the proper mindset for the game.

Choking

All mistakes are not chokes. Every time someone fails at a critical time, it is called a choke. It should be noted that the best baseball hitters hit .300 or a little better. This means that the best hitters fail 2 out of 3 times. The percentages tell us that they are not choking, just playing to their percentages. Golfers also play to their percentages and natu-

rally the better players have better percentages; however, no golfer has a 100 percent perfect rate of execution. Do not believe every mistake is a choke. Often it is merely the percentages falling into place. Do not believe you are a choker, it may just be the percentages falling into place or catching up with you.

Choking does happen, and it is usually the result of worry over what others are thinking about you and how you will perform to their expectations. In crucial situations, the choke occurs with you focusing your attention on what others are thinking of you and how others are evaluating you, rather than focusing your attention on execution of the shot. The mental strategies in this book will help you deal with any choking (anxiety) problems.

The Five Stages of Accomplishment

Billy Andrade won the 1998 Canadian Open Golf Championship after many years of turmoil. His years of turmoil had put him in position to lose his tour card and force him back to qualifying school.

After his win, congratulations came in from the other golfers. One congratulatory post card came from Jeff Sluman, who had gone through a similar turmoil of no wins. Fortunately, Jeff recently won and sent his friend a post card with the following text:

Forget the Past,
Do Not Think of the Future,
Perform in the Present

There is a big difference in saying you will win and believing you will win.

Winners never say it, because winning is a matter of fact to them. Besides, they are focused on the present, not the future. Declaring to win is focusing on the future. Winning is a quiet acceptance of the fact. Real winners do not have to rely on bravado, taunting or trash talk. Their confidence is secure, as they know nothing can stop them. They give maximum performance to the present and let winning take care of itself.

Table 13-2. The five stages of accomplishment

1. Denial: I can't do it.

2. Uncertainty: maybe I can do it.

3. Resistance: no way I can do it.

4. Panic: what if I can't do it?

5. Acceptance: I believe it. It is a fact.

Part V
Advanced Techniques

14
Does Your Golf Ball Know What Your Body Is Doing?

This chapter gives a little insight into how the professionals are swinging to their natural movements and not to a theoretical swing analysis. Although they swing with different characteristics, they all scrape the grass under the ball in line to the target. They are all correct at ball contact. Remember that this chapter is not advocating deviations to the swing or to purposely do things incorrectly. This chapter is designed to make you aware of the variations to the golf swing.

The Grip

The grip has been referred to as the key to good golf. Very few teachers and pros will debate this. Yet, despite this widespread belief, there seems to be a lack of consistency as to what constitutes a good grip. Most teachings stress that the two palms should be opposite each other and in line with the direction of flight. The V's of the thumb and forefinger should point to the head. This grip gives the left hand the so-called weak grip position that is popular with many pros. Many other pro golfers use the strong left hand grip, with the left hand V pointing to the right shoulder. Paul Azinger and Bobby Clampett have had great success with the strong grip, while Bernard Langer

uses such a strong grip that the back of the left hand is pointing to the sky.

Tom Watson, like most golfers, holds the club shaft grip diagonally across the palm of the left hand, but for Mike Dunaway, the 1985 longest driver in golf, this position is insufficient. Mike uses a strange grip as the club does not lie diagonally across the palm of the left hand; instead, it lies squarely across the end of his palm. This grip places the shaft across the end of his palm and in the joints of all the four fingers of the left hand. His fingers are then curled around the shaft. All of his "long" thumb lies flat on the shaft and not like the conventional grip where just the thumb tip is on the shaft. The rest of his grip is the familiar interlocking grip.

Al Wagner carries the conventional overlap grip a little further. If one overlapping finger is good, then two overlapping fingers should be better. Al has his students use a double overlap grip with the last two fingers of the right hand overlapping the first two fingers of the left hand.

And how can you argue with the grip of Charles Owens, who won $200,000 and two tournaments on the Senior PGA Tour in 1986. Charles uses a cross-handed grip and a stiff-legged swing to defy all teachings.

Finally, let's not forget Moe Norman the great golfer who many of the top pros claim to be the best ball striker in golf. Moe has been compared to Ben Hogan. Moe uses the ten-finger grip, but with the club in the palms of the hands. He claims that is how you hold a hammer to strike a nail.

It must be evident that there is no one grip to better golf. Teachings do not agree as to where the V's should point or whether the weak or the strong grip is best. The interlocking, ten-finger, baseball, overlap, double overlap and even the cross-handed grip have all been successful. It is hard to define one grip as the correct grip when the top touring pros use different grips. There is no doubt that the best grip is a grip that coordinates the two hands to act as one. How this criterion is achieved depends on you, your feel, your musculature, your palm and finger size and your confidence.

The Stance

In most teachings the stance has the weight evenly distributed on both legs, or with a little more weight to the left leg. Bob Toski, however, teaches that the weight should be mostly on the right leg. Whitney Crouse claims that it is easier to shift the weight to the right side if 60% of the body weight is on the right leg prior to the weight shift. John Mahaffey credits his success to his ability to achieve a fuller body turn by placing his body weight on the right leg during the stance. This weight placement has added an extra 20 yards to his drives.

Jim Flick says that the new golf stance has the knees and hips cocked laterally toward the target, with the left knee outside the left shoulder for the stance as well as throughout the swing. The right eye is lined up over the right knee and 60–70% of the weight is on the inside of the right foot.

Don Trahan teaches an interesting concept of different weight distribution for different shots. For the short lob shot, the weight distribution is 90% on the right leg and 10 % on the left leg; the long iron hook is 70% right and 30% left; the high drive is 60% right and 40% left; the low drive is 40% right and 60% left; and the low running chip is 10% right and 90% left. What this all comes down to, is that the higher trajectory shots place more weight on the right side, while the lower trajectory shots place the weight more toward the left side.

Long ball hitter Mike Dunaway says, "Put a little more than half your lower body weight on the left hip, with the upper body slightly favoring the right side."

Ben Hogan, like many other pros, places his right foot perpendicular to the flight of the ball. Charles Owens, the cross-handed player, turns his right foot well out to give his body a freer and bigger turn for his backswing. The right foot positions vary with most golfers and can be an aid to controlling the body turn and backswing.

In the stance position, the left arm and the golf club form a line to the golf ball. With some golfers, this line is straight, with others, it is bent. The line varies so much from golfer to golfer, it is difficult to determine a consistent pattern.

Ball placement is also a source of inconsistent teachings. Some golfers play the ball off the front heel for all shots, while others play the ball one or two inches off the front heel for all shots. Some golfers play the driver off the front heel and progress through all the clubs backward until the wedge is played from the middle of the stance. Some golfers play the driver off the front heel and progress backwards with all the clubs until the wedge is played off the right heel. Peter Jacobson plays all shots off his left heel. John Miller moves the ball around in his stance.

In the alignment of the stance, golfers may use a square stance for all shots or they may use a closed stance for the drive, a square stance for the midiron, and an open stance for the short shots. Some golfers use combinations of square, open, and closed stances.

Almost all golfers can be identified by their stance position, as they all vary to some degree. Perhaps the one consistent pattern all good golfers show is that the body is in the "ready" position—ready to explode into action.

The Backswing

The one-piece takeaway is the rage of teaching, but it seems to be ignored by many successful golfers. Gretchen Byrd teaches that the backswing should be started with a push of the left arm and hand. Bobby Clampett uses a hands-arms-clubhead takeaway with the shoulders turning as flat as possible but independent of the hands-arms-clubhead takeaway. Gene Littler says that it is really the right arm that takes the club back to the top.

Many pros state that in order to start the backswing, you should move the club back with the body and not the hands. Simply turn your body and arms away from the ball. Don Willingham claims that to achieve proper shoulder turn, think of turning the right shoulder back instead of the left.

It is interesting to note that there seems to be no consistency in the teachings as to how the wrists should break. Some teach that the wrists break immediately on the takeaway, some say after the hands reach waist height, some teach that the wrists break at the top of the swing and some say just let it happen and don't worry about it.

Ben Hogan, who many claim has the most perfect swing in golf, took time off the tour to shorten and flatten his swing arc. Jack Nicklaus also did the same thing recently.

Gary Player, like many other pros, fans the clubhead open during the takeaway. This is against the teachings of keeping the clubface square during the backswing. Some golfers even close the face during the backswing.

Golf teachings emphatically state that the weight must not move past the inside of the right foot; however, Charles Owens, on his takeaway, moves his weight to the outside of his right foot. It is believed that if the weight goes past the inside of the right foot, the body will sway on the backswing. This swaying on the backswing is considered another no-no in golf; however, Craig Shankland feels that a little lateral sway of the body won't hurt the overall swing. It may even be helpful. Some of the tour players sway when they swing at the ball.

Bernard Langer keeps his left heel down when at the top of his backswing while Jack Nicklaus raises his heel considerably more than most golfers. Some golfers just roll the foot inward instead of lifting the heel. It is also interesting to note that Nicklaus places his left toes out at address; on the backswing he raises the heel, but on the downswing he moves the heel forward so that the heel returns to the ground, with the foot now perpendicular to the line of flight. This perpendicular position eliminates the chance of body spin and gives Jack a solid left side.

At the top of the backswing, Charles Owens, wraps his left arm around his neck to give the elbow a 90 degree bend. Everyone knows this is never taught or accepted.

Peter Beames claims he benefitted greatly from an article on a Ben Hogan secret, where the left wrist is slightly cupped (concave) at the top of the swing. Most teachings say this wrist position should be flat, like that of Johnny Miller and most of the other pros. But Arnold Palmer, like many power golfers, puts his wrist in a slightly convex position when at the top of his swing.

With all the teachings and problems with the backswing, it would seem that the Andrew Mullin theory of eliminating the backswing altogether may be the best solution to backswing problems. Andrew says that in order to place the club at the top of the swing, make sure it is in the correct position and then just start the swing from the top. This method puts the left side in control of the swing and eliminates the dominant right side. On first thought it seems like a crazy idea, but the baseball swing does not have the long backswing either. Also, in scientific principles, motion in one direction cannot increase motion in the opposite direction, therefore the backswing has no bearing on the downswing. So why not start the swing at the top and eliminate half your problems?

It is getting complicated in picking the correct backswing. Success has been achieved by taking the club back with the body, the arms, the shoulders, or the hands. The clubface can be open, straight, or closed on the backswing. The wrists can break early, medium, or late. At the top of the swing, the hands have been placed in the cupped, flat, and convex position. The upright swing is being changed by some for a flatter plane. The left foot has been raised, rolled, and stayed in place. The left arm can be straight or bent 90 degrees, and lateral sway can now be accepted. Perhaps eliminating the backswing has merit.

The Downswing

Most of the teachings stress left-side control for striking the ball. There are some experts, however, who stress right side control for the downswing. Peter Jacobson claims that for maximum power and control, you should hit the ball with the right side. Just grip the club, turn the big muscles, and forget your hands and arms, as they'll follow. Ernie Vossler teaches the downswing as a "just hit" the ball. The whole right side hits the ball—right hand, right arm, right hip, right shoulder—the whole right side flows through the ball. Joe Nichols, who developed the "Rotor Method" (to be discussed later), stresses the right side on the downswing, so that the clubhead will catch up to the hands and pass the hands.

Time and time again, the golf swing is referred to as a centrifugal force action. Mike Dunaway believes this and advises not to pull down with the arms but to let centrifugal force swing the club.

All golfers are taught to swing with the delayed hit, or delayed uncocking of the wrists. It is believed that this delayed action is mandatory for full swing power. Ernie Vossler says that the earlier you uncock on the downswing, the better and farther you will hit the ball. He believes that no one can hit too soon or release the clubhead too early. The earlier you release or uncock in the forward swing, the better your chances of meeting the ball square and with maximum force.

Paul Bertholy claims the secret move is a horizontal "tug" from right to left by the muscles of the upper left arm. This tug increases clubhead speed at impact, it keeps the clubhead in line with the target, and it prevents the right hand from hitting prematurely. This is in line with T. P. Jorgensen and his demonstration with the ruler on the table top described in Chapter 1.

The downswing can be controlled by the left side or the right side. Your body has only two sides, so take your pick. Uncocking of the wrists is usually late, but an early uncock may even help you. If it doesn't matter whether you use your left or right side, or uncock early or late, then perhaps you have nothing to worry about—swing away confidently.

Contact

At contact, most golfers have the right heel off the ground as the body is moving forward, but Scott Verplank, like many other modern pros, keeps his right heel down at impact to prevent the upper body from spinning away from the ball and causing a slice or a pull. The right heel on the ground discourages a sway by keeping the head and upper body behind the ball at contact.

Golfers are taught to hit the iron shots on the downswing and the drive on the upswing. Phil Rodgers teaches to move the club face parallel to the ground for ball contact with all irons and woods. This parallel-to-the-ground swing action gives better control and distance, as the ball is not pinched into the ground when struck on the downswing.

Dr. Ralph Mann, in his study of biomechanics of the golf swing, has found that with better performers the hands are going very slowly at impact, but the clubhead is going very fast. Jack Nicklaus' "hands are virtually stopped at impact, acting as a lever. Actually, it may be that the wrists are doing nothing but being a hinge."

When comparing golfers, the body position at contact may well be the most consistent similarity with all golfers. Golfers look very individualistic on the grip, stance, backswing, downswing, and follow-through—but at contact, they all look similar.

The Follow-Through

Probably the biggest change in the follow-through is that many players on the tour are finishing their swing low and around instead of high and straight ahead. The left arm bends quickly after contact, which is unlike the conventional theory of a straight left arm well after contact.

Peter Beames claims that he was able to get more distance to his shots by using the Gary Player "walk through." The walk through is striding or walking forward with the right leg as the body goes into the follow-through.

The follow-through means nothing, as the ball is already on its way. The value of the follow-through is to check the downswing and contact positions.

The Overall Swing

Desmond Tolhurst has broken the teaching methods into five groups—the swingers, the left-siders, the right siders, the mechanical, and the mentalists. Other teaching theories range from the extremes of the mechanics or theorists to the feelers or mentalists. The mechanics are the golfers who are very mechanical, robot-like and precise in their body movements. The feelers and mentalists are the golfers who play by feel and/or the subconscious. All methods have been successful.

Joe Nichols' "Rotor Method" is a new kind of arm swing with excessive wrist action. "Nichols preaches virtually no takeaway, very little follow-through, an action where the club is nearly vertical through most of the swing, and an almost negligible amount of lateral leg drive." Nichols

disciples are on the PGA tour and at various clubs as teaching pros.

Some teachings claim that you can use any swing you want, providing you follow a simple move. Alex Morrison claims that all you have to do is point the chin to a spot just back of the ball and keep it pointed there until well after the ball has been hit. "No matter what method of swinging a club you may use, you cannot make a successful shot unless you do this."

Eddie Merrins teaches to swing the club handle. Tom Purtzer says to practice the golf swing with a ball tucked under your right armpit. Hank Johnson uses a broom to teach the golf swing, as swinging the broom gives the feel of how to swing a golf club. Ben Doyle uses additional props from a junkyard to teach the golf swing. His students swing while balanced on milk crates, swing mops, swing open umbrellas, swing hockey sticks, etc. Manuel de la Torre teaches that the swing is executed by swinging the clubhead back with the hands, but forward with the arms.

Many teaching professionals stress that the golfer should go to the three-quarter swing for more consistency and control. Doug Sanders was one of the first to prove the viability of the short backswing in his play and book "Compact Golf." He feels that the short backswing, or the compact swing, is the key to better golf, as it will give the golfer distance, consistency, and ball control. His theory is that the longer the swing, the more things that can go wrong.

Henry Cotton claims that the most important factor in learning golf is not in the swing but in the hands. The hands are trained to find the back of the ball with a square clubface and to whip the club through the ball for distance. He believes that golfers should train and strengthen the hands and the arms first without any specific swing action. When good contact is acquired, then the golfer may work on a swing method. Henry is against the "leftist" golf thinking. He feels that the right hand is the "finder hand." He is little concerned about the position of the hands or wrists at the top of the backswing, as the right hand will naturally come back from any position to hit the ball squarely and the right hand will find the correct position for contact. All that matters is letting the right hand find the ball.

David Lister claims to have found the missing link to the golf swing. Basically, the missing link, is to draw back the right shoulder during the backswing. This action gives the body a fuller and freer use of the right side for the forward swing. Pulling the right shoulder back facilitates in making a bigger shoulder turn for power and for forcing the right side into position to properly strike the ball from inside the target line.

James Haber, in his book *Golf Made Easy* feels that the golf swing should be spot-focused through the left foot arch. His theory is to control the clubhead by focusing your attention on this spot-focus on the left foot. A chain reaction from the spot-focus, up the left side, to the left shoulder, and down the left arm to the clubhead, helps the subconscious to control the swing correctly. Haber also stresses the square clubface two inches in back of the ball and three inches in front of the ball as a key to the swing. This key was also the backbone of the J. Victor East golf swing theory (*Better Golf in Five Minutes*). Both teachers stress the impact zone and leave much of the other swing part theories to occur as a result of achieving impact zone squareness.

Carl Lohren, in his book *One Move to Better Golf*, claims that the rotation of the left shoulder as the first move in starting the backswing is the key to better golf. This move alone will be sufficient in creating a successful golf swing.

Mr. X says that timing and tempo of the golf swing can be aided by the count of "one-and-two." The count of one—two is not correct as there is no count for the top of the backswing. Oliver Brizon may be a little more sophisticated as he claims that to develop tempo for the swing the count should be one-two-three in French. "Un" for the takeaway, "deux" for top of the swing, and "trois" through impact. Using an unfamiliar language promotes a slower pace.

Sam Byrd, a former Yankee baseball player and now a PGA pro, says that golf is not a left-side game. He claims that hitting a golf ball is like hitting a baseball, with the right hand supplying the power. He teaches that the backswing is

started by a slight push with the left foot and by the lifting of the right side to move the club back to the top of the swing. The downswing is a pushing down of the right side and a lifting up of the left side.

Desmond Tolhurst claims that to increase distance, you should use a karate breathing skill. Before the swing, take a deep breath and fill the abdominal area, then the chest and then the upper chest. The breath is held and forcibly released during impact.

Sometimes golfing problems can be a result of the equipment. Many pros claim that if you want more distance, you should get a longer driver, shallower clubface, and greater loft.

Perhaps Al Barkow has solved the improvement problem: Better concentration and better play is simply the result of faster play.

The Short Game

Like everything else, the short game has its inconsistencies. Most short game teachings stress the left side, but Dick Farley and Rick McCord say that for pitches, chips, and putts, you should control the shot with the right arm. Better control and cleaner contact will result by keying on the bending and straightening of the right arm, while keeping the left side solid.

Many of the top golfers let the right hand/arm roll over the left hand/arm after contact; however, Tom Pullman believes in the reverse release on the follow-through of pitches and chips. The reverse release is flipping the right hand under the left at impact.

Ken Venturi teaches the stiff-wrist method, where the chip is stroked by the movement of the shoulders and arms, while Isao Aoki uses the wristy stroke style for chipping.

Ball placement in the chip varies between the front foot and the back foot. On chip shots, Hubert Green doesn't even place the ball between the feet. He plays the ball way back in the stance, with the ball to the right of the right foot. Hubert uses a wristy stroke, with the hands well down to the metal shaft. With this ball position, it is only natural that the hands are well ahead—in fact way ahead, of the ball.

Phil Rodgers disagrees with spinning the ball for the short game. He feels it is impossible to spin the ball the same amount every shot. The spinning technique breeds inconsistency in regard to distance, as some shots will back up and others will skid forward. Naturally, he teaches the no-spin shot for a consistent roll pattern:

❑ For chips with the pitching wedge, it is 1 part carry and 2 parts roll;

❑ with the 9 iron, it is 1 part carry and 3 parts roll;

❑ with the 8 iron, it is 1 part carry and 4 parts roll;

❑ with the 7 iron, it is 1 part carry and 5 parts roll;

❑ with the 6 iron, it is 1 part carry and 6 parts roll.

Dave Pelz has taken the judgment of distance from a feel process to a mechanical process. Distance is determined by the length of the backswing and a similar length to the follow-through. You determine distance by a backswing when your hands go to the eight o'clock, to the nine o'clock and to the 10 o'clock positions. When playing the course, all you have to do is determine the distance to the green and then take the backswing to the clock position of 8, 9, or 10 o'clock.

Like the rest of the golf swing, the short game can be a left-side swing or a right-side swing. The hands can roll over or under each other. The stroke can be wristy or stiff. The ball can be played anywhere between the feet or even behind the right foot. The approach shot can use backspin or no spin. Distance can be determined by feel or by mechanical positioning of the backswing.

Putting

Despite all the theories and mechanics on putting there are only four factors for accurate putting:

1. keep the head steady;

2. stay in balance;

3. make a low, smooth takeaway; and

4. keep the left side firm.

Phil Rodgers has an interesting concept for determining how hard to hit a putt: "For every inch you swing the putter back, the ball will roll one foot." This means that for a 6-foot putt, you should use a 6-inch backswing and a 6-inch follow-through.

Dr. Robert E. Kraft, in studying the research on golf putting, was able to conclude that there are more differences than similarities. The only consistencies were that most golfers placed the ball opposite the left foot and the eyes were directly over the ball. Spot putting to a three-foot mark, seems to be better than aiming directly at the hole. It made no difference whether the putting stroke was smooth-flowing or a short tap, or whether it was a wrist stroke or an arm stroke method, or whether the golfer used a blade, a mallet, or a center-shafted putter. He did find that the weight on the putter should be at both ends of the blade, which is prevalent with most putters today. He also found that it really doesn't matter which type of putter to use, as proficient golfers can adapt to any putter.

In putting, ball contact theories range from striking the ball on the downswing to striking the ball on the upswing. New putting research shows that the ball must be struck at the exact bottom of the swing arc. It does not matter where the ball is placed in the stance, provided the shaft is precisely vertical at impact. When the ball is struck from this vertical club position, it will achieve its best rolling action. When the ball is struck with the hands ahead of the ball, it takes an irregular roll with some bouncing. When the hands are placed behind the ball, the ball has extensive skidding action, and when it starts to roll, the revolutions are inconsistent. The most consistent roll is achieved when the shaft and the hands are precisely vertical over the ball.

Putting, although half the golf game, is the least taught skill. This may not necessarily be such a bad idea.

Summary

The golf ball is not aware of how the body moves, but the golf ball is well aware of how it is struck by the clubface. It is the position of the clubface at contact that is important—not how the body has moved to put the clubface into contact position. Although the pros may move differently from each other, they all have a similar clubface position at the point of contact. *Remember, it's not how you move the body but how the clubface moves into the ball at contact.*

Most golf teachings stress how to move the body in order to get the clubface square at contact. This type of teaching has you focus your attention on the body to the exclusion of the club. The focus of attention must be on the club, and particularly on the face of the club. If your thoughts are on the clubface then your body will adjust naturally to move the club into the desired clubface position. This is why the good golfers visualize the ball's flight, and then swing at the ball. By doing this, you are focusing on squareness of the clubface and letting your muscles react to create this squareness.

15
The Practice Swing Is Always Better

Have you ever noticed how some of your golfing partners take the nice and easy practice swing that looks so good, but when they go to hit the ball, they take a swing that may not even resemble the game of golf? Have you noticed that this may also be your problem? A good practice swing confirms your ability to physically perform the golf swing. Failure to carry over a good practice swing to the golf ball is a mental problem.

The Ball

And what causes this mental problem? "Well, it's the damn ball." As soon as you step up to the ball, you become tongue-tied, muscle-tied, scared, forgetful, weak, and anything else that may interfere with your swing. Stepping up to the golf ball triggers your breakdown.

When you take your practice swing, you "freewheel" the swing. You do not get tied up with thoughts of body mechanics, contact or direction of the ball. You simply swing the golf club. Often this practice swing is done with no focus of attention or concentration. Your mind is clear. You feel the swing. You let it happen.

When you attempt to hit the golf ball, your mental approach changes. You now think about body mechanics, force, direction, and trajectory. You concentrate and focus your attention on all these aspects. You become mentally confused. You short-circuit. You may even blow a fuse. Concentration appears to be essential, but it can be the one factor that ties the body in knots. *Forcing the concentration factor can restrict body movements.* You concentrate so hard that we tighten our muscles. Often, we are unaware of this tensing of the muscles. Have you ever noticed, while watching a thriller movie, how you concentrate and focus your attention so hard on the movie that your muscles tighten up? Sometimes, when absorbed in writing, you squeeze the hell out of the pencil. Concentration should be an easy and natural response. It cannot be forced.

Concentration must be practiced without letting the muscles become tense. Practice for concentration can be done anywhere, and under various conditions. You should practice concentrating (focusing your attention) on various objects, while continually checking your muscles for maintaining a relaxed state. Let yourself become engrossed in a movie without letting your muscles tighten. Practice relaxed movements while concentrating during activities like walking, jogging, tossing pennies, throwing a football, etc.

If you can type, practice typing by intently concentrating on the movement of each key or finger. The results are not very good. Your fingers probably mov slowly, awkwardly, and with some mistakes. Notice how when you type efficiently, you do not really concentrate on your typing. It just seems to happen. Good typists can even talk to you while they are typing. If a good typist can talk to you and type a report at the same time, then perhaps the concentration factor is not such a big deal. If you just let your golf swing happen, then perhaps we do not have to concentrate so intently.

To get the feel of concentration, get a golf ball, or any small object, and toss it in the air and catch it. Now, did you notice how easy this was? You focused on the ball while it was in the air. You noticed no distractions. You concentrated on the ball going up and down. There were no forced mental activities. It was natural.

Although we seem to stress a lessening of concentration, you must be careful not to become careless in your manner. It seems like double talk, and in a way it is. You must concentrate and be aware of the situation, but you must not become so intent that you tie up. Mental practice will help you develop this fine line of performance and concentration. Have you noticed when you played well or hit the good golf shot, how easy and natural it was? You did not force your swing or your concentration. It just happened. This is the feeling you must recall for future golf shots. When you step up to the ball, recall your past successful shots and how natural it felt. Let this feel govern your swing.

Swing with feeling—not concentration

In summary, it appears that the best way to hit a golf ball is to sneak up on it and hit it with your practice swing.

Don't Aim

If you want to hit a golf ball to the target—don't aim! Many golfers on the practice range hit shot after shot consistently straight ahead. But when they hit the same shot on the playing course, the shot goes right or left of the target. The accuracy is gone. Since the practice range shot proves that the you are capable of hitting the ball straight, any failure for accuracy on the playing course must be mental.

Alignment Obsession

While hitting balls on the practice range, you do not become obsessed with alignment. You line up the club, adjust the body, and then you swing. If this simple alignment procedure is accurate on the practice range, then it should be used on the playing course. The procedure is simple. Just line up the club in the position you want for ball contact. Freeze the club in this position, and then grip with the left hand. Now grip with the right hand, and then adjust the feet to the positioning set by the arms and upper body. While adjusting the body, be careful not to move the club out of its original position. Also, it is necessary to adjust in the order of left hand, right hand, and then the feet.

The left-hand grip sets up the swing radius from the shoulder to the club head and helps to set up the body's distance from the ball. The right-hand grip helps to put the body in alignment. The feet must be adjusted last to complete the stance with correct distance from the ball set-up through

the reach of the arms. This alignment procedure sequence adjusts the body to your natural feeling for straightness, a personal feeling, and not a text-book feeling of lines and angles.

If you toss pennies to a wall, you do not think of adjusting the body by means of imaginary lines and angles. Your body alignment is a personal feeling that allows a free arm swing to the target. Your mind focuses on the target, and your muscles react to the instructions your mind visualizes. You feel the toss as a simple natural movement, as the arm automatically swings to the target and not away from the target. Tossing pennies is similar to hitting a golf ball straight. Once you have the skill ingrained in our muscles, you must let your muscles function—without confusing thoughts from the mind.

For some reason, even experts have told you, that to hit a golf ball straight, you must line up your shoulders, hips ,and feet square to the target. Really now! How many times have you lined up square and not hit the ball straight. Lining up square is no assurance of straightness. The squareness of the clubface at contact determines the ball's flight straightness. The body does not determine the straight shot. Some golfers line up square and still take an outside-inside swing to cut or pull the ball. Perhaps such golfers should adjust a little to a closed stance position to help bring the swing in square to the ball for contact? Trevino, and many other golfers, do not line up their body square to the target, as they use an open stance but swing the club square to the target. Johnny Miller shot a 63 in the final round of the 1973 U.S. Open by opening his stance so that he aligned his body 40 to 50 yards left of the target. He claims this alignment forced him into a tighter one-piece swing through a shorter backswing.

Squareness on the Swing

It is the squareness of the swing at contact, not the squareness of the body, that is the key to the straight shot. When swinging at the ball, *the ball does not know what your body is doing, nor does it care what your body is doing. The ball is only concerned with the face of the club at contact.*

If you are in doubt about this philosophy, then go to the practice range and hit golf balls with varying body positions. Experiment with a closed, a square, and an open stance for many shots, but always swing to the target. Years ago, tennis players were taught to stand with feet parallel to the flight of the shot for the basic forehand stroke. Years later, they found that the good players ignored this teaching and stroked the ball with an open body and an open stance position. Like Miller's golf swing, it gave a tighter one-piece swing through a shorter backswing. The tennis ball went where the racket was swung—not where the body was aligned. Body position does not determine direction of the shot. Body position may give balance, feel, and power to the shot, but not direction. The club face and the swing path at contact determine direction. Just like tossing pennies, the body position does not determine the penny's direction. The arm swing does.

To hit the ball straight while on the golf course, you must use the same mental strategy as on the practice range. Do not aim the shot. Aiming leads to steering the club. Baseball pitchers lose control when they start aiming their pitch. When the pitcher loses control, especially in a tight situation, the manager or catcher goes to the mound and simply tells the pitcher to throw the ball— don't aim or steer the throw. Let it go. Trust it. On the golf course, you should line up the club to the target, adjust the body to the club, and swing to the target. That is all. Forget all the alignment theory and drawing of lines and angles and laying clubs down for squareness and direction. Just swing to the target.

17
Don't Hit the Ball Straight

In a golf magazine, a reader requested simple instruction on how to hit the ball straight rather than complicated articles on fading and drawing the ball. On reading this, I immediately thought of my students, as they start out with the same desire of learning to hit the ball straight. Unfortunately, it is this obsession with straightness that causes so many learning difficulties, frustrations, temper tantrums, obscenities, lack of fun, and a desire to quit the game.

The Most Difficult Shot

Hitting a golf ball straight is the hardest shot in golf. Experience and talent make it easier, but it is so difficult that even the tour professionals play the ball either right to left or left to right. If you play your shot with a predetermined right or left spin to the ball, then you can be fairly confident the ball will bend in the desired direction. By knowing the spin on the ball, it becomes easier to aim the shot. Golfers with consistent flight patterns know where to aim the ball. It is not so important as to whether the ball goes straight or bends. What is important, is that the flight pattern be consistent, so that the golfer knows how the ball will fly and where to aim the shot.

To hit a golf ball straight, the ball must be struck without sidespin. If the ball is struck with a spin to the right, then the ball will bend to the right; if the ball is struck with a spin to the left,

then the ball will spin to the left. Naturally, the more the sidespin, the more the bend in the ball's flight. Controlling spin for the straight shot means precise contact. In most cases, the ball will receive some sidespin from contact. The problem is not in the spin imparted to the ball. The problem is not knowing which way the ball will spin. By opening or closing the face at contact, you can increase your certainty of which way the ball will spin and in turn how the ball will fly. By knowing which way the ball will bend, you make it easier to aim the shot with some certainty.

Learning the Straight Ball

The best way to learn the straight ball is to learn the basic swing fundamentals for making consistent contact with the ball. Once consistent contact is achieved, then fading and drawing the ball is accomplished by simply aiming the ball straight and opening or closing the clubface for contact. As you learn the flight characteristics caused by the open or closed clubface, it becomes easier to control the clubface for feeling the straight shot.

When you have achieved some proficiency in ball control, it is a simple process to apply the fade/draw mechanics to the golf swing. When playing the tee shot, most golfers aim down the middle and hope to land the ball in the middle. On a 50 yard wide fairway, the golfer who aims down the middle will have only 25 yards of fairway to land the ball if the ball goes to the right or to the left of the middle.

The better strategy is to tee the ball on the right side of the tee box, aim the ball about 250 yards down the opposite side of the fairway, and slightly open the face of the golf club. If the ball goes straight, then it is still on the fairway, but near the edge. If the ball bends (fades) because the clubface was opened at contact, it has 50 yards of fairway to fall on. The chances of the ball hooking are diminished in relationship to the openness of the clubface. The more open the clubface, the less chance of hooking, although the more the face is open, the more the ball will bend. To draw or hook the ball, the procedure is reversed.

18
Club Selection

Selecting the wrong club has caused many golf rounds to be scored higher than necessary. Such mistakes are often the result of a lack of knowledge about your club's distance and dispersion. Using the correct club for your shots is essential to scoring. Experience and training help in selecting the correct club; however, learning club selection can be quickened by practicing the following simple guidelines.

Distance and Dispersion Pattern

The first requirement to club selection is learning the club's distance and dispersion pattern on the practice range. The signs on the range will give you an estimate of the distance. Hit 10 shots for easy calculation, note the distance, and then compute the average. It is important to realize that your distance for the club is determined by your *average* and not how far you hit your best shot.

For instance, ten 5 iron shots with distances of 170, 160, 155, 155, 150, 150, 150, 145, 145, 140 give an average of 152 or 150. Your distance for the five iron is 150—not 170. Only one shot reached 170 yards, so when playing the golf course, do not think you are a 170 yard 5 iron player. Such reasoning is an ego trip and will bring you short of 170 yards nine out of 10 times. With your 150-yard average and range consistency of 145 to 155 yards, you should reach the pin within five yards, long or short, 7 out of 10 times. Your five iron distance is 150 yards or in the 145 to 155 range.

To establish your dispersion pattern, aim 10 shots to a target and then count the balls that go right and left of the target line. If 7 out of 10 balls go left of the target line, then you can allow for this variance when lining up your shots while playing the course. The amount of deviation from the target line will help you decide how much to allow in your alignment when playing the golf course.

A similar procedure applies to the driver. Hit 10 drives and take your average. Drives of 250, 230, 215, 195, 190, 190, 185, 180, 120, 120—gives an average of 187.

These scores do not make you a 250-yard driver. One shot out of 10 is 250 yards, and only 3 shots in 10 are over 200 yards. Your consistency for the driver is very poor. Hit 10 shots with the 3 wood. Distances of 230, 230, 225, 220, 205, 205, 200, 200, 180, 175—that's an average of 207.

Notice that the distance average for the 3 wood is higher than the driver's average. Distance consistency for the 3 wood is fairly good, and much better than with the driver. In fact, eight out of ten three woods shots are 200 yards and over, while the driver has only three shots over 200 yards. For many golfers, this is not unusual. It is just that many golfers are not aware of this possibility, as they always think the driver goes farther. The driver is capable of going farther, but it is not always the best for average distance.

Notice your dispersion pattern for the 3 wood and the driver. Is the driver placing more shots off line than the 3 wood? Many golfers do not realize it, but they are more consistent with the 3 wood than with the driver. The 3 wood's shorter shaft, with more loft, often gives it a greater consistency and a higher distance average to the shot. When playing the golf course, it may be better to use the 3 wood instead of the driver for the tee shot. Many tour pros are now going from the flatter 7-, 8-, and 9- degree lofted drivers to the greater lofted drivers in the 11- and 12-degree loft range. The higher lofted drivers are closer to the 3 wood's loft of 16 degrees and give the pros more consistency and accuracy off the tee.

Short Irons

Now let's try to find your distances for the pitch shot with the wedge. Figure out your average distance for the wedge with a full swing while griping the end of the club. Next, find your average distance by taking a full swing while griping the club 2 inches down from the end of the grip. Repeat the above for swings with a three-quarter backswing, a half backswing, and a quarter backswing. Some use the hands of a clock to determine backswing length. For example, 6 o'clock would be the ball position. The backswing would go to a 7, 8, 9, 10 o'clock swing length. Do not swing harder as you shorten your backswing. Maintain the same swing pace and rhythm for all shots. Distance will be determined by the length of the backswing. Be sure to use the same swing length for the follow-through and the backswing. As you shorten the length of your backswing, notice how the ball's distances become shorter by about 10 to 20 yards for each swing. This procedure establishes your wedge distances. When you have a required distance to fly the ball, you will now know what swing length and grip position to use.

A similar technique is used to find your chip shot distances. By this we mean how far the ball

Table 18-1. Sample of Golf Club Distances

Distance in yards	Club
200 plus	driver
190–200	16-degree wood
170–180	7 wood
160	4 iron
150	5 iron
140	6 iron
130	7 iron
120	8 iron
110	9 iron
100	Pitching wedge
90	49-degree wedge: 9:30 backswing
80	49-degree wedge: 8:30 backswing
70	49-degree wedge: 7:30 backswing or 55-degree wedge: 9:30 backswing
60	55-degree wedge: 8:00 backswing
50	60-degree wedge: 9:30 backswing or 55-degree wedge: 7:30 backswing
40	60-degree wedge: 9:00 backswing
30	60-degree wedge: 8:00 backswing
20	60-degree wedge: 7:30 backswing
Out of sand	
Distance to pin in yards	**Club**
8–10	60-degree wedge
12–15	55-degree wedge
18–20	49-degree wedge
25–30	Pitching wedge
30	9 iron
35	8 iron

Table 18-1, continued

Chipping	
Club	Fly-to-roll ratio
4 iron	1:5 (fly one part, roll five parts)
5/6 iron	1:4
7/8 iron	1:3
9 iron	1:2
PW	1:1
SW	1:1½

will roll in relation to the distance the ball will fly. Pick a flat part on the green. Place your golf balls about 5 yards off the green. Take a tee and measure or pace off 10 yards toward the green and place the tee at this spot in the green. The tee will be about five yards from the fringe. Continue walking in a straight line and stick tees every five yards from the first tee. Now hit your chip shots to fly in the air and land at the first tee. Using the 5-yard tee placements, measure how far the ball

rolls. If the ball flies 10 yards and rolls 30 yards, then the ratio is fly one part to roll three parts, or a 1:3 ratio. Do this procedure for all clubs you could use for chipping to establish your fly/roll ratios. When playing the chip shot, simply determine the following: distance to the hole, club choice, and landing spot. Naturally, you must make adjustments for grain, wet or dry greens, uphill or downhill slants, etc.

Your Ego

Do not let your ego interfere with your reasoning for club selection. Many golf scores are ruined by nothing more than the ego overriding the player's reasoning ability. Trying to outdrive the other golfers, using a 5 iron instead of a 3 or 4 iron, overestimating your accuracy, are all ego mistakes. *Think intelligently.*

The accompanying table 18-1 is a sample of a chart on distances. Such a chart can be kept in your pocket; simply refer to it when needed. In time, it will be easily remembered.

19
The Role of the Right Elbow

In the full golf swing, the role of the right elbow is an ongoing controversy. Do you keep it in or do you let it fly? Great golfers keep it in and great golfers let it fly; but for power and accuracy, all great golfers bring the elbow in during the downswing. Here's why.

Throwing Action

Take a ball and throw it. Did you notice that as your arm moves forward, the elbow is in front of the hand? As the arm continues forward, the hand whips forward past the elbow for release of the ball. It is this whipping action, or leverage, of the forearm off the elbow that gives velocity to the ball. By positioning the elbow well ahead of the hand before release of the ball, you are able to achieve maximum forearm leverage. Baseball pitchers are particularly adept at this skill (Fig. 19-1). This time, throw the ball with the hand ahead and leading the elbow. Did you notice how weak the throw was executed? The reason for the weak throw is that your arm is positioned for a pushing action rather than a whipping action. This pushing action is a weak and inefficient action because it prevents the build-up and release of leverage.

Now find a stone and throw it to skip on water. No water? Then throw the stone to skip on imaginary water. Again, you will notice how the

elbow leads the hand as the hips slide forward to give clearance for the arm action. If you have ever thrown your golf club, you will have noticed that the arm action is the same as throwing the stone

Fig. 19-1. The baseball pitcher's right elbow leads the hand holding the ball.

to skip on water. The elbow must lead the hand to create leverage for maximum efficiency. Try throwing the skipping stone or the golf club with the hand leading the elbow. Again, you will notice the weak throw as a result of the pushing action. These experiments should give you an understanding of the role of the elbow, forearm, and hand in throwing an object. This throwing action of the elbow leading the hands is required for a successful golf swing, as the golf swing is similar to throwing a golf club or skipping a stone on water.

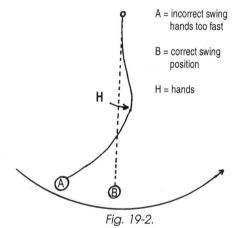

Fig. 19-2.
Hand movement in correct and incorrect swing.

Lead with the Elbow

When you swing a golf club, your right elbow can do what it wants on the backswing. At the top of the swing, the elbow can be positioned in or out (flying). It is the start of the downswing, not the backswing or the top of the swing position, that determines the success of the swing. At the start of the downswing, the right elbow, regardless of position, must drop to the right hip and lead the hands into the contact zone. It is only when the elbow leads and the hands lag behind the elbow, that forearm leverage can be created.

The release of this leverage gives the golf swing the whipping action through the contact zone. The release of this whipping action is called the "delayed hit." The delayed hit used to be the uncocking of the wrists. In the modern golf swing, the delayed hit is the uncocking (leverage) of the forearm off the elbow. The uncocking or leverage off the elbow creates greater leverage than the uncocking of the wrists. This is why the modern-day pro is able to achieve a powerful swing even with the short backswing and/or with the stiff or minimal wrist action swing.

Execute a golf swing with the right elbow out or flying on the downswing (the right hand leading the right elbow), and notice the loss of whip and power to the swing. This elbow out or hand leading the elbow position causes the right arm to push the club because there is no build-up of leverage. As previously explained, the right arm

Fig. 19-3. Right elbow tight to the body, ahead of hand.

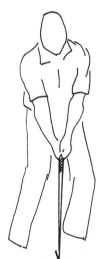

Fig. 19-4. Right elbow tucked into the hip during address.

pushing action lacks power, but ironically it gives the feeling of power to the swing. Unfortunately, this feeling of power causes confusion to the golfer as distance and power seem so minimal to the amount of effort put into the golf swing. Also, this right arm pushing action is often the reason why golfers fail to execute the instructions to lead with the left and hit hard with the right. Such golfers usually lead and guide the golf club correctly with the left arm and hand, but mistakenly feel their right arm power by pushing the club. Golfers who lead and guide the golf club with the left arm and push for power with the right arm naturally conclude that they are swinging as advised, but since the results are bad, they conclude the advice is no good. Although the pushing action has given the feeling of power, such action has nullified the forearm leverage. It is only when the right elbow leads the hands on the downswing that the instructions to lead with the left and hit hard with the right have any meaning. Surprisingly, when the right elbow action is executed properly, there is no feeling of effort, as the swing is easy and comfortable.

Right Shoulder Problem

Another problem that usually occurs when the right arm pushes the golf club into the downswing, is that the right shoulder rolls forward instead of down and into the swing plane. When the right shoulder rolls out, the arms and hands are directed out of the swing plane and into the

Fig. 19-5. Top of the swing (right arm not shown).

Fig. 19-7. Elbow positioned for forearm whipping action.

Fig. 19-6. Swing starts down with right elbow dropping to the hip, hand lagging behind elbow.

Fig. 19-8. Beginning of hand whipping action.

137

Fig. 19-9. Hand whipping past elbow position.

Fig. 19-10. Completion of whipping action.

dreaded problem of cutting across the ball. If you drop the elbow to the hip at the top of the swing, and lead the downswing with the right elbow, the right shoulder will remain back on the swing plane and direct the arms and hands along the proper swing plane path.

Learning the Move

To facilitate the elbow leading position, some golfers will point the inside right elbow straight ahead at a 90 degree angle from the target during the address position. On the backswing, by maintaining the elbow's 90-degree angle away from the target, the elbow will stay close to the hip and be in position at the top of the swing to lead the hands into the downswing. If the right inside elbow turns to point at the target on the backswing, then you will have a flying elbow at the top of the swing. The flying elbow is no problem if at the beginning of the downswing you drop the right elbow toward the hip. This dropping action positions the right elbow to lead the hands into the contact zone. If the inside right elbow points at the target during the downswing, then there will be a pushing action on the golf club rather than a swinging action of the golf club.

In diagram 19-1, notice how the baseball pitcher's right elbow leads the hand holding the ball. In diagram 19-2, notice how the right elbow leads the hands in the downswing and into diagram 19-3 where the right elbow is tight to the body but still slightly ahead of the hands. The elbow leading the hands in the downswing has built up leverage for the forearm and hands so that the hands can whip past the right elbow for a powerful stroke on the ball. In diagram 19-4, the golfer has tucked his right elbow in to the hip during the address position. Diagrams 19-5 to 19-10 have eliminated the left arm and golf club in order to emphasize the right arm action. Diagram 19-5 is the top of the swing. In diagram 19-6, the swing starts down with the right elbow dropping to the hip while the right hand is lagging well behind the elbow. In diagram 19-7, the elbow is positioned for the forearm whipping action as the elbow is in almost the same position as in diagrams 19-8, 19-9 and 19-10. In diagram 19-7, the hand is still lagging well behind the elbow, but in diagrams 19-8 and 19-9 notice how the hand is whipping down, through, and past the elbow into the position of diagram 19-10. Now, if you will look at diagrams 19-5 through 19-10 again, you will notice that the golfer's action is the same as throwing a stone to skip on water.

Analyzing Your Game

To make progress in any pursuit, it is necessary and useful to analyze the your current status. This will help you determine what to work toward and how you have been progressing to date. In analyzing your game, there are four factors to consider. These factors are simple and are easily recorded on your scorecard (Fig. 20-1).

Drives on fairway: Give yourself one point if your tee shot is in the fairway or on the green. Use a "0" (zero) if you miss the fairway.

Greens in regulation: Many consider this the best factor for an evaluation of your game. Give yourself one point for each green you reach in regulation. The ball must stay on the green for the point. Use a "0" (zero) if you miss the green in regulation.

Putts on the green: one point for each putt on the green.

Up and downs: give yourself one point if you miss the green in regulation but you chip, pitch, blast, etc. onto the green and one putt for your par.

Score: There is no doubt that your score is the best indicator of your game. Our score is based on 18 hole par. Give yourself one point for each stroke over par; zero points for par and minus points for each stroke under par.

Table 20-1. Sample score card

Hole	1	2	3	- - - - -
Drv	1	0	1	- - - - -
Gir	1	0	1	- - - - -
U+D	0	1	0	- - - - -
Putts	1	2	2	- - - - -
Scr	−1	+1	0	- - - - -

Table 20-1 Represents a sample score card

Table 20-2. Regulation play consists of:

Par	Tee Shot	Approach Shot	Putts
3	1	0	2
4	1	1	2
5	1	2	2

From these scores, it is easy to determine your percentages.

$$\frac{greens\ in\ regulation}{holes\ played} \times 100 = percentage$$

$$\frac{10}{14} \times 100 = 71\%$$

Table 20-3. Bar chart

This is a sample of a bar graph, or chart, that can easily be done on a computer or a sheet of graph paper. This sample is for scores, but it can also be done for many other statistics. The horizontal numbers can be the dates played. The vertical numbers can be percentages for other statistics. Graphs like these are easy to set up and maintain and offer an excellent visual effect and understanding.

Computer Spreadsheet Analysis

Setting up a spreadsheet for your analysis is fairly easy. The following are the formulas for various statistics.

Fairways in regulation

This is a simple percentage formula:

$$\frac{fairway\ hit}{attempts} \times 100 = \_\%$$

e.g. 10 fairways hit out of 14 attempts is:

$$\frac{10}{14} \times 100 = 71\ \%$$

Greens in regulation

This is also a simple percentage formula:

$$\frac{greens\ in\ regulation}{holes\ played} \times 100 = \_\%$$

e.g. 10 greens in regulation out of 18 holes is:

$$\frac{10}{18} \times 100 = 55\%$$

The above percentage formulas can be used for a number of other statistics that you may want to record. For example, you can keep track of chips, pitches, sand saves, up and downs, etc.

The basic formula for percentages is:

$$\frac{number\ of\ successes}{number\ of\ attempts} \times 100 = \_\%$$

Putts Per Green

Putts per green is calculated by recording the number of putts and dividing by the number of greens.

$$\frac{39\ putts}{18\ greens\ played} = 2.167\ putts\ per\ green$$

Putts per distance

Putts per distance informs you of your average length of putts made. Simply estimate the length of your first putt visually or by pacing. Pacing your putt length may be easiest to record, as it is in line with yardages, and golfers often walk along the putt line to study the putt. Feet, yards, and paces all work. Use what is easiest. Record on your score card as length/number of putts. For example, two putting a 10-pace putt would be 10/2. The average length of putt would be 5 paces. At the end of the round, just add your dis-

Table 20-4. Sample computer analysis in detail

1	A	B	C	D	E	F	G	H	I
2		Per round					For the year		
3	Fairways in regulation					Fairways in regulation			
4	% age	attempts	hits			%age	attempts	hits	
5	66%	12	8			62.5%	24	15	
6									
7	Greens in regulation					Greens in regulation			
8	%age	attempts	hits			%age	attempts	hits	
9	55.6%	18	10			58.3%	36	21	
10	Putts per distance					Putts per distance			
11	dist/per pt	distance	putts			dist/per pt	distance	putts	
12	3.85	150	39			3.80	300	79	
13	Putts per green					Putts per green			
14	put/green	# greens	putts			put/green	#greens	putts	
15	2.166667	18	39			2.19444	36	79	
16	Chip saves					Chip saves			
17	%age	attempts	hits			%age	attempts	hits	
18	50.0%	6	3			58.3%	12	7	
19	Pitch saves					Pitch saves			
20	%age	attempts	hits			%age	attempts	hits	
21	25.0%	4	1			50.0%			
22	Sand saves					Sand saves			
23	%age	attempts	hits			%age	attempts	hits	
24	50.0%	2	1			25.0%	4	1	
25	Holes per penalties					Holes per penalties			
26	hls/pen	hls plyd	strokes			hls/pen	hls plyd	strokes	
27	9	18	2			18	36	2	
28	Scores per holes played					Scores per hole played			
29			hls plyd	number				hls plyd	number
30	0.0%	eagles	18	0		0.0%	eagles	36	0
31	5.6%	birdies	18	1		8.3%	birdies	36	3
32	61.1%	pars	18	11		58.3%	pars	36	21
33	22.2%	bogies	18	4		19.4%	bogies	36	7
34	5.6%	doubles	18	1		2.8%	doubles	36	1
35	5.6%	other	18	1		2.8%	other	36	1
36									
37		score	hls plyd	ttl strks			score	hls plyd	ttl strks
38		4.444	18	80			4.389	36	158

tances and numbers of putts. Apply to the formula.

$$\frac{150 \; paces}{39 \; putts} = 3.85 \; \text{paces per putt}$$

Penalties per holes played

The number of holes played for every penalty stroke can be calculated as follows (example):

$$\frac{18 \; holes \; played}{2 \; penalty \; strokes} = 9$$

Percentage of pars, birdies, bogies, etc.

This is the simple percentage formula. Just substitute for birdies, bogies, etc. (example):

$$\frac{11 \; pars}{18 \; holes \; played} \times 100 = 61.1 \; \%$$

Average strokes per hole

This is based on 4 being the average score per hole (72 par divided by 18 holes = 4.0 strokes per hole. In the following example, a score of 80 for 18 holes is 4.44 strokes per hole.

$$\frac{80 \; strokes}{18 \; holes \; played} = 4.44 \; \text{strokes per hole}$$

Average strokes for par 3, par 4, and par 5

This is the same formula as the strokes per hole (example):

$$\frac{15 \; strokes \; for \; par \; 3 \; holes}{4 \; par \; 3 \; holes} = 3.75 \; \text{strokes per par 3}$$

There are hand-held computers that can be used for statistical analysis. Stat Tracker II is such a devise available at a very reasonable price. It will keep track of stats for four people for about 100 rounds. It is simple and easy to use. The authors have bought one and have used it with great satisfaction. Along with the Stat Tracker II, there is a software program for your computer to receive the stats by download for more detailed analysis. The stats input are drives in fairway, driving distance, greens in regulation, up and downs, sand saves, putts, penalties, and score. The software analysis will give you the percentages for the above data, and also your putts per green and putts per green for greens reached in regulation. Your handicap will also be computed. Their web site is www.stattracker2.com. This or a similar device is well worth considering for anyone who wants to keep track of his or her progress.

21
Golf Drills for Feel

For improved performance, it is important to work on all aspects of your play, and a great, yet too often ignored method is by carrying out a systematic program of exercise drills that can be done anywhere away from the golf course. In this chapter, we'll suggest some useful drills to practice your feel for the golf swing.

1. Half-swing scrape the grass drill. Feel the arm roll and pass the head. The head is relatively stationary. Flow with the movement. This drill can be done at home, with the club head scraping the carpet. The scrapes must be clean and consistent.

2. Swing a broom, mop, or an open umbrella. The swinging of a broom is perhaps one of the best drills to acquire the feel of the golf swing. Swing the broom so the broom head is flat to the direction of travel. This gives air resistance to the bristles of the broom. Since the broom is quite long and fairly heavy, you will feel the broom head whip through the contact area. Swinging a mop or an open umbrella is performed in a similar fashion. When swung like a golf club, the open umbrella gives a slow arm swing at the start of the downswing and a whipping action through the contact area. This is very similar to the real-life golf swing.

3. Use a yardstick to get the feel of the grip. Hold the yardstick so the flat side is facing the imaginary line of flight. Place the left hand and then the right hand on the yardstick. The yardstick will give the feeling of how the hands face opposite each other and down the line of flight.

4. Swing a ball on a string like a golf club swing. The purpose of this drill is to get the feel of centrifugal force and how the string and the ball must stay on a smooth course by timing the swing with the arm movement.

5. The baseball drill for "release" feel. Release means the action through the contact area. Grip club and swing at waist level like a baseball bat at an imaginary approaching baseball. After the follow-through, just swing the club back into position for another swing forward. As you continue to swing back and forth, gradually bend forward at the hips so as to lower the swinging club to ground level. As

the swing continues to an imaginary golf ball, you will notice how the baseball swing and the golf swing are similar.

6. Swing the golf club from waist high to waist high, with the arms and hands remaining almost stationary, while the wrists do the swinging. Strong and flexible wrist action is needed for this drill, as it is basically all hand action. This drill is good to get the feel of the delayed hit and how the hands react in the contact zone.

7. Hold a golf club in each hand and swing the clubs so that the both clubs move parallel to each other in the pattern of a golf swing. This drill is beneficial to the whole swing feel.

8. Without a club, assume the stance position. With the right hand, rotate the shoulders to shake hands with someone to the right of you. This drill gives the feel of the backswing with emphasis on golf's necessary shoulder rotation. This drill can be done with the left hand doing the shaking.

9. Stand like a football quarterback receiving the ball on the snap from center. From this position, the move is to make a handoff to an imaginary halfback on the right side. This move is similar to the starting action of the backswing.

10. To determine how fast you should swing a golf club, practice the golf swing with the left arm only. Slowly execute the full swing several times and then increase the speed of each succeeding swing until it breaks down. The speed of your golf swing should be a little under the breakdown speed.

11. With a golf ball in the right hand (for right hand golfers), swing the arms as if hitting a golf ball. When the hands are in the contact zone, throw the ball at a spot on the ground in front of you. This drill will give you the feel of the hands in the release or contact area.

12. Swing a golf club with one hand, while the other hand grips the forearm of the swinging arm. Alternate swinging arms. This is not only a feel drill, but a good arm and hand strengthening drill.

13. Take your golf stance and then take continuous full swings with your golf club back and forth from downswing to follow through and back to downswing. Be sure to achieve good shoulder rotation. Start this drill in a slow swinging action and then increase speed in several stages until you have reached a fast swinging action.

14. Swing a golf club with the feet together or even crossed. This is a good drill for developing balance.

15. Swing a golf club while on one foot. This is another good drill for balance.

16. Place a golf club across your thighs and keep it there while making the golf swing motion back and forth.

17. To get the feel of a pitch shot, hold a golf club at the grip end at arms length with the left hand. Let the head of the club rest on the ground with the shaft in a vertical position. Hold a ball in the right hand and with a swinging motion or the right arm similar to a golf swing, toss the ball under the left arm.

18. To get the feel of moving the body into the swing, try this step-in drill. Place the two feet together and then hit the golf ball while striding forward with the left leg, like a baseball batter.

19. Similar to the step-in drill. Take your stance and then, as you move into the backswing, swing the left leg past the right leg on the backswing, and then swing it forward with the downswing while trying to hit the golf ball. The left leg should make contact with the ground prior to ball contact on the golf club.

20. Another variation to the step-in drill. On your backswing, lift your left leg off the ground and swing it back to your right leg. As the down-swing begins, the left leg swing forward and is placed on the ground for impact. At impact, the right leg lifts up and swings forward with the momentum of the swing into the follow through.

21. Stand facing a wall or an imaginary wall. Throw a golf ball with the right hand in the manner of a golf swing so that the ball flies parallel to the wall. Do some easy tosses and gradually throw the ball in increasingly far-ther distances. As the arm swing increases in length, and the swing gets faster, notice the re-action of the legs and feet. This is the feel of the lower body for the golf swing.

22. Stand a few inches from a wall and lean for-ward to place your head on the wall. Let the arms hang down and clasp the hands. Take a golf swing. With the head placed against the wall, you can feel how the head remains rela-tively stationary throughout the golf swing, while the body rotates.

23. This drill is often used as a warm-up drill but it is also excellent for giving the feel of shoul-der rotation and body coil for the golf swing. This drill is to be done by rotating the body and not letting the body sway. Place a club be-hind the back and then swing each arm in turn back so as to circle the club with the elbows. With the elbows around the shaft, bring the hands forward and place them on your stom-ach as close together as possible. From this po-sition, bend forward slightly at the hips, and then rotate the body as if taking a swing at a golf ball. Rotate the body back into the swing position and continue to rotate the body back and forth.

24. Place balls in a row and then walk down the line, hitting each ball by swinging forward and backward. Only hit the ball on the for-ward swing—the swing back is just to put the club in position for the next swing.

25. Swing the arms from right hip to left hip level, with the arms and hands controlled or swung by body rotation. Do this drill on one leg. Al-ternate legs.

26. See how far you can hit a golf ball by swinging the arms and the body in the slowest possible motion. Imagine you are performing the cor-rect swing technique but in super slow motion.

27. Swing with your eyes shut. This can be done while hitting golf balls or just practicing the correct swing techniques without ball.

28. From the address position, swing a golf club over the ball about a foot or so and into the follow-through. Let the right side release like a regular swing. Then swing back into the top of the backswing position, and then swing down to hit the ball.

29. Swing at a golf ball while sitting on the edge of a chair. This drill gives the feel of strong shoulder rotation with a limited hip rotation.

30. Grip a golf club with the hands about one inch apart and swing the club at an imaginary golf ball to get the feel of the hand action at impact. You will notice how the hands slow down but the club head whips through the ball.

22 Practice Workbook

This chapter consists of a full checklist with the various golf drills arranged in progressive order, as in the book. Start at the beginning and progress to the next drill when you are capable of executing the drill you are on. Be sure you have a thorough knowledge and/or ability with each drill before progressing. It is best to have muscle memory before moving into the next drill.

Learning check list

____ Understanding of mechanics

____ Understanding of golf swing problems

____ Scrape the grass drill, without golf ball

____ Grip, stance & alignment

____ Establishing the swing's center

____ Chin position

____ Basic swing

____ Is the chin pointing to the ball area?

____ Is the swing's feel smooth and easy

____ Do you have a good picture in your mind of the club face being square to the line of flight and scraping the grass accurately?

____ swinging with tension and then relaxation.

____ Are you able to clearly notice the difference in swinging with tension and with relaxation?

Nonvisual basic swing practice

____ With the short basic swing eyes closed drill, are you able to feel the swing, visualize the square clubface, and scrape the grass or the carpet accurately?

The Full swing, without golf ball

____ Repeat the basic swing drills with a backswing of the hands going waist high and a follow-through with the hands going waist high (half swing). Eyes open.

____ Repeat the basic swing drills with a backswing and follow-through with the hands going waist-high. Eyes closed.

___ Repeat the half-swing drills but increase the swing length to the three-quarter swing length or the full swing. Eyes open.

___ The above drill with eyes closed. Remember, straight left arm, swing center, chin pointing to golf ball contact area, and good shoulder and body rotation.

On the full swing drills, you must achieve the following before moving onto the next drills:

___ Excellent scrape on the grass or carpet

___ Chin pointing at the ball contact area when swing is well past the contact area.

___ Weight shift

___ Arm and hand roll

Scrape the grass with a golf ball using a 5, 6, 7, or 8 iron

___ Hitting the golf ball with a half swing. Eyes open

___ Hitting the golf ball, half swing, eyes closed

___ Hitting the golf ball, full swing, eyes open

___ Hitting the golf ball, full swing, eyes closed

___ Determine ball placement

One-leg stork stand drill

___ balance good

___ body rotation good

___ contact good

The string drill

___ Full string extension on backswing

___ Full string extension just after contact

___ Full string extension on follow through

___ Full execution of swing in balance and with excellent ball contact.

Putting

___ Stand about 10 paces or yards from the hole and roll the ball with your hands to the hole much like a bowling ball. Repeat this several times until you have a good feel for the roll of the ball and how hard to roll the ball.

___ With a putter, putt the ball to the hole by using a backswing that is the same length and with a force similar to the roll of the ball with the hand.

___ Do you have the feel for the 10-pace putt?

___ Do you have the feel for the 7-pace putt?

___ Do you have the feel for the 5-pace putt?

___ Do you have the feel for the 3-pace putt?

___ Do you have the feel for the 1-pace putt?

Chipping

Chipping is the same as putting, only an iron is used instead of a putter. Practice the roll of the ball with the hand ,and then chip the ball much like a putt.

Pitching

Pitching is the same as the full swing. Once again the scrape of the grass is essential. Following the drills above will give pitching practice and learning.

Part VI
The Spiritual Side of Golf

23
Golf and Life: The Final Stage

Zen is simplicity. It is a way of achieving self-control through simple procedures. Throughout this book we have discussed various controlling methods. Such methods are not as difficult to learn as you may believe. It is not the learning that is difficult, it is putting in the time to practice. Practice is the key to Zen. The following will be of help in learning to practice Zen Golf.

Practice

To learn Zen, simply practice Zen. If you are learning to concentrate, practice concentration. In time, you will learn to concentrate unconsciously. There is no wrinkled brow and squinting eyes. When concentrating, there is no tension of the mind or the muscles. Unconscious concentration is easy, relaxed, and not forced. It just happens. If you want to better focus or concentrate on a certain aspect, then just simply practice focusing on the aspect. Logic will dictate many practice methods.

The mastery of Zen occurs not only on the golf course but in life. Everyday life is Zen. Eating, walking, working, etc. are all a part of the body's awareness. An awareness that extends from everyday occurrences to the golf course. If your body cannot focus on life, do not expect it to focus on the golf course. If your body cannot be in a state of awareness with life, do not expect body awareness on the golf course. If you cannot control the mind in life, do not expect mind control on the golf course.

Time and time again, people have stated that they can learn more about a man in one round of golf than working with him for a year. Others claim that a man's character is revealed on the golf course but hidden in life. These statements are not just words of wisdom. These statements simply reflect the Zen philosophy that man reveals himself in everything he does. His weaknesses are revealed in his decision making on the golf course. His ego hampers his progress. If you want to improve your golf, improve your life. Practice your life. Practice your awareness at all times. Practice concentration all the time. Practice letting the ego go. Practice, practice, practice. How long do you practice? Until you die.

To reach the ultimate in golf, you must not practice golf solely for hitting the target. Technical skill is not enough. You have to expand beyond the technical phase into the final stage of learning to perform in the unconscious stage, the spirit stage, the intuition stage, the third stage of learning (explained further on). The game of golf becomes an art, a spiritual art of where the golfer and the target are one and not two opposing forces. The mind is free and "empty" of conscious thought. There is no thought of the self or the ego to hinder the skill. The mind is completely focused on the moment. Skill, execution, the body and the mind are all one.

It may be difficult to understand, but the target and the golfer are one. The golfer is aiming at himself. The battle is with himself. The golf course, the golf club, and the golf ball are merely tools for testing the self. Mastery of golf is more than a game. It is mastery of life and the self. The tools are merely a means to achieve this mastery.

Learn to use your tools. Do not let one club become too much a favorite. Too much use of a favorite takes time from the other clubs. Lack of use with the other clubs brings loss of confidence in these clubs when they are needed. If the sand wedge is a problem, practice and learn it. The golf course is a complex and demanding enemy (or partner). All your skills, physical and mental, will eventually be needed. You cannot defeat the golf course with one club. All clubs are needed. Learn them.

According to Suzuki, in the *Introduction of Zen in the Art of Archery* (page vii), Zen is nothing more than the "everyday mind." Sleep when tired and eat when hungry. As soon as you

> "reflect, deliberate, and conceptualize, the original unconsciousness is lost and a thought interferes… calculation which is miscalculation sets in. The whole business of archery goes the wrong way. The archer's confused mind betrays itself in every direction and every field of activity. Man is a thinking reed but his great works are done when he is not calculating and thinking. "Childlikeness" has to be restored with long years of training in the art

of self-forgetfulness. When this is attained, man thinks yet he does not think.

This is the spiritual, or intuition, stage of learning in Zen.

The Self

Zen is the study of the self. It is a "way" of life, the self. The ironic study of the self requires one to forget the self, to forget the ego. The self flows from one event to another in harmony with the universe. Problems on the golf course or in life are not to be taken as personal. You are not the target. A ball stopping in a divot is not a sign that life is out to get you. A ball in the divot is just part of life. Crying, moaning, groaning, and temper tantrums will not solve the problem. The self must be in control and react to the situation. You have to play the shot, so play it. Do not take it as an ego threat. Flow with the problem. Do not push the river.

When our minds are upset, our bodies become dysfunctional. When our minds are calm, our bodies can respond to action, quickly and accurately. When we move unconsciously it is as if the body thinks. In a way the body does think. Our muscles react through muscle memory. The typist uses muscle memory. Ask a typist where the "k" key is and they cannot tell you where it is unless they move their fingers in a typing manner. The mind does not know where the "k" key is but the body does. It remembers. The body thinks and reacts correctly. In time this unconsciousness develops into intuition. The ultimate stage.

Zen Learning

Learning a skill, under the Zen philosophy, is a three-stage process. The first stage involves the use of the conscious to learn and understand the skill.

The second stage puts the skill into the automatic stage, or the unconscious. This is the stage of performing the skill automatically, or unconsciously. In fact, it is very similar to a reflex action. This second stage is also the stage of learning to "let go of yourself." This is a difficult stage, but it is necessary for development into the third stage. At this stage, you become purposeless and aimless. If you aim too hard with a purpose, your muscles suffer tension and confusion. Your execution of the shot is failed. The golf shot is not forced to happen. It happens if you let it.

The third stage of learning is the spirit, or freedom ,stage. This is the ultimate stage, were no planning or thought occurs. It is the intuition stage of reaction through intuition. The body is in complete awareness of self-mastery and control.

In golf, you learn mastery of the self. A mastery that carries over into everyday life. Golf is life. Life is golf. Both are one. The body is in harmony with the golf course, the golf ball, the golf club, the weather, the opponents, everything. When you achieve this, you are in a state of flow—the magic state where everything just flows correctly. You seem to be in slow motion, in perfect harmony with everything.

Intuition, the third stage of learning, is harmonized with action. Practice develops the skill and stores it in the body until intuition calls it into action. You analyze the shot before execution and then, as you step up to the ball, your body goes into the pre-shot routine. During this routine, the body goes into its intuition mode. Intuition takes control of the mind and the body. You are focusing on the target, while the body is feeling the action for the shot. Intuition is in control—if you let it take control.

Often you think you cannot trust your intuition. The shot is so important, you feel you must totally think his way through the shot so that you do not make a mistake. This thinking is the mistake. The body knows what to do, and intuition will let the body take control and execute the shot precisely. It is difficult and takes practice, lots of practice, to acquire the skill of "letting go" with the mind (no thinking) and letting intuition take over. It takes trust. You must trust yourself. This is where the battle is—with yourself, trusting yourself.

As you develop into the higher levels of the second stage and into the third stage of learning, you will learn to aim without aiming. Your aim will be by intuition. No conscious effort is involved. No lines and angles are drawn in the mind. As a golfer, you do not have to draw the imaginary parallel lines and angles with the feet, shoulders, hips, and ball. The body feels the shot. The body feels the direction. Accuracy is built into the shot. It is a natural evolution of practice.

The Moment

Everything is *here and now*. The mind must focus on the here and now. Our actions must be geared to the here and now—not in the future or in the past. With the shot to the green, the focus is on the green—not whether the shot will beat the opponent or win the tournament. Or whether the shot will be like the last round shot that failed. The mind is clear of the past and the future. It is the *moment* that counts. It is the moment that takes all your energy. It is this moment that you take the situation to the maximum in ability. There is no let up. Reacting to the moment and playing to the moment must be practiced continually.

Breathing

Breathing helps control the body. The body is strong breathing out and weak breathing in. Moments of effort or exertion require the body to breath out, exhale. The karate chop is executed with a yell as the arm swings into the chop. This yell expels the air from the lungs for maximum power. The golf swing is best performed in the same manner. Exhale during the downswing. No need to yell: just a simple release of air from the lungs.

Herrigel, the author of *Zen in the Art of Archery*, took several years to fully understand this. Once he was able to execute this breathing skill, he was able to "let go" with the arrow for accurate flight. Some golfers have even found that breathing out takes the mind off shot mechanics and helps in feeling the smooth flow of the swing. Go to a driving range and hit balls with the lungs full of air at contact. Next, hit balls while slowly breathing out on the downswing. The difference is readily noticeable. Zen masters claim that exertion of the body with the lungs full of trapped air is a dangerous practice.

Breathing will also help you in moments of tension or fear. Golf will present many moments of anguish when the heart beats faster and the breath is shorter, quicker and shallower. At these moments, utilize the long breath out. Take a deep breath and release the air slowly to a count longer than the breath in. While breathing, visualize and feel the body relaxing and calming. If necessary, repeat several times. When anxiety presents itself, keep control and execute the breathing technique of a longer exhale.

Act "as if" in Control

Never show your weak points or defeat. No matter how bad things are going, act as if everything is under control. Carry on as if you are winning. Never let the opposition think they have you beat. Put your head down when things are going badly, and your opponent knows you are beat. When your opponent thinks or knows you are beat, the pressure is off him. He can relax. He is secure in the contest. When things are bad and you act as if everything is great, your opponents will recognize and even respect your determination and your fighting spirit. Your opponents cannot relax, because they suspect that you may triumph over your problem. They cannot relax, because they think that perhaps your problem is only temporary and you will pull through in the long haul. They cannot relax, because they do not know how to read you. No matter how bad thing are, you look invincible. This look and attitude is a problem to your opponents. They cannot read you. This will scare them.

When performing on the golf course, or even in life, never let your spirit deviate from normal. Too high a spirit may bring tension and loss of focus to the situation. This happens to the warrior who celebrates before it's over. Too low a spirit, and the body may become careless or even give up. This happens to the golfer who thinks he is beat, gives up and then finds out he still could have won. When the challenge presents itself, remain normal, calm, and not reckless. Remain spirited, but not over-spirited or under-spirited. This is control; practice it.

Fear

Fear is the first enemy. Fear is what you make it. Past experiences and thought processes give you your fear. Your perception of the situation creates fear. In golf, fear is a constant companion. Fear is a battle with the self. All golfers know and experience fear—the "must putt," the narrow fairway, the water hazard are all part of the game. There is no reason for fear. Think about it. Why are you afraid? Fear is like a shadow—it is there, but it has no substance. Often your fear is because of the uncertainty of the situation. Your inability to cope with the situation. The situation is a threat to your ego—you may look bad, you may fail. The fear of failure prevents you from letting yourself go. Let go of your ego, and your ego cannot be under attack. Free yourself and take control. Become the situation. Be the situation. Be one.

Tension, both mental and physical, deteriorates skill execution. When playing golf, you must be able to recognize when tension is creeping into your muscles. Extreme tension is readily noticeable, but subtle tension is often ignored. Learning to recognize tension can be practiced very easily. Away from the golf course, tense your muscle and feel the tension of the muscle. Relax the muscle and feel the relaxation. Do this several times, and soon you will be able to recognize a tense muscle and a relaxed muscle. Practice this with various parts of the body, like the arms, the legs, the forearms, etc. As you acquire the feel for tension and relaxation, adapt the same procedure on the golf course or the practice range while hitting golf balls. Hit some shots while under tension to various parts of the body, and then hit some shots while completely relaxed. Soon you will be able to recognize the tense golf swing and the relaxed golf swing. With this recognition, you will be able to notice tension creeping into your golf swing, and you'll be able to correct it. As you walk down the fairway to your ball, you will also be able to recognize if your body is relaxed or tense. Learning this tension/relaxation skill is not difficult. Just be willing to take a little time to practice.

Patience

Good players know patience. Patience is simply not being slow or lazy. Being slow and lazy cre-ates an atmosphere of carelessness. Patience is moving to a pace that is comfortable to you. It is moving to your own internal clock. There is no wasted time while deciding the golf shot. The analysis flows smoothly and efficiently. Patience must not only be practiced on a short-term basis like the shot at hand but patience is also needed for the long term. You must have patience for learning to ingrain physical and mental skills into the body. Learning cannot be forced or given a certain time limit. Learning moves to the drum beat of the individual. The beat varies from individual to individual. Disturb the beat, and you disturb the learning. Flow with the river.

24
Enlightenment

Talent, equipment, and technology have been a tremendous factor in the improvement of golf and in life. However, the use of your talent, equipment, and technology is still dependent on the mind. The mind controls all the factors. The mind decides how to use these factors to advantage. The ability to win or succeed is, and will continue to be, decided by the mind. The use of the mind determines your final success. Better warriors think better. Better warriors have better mind control. The best warrior has the best mind control of all the warriors.

Mind Control

Mind control is the key to golfing enlightenment. The great Japanese swordsman Munenori claimed that he used swordsmanship to learn how to control the mind. As his mind control developed, his swordsmanship was able to perform through the will. Golf is the same way. Use golf to learn to control the mind and then let golf be performed by the will. Performing by the will is the enlightened stage.

The mind controls the body. It is the mind that moves the arms and the legs. When you use the will, you are using your intuition. It is important to know that the mind is not the brain. The mind is the mind. The brain is the physical organ in the head. The mind is in the muscles, bones, skin, etc. The mind is in the body, the whole body. With the mind in the body, the body is able to react quickly,

without thought. Thinking takes time. Thought impulses must travel from the brain to the muscles of the body. This is too slow for quick movements like the golf swing. The brain is inactive, empty, and flowing. The mind is ready, always ready, if the mind is aware and alert. To reach the stage of enlightenment, you must let the mind move from the brain and into the body—the entire body.

To reach the stage of enlightenment, you must master all things you do. If you have not mastered all things, then you cannot do it. When you have not mastered a skill, you will have doubts about how to do the skill. Your mind has doubts. Since the mind controls the body, the doubting mind transfers the doubts to confuse the body. Develop your skills to eliminate confusion in the mind. When you perform, be clear in your mind. In the book *The Sword and the Mind* by Yagyu, Munenori, translated by Hiroaki Sato, page 60, the following quote is very applicable to the golfer's situation:

> That is the ultimate end of all disciplines. The final state of any discipline is where you forget what you have learned, discard the mind, and accomplish whatever you set out to do without being aware of it yourself. You begin by learning and reach the point where learning does not exist.

Obsession

❏ It is a disease to be obsessed with the thought of winning.

❏ It is a disease to be obsessed with the thought of failure.

❏ It is a disease to be obsessed with the thought of anything.

Obsession sickens the mind. The obsessed mind is clouded. The enlightened mind is alert and aware of all factors. Obsession on a factor does not develop the full picture. The warrior's obsessed mind is on a single factor and not on the big picture. The obsessed mind has become attached. The mind must never become attached. This is not the way of the warrior. The attached mind is a stuck mind, a slow mind, a diseased mind. The enlightened golfer must not let his mind become obsessed.

When enlightened, you see with your mind. When your mind sees it, your eyes notice it. Your mind controls your body, even your eyes. Your arms and legs see with the mind. Your arms and legs perform their skills through their own eyesight. This is the ultimate stage of learning—the intuition stage.

To be a golf warrior, you must practice all the principles in this book. Reading alone will not do it. Reading and practice must go together. Without practice, you cannot find the Way. The Way is the way of the Golf Warrior.

25 The Tao: Nature's Flow of Golf

Every shot in golf is a unique and individual stroke that a mechanical pattern cannot perfect. A golfer is invariably subjected to shots that require adjustments and deviations to the robotic stroke which instructors are trying to mold. Instructors are struggling to construct their own movement pattern to discover the all-inclusive stroke that can solve all the cures of all the golfers. They are fighting the winds of nature, for no stroke is omnipotent. Too many golfers are so boggled with instruction and mechanical structure that they lose touch with the nature of golf, they lose touch with the direct experience with the swing. Their swing is externalized. This externalization results in decreased performance and increased frustration.

The Prime Mover

Instruction and recommendations are very useful tools, and sometimes they should not be ignored. But when it comes down to it, only you (the one hitting the ball) is in control. You are the prime mover of the golf club. You are in sole possession of the unique and individual situation, both internally and externally. Internally, we have different bodies requiring slightly different movement patterns. Externally, we have a different environment for every stroke of the game. It may be the weather. It may be your psyche, involving the slower golfers in front of you, the faster golfers behind you, or the cunning comments from those you are with. It could be almost anything.

So take instruction and recommendations for what they're worth. Stand at a driving range and develop a structured swing. But when it is time to swing, don't reference your way through the swing. Don't be boggled with all the tidbits of information you have acquired. Use the tips to make adjustments to the natural flow of *your* swing. Let the instructions flow into *your* swing. Keep instructions in the back of your head, but don't let them take your mind off your swing. Learn to feel your swing and correct it accordingly. Partake in the moment of your swing and don't let it be dominated by instructions from the past.

As you look around the golf course, you'll see golfers who are not in the moment of their golf. They finish their round and they were never here. They lived their round of golf elsewhere, in the instructions from another time and space. They lived their round of golf in the instructor's mind. You paid for your round of golf, and you should partake of it. If you hit a bad shot, there is a reason for it. Instructions and recommendations can help, but don't let the instructions and recommendations annihilate the natural flow of your golf swing.

Partake in the higher experiences of *your* golf and not the lower level of someone else's molded structure of golf. Structured thought can be useful, but golf will never be enjoyed unless you step above the robotic structure and into nature's flow of golf.

A Round of Golf

Can a mechanical robot be programmed to play a precise game of golf? And if so, who really plays the game and would you like to be that robot?

The first hole of golf, I use to bring past experiences into the present moment. All I have been instructed, learned, and developed loses its still, static, absolute nature and becomes my new game, always open to more changes and modifications. Before today, I have thought about different methods, I have tried to develop certain structures of my swing, and I have even tried to modify certain aspects of my game into what will take place today. But today, different from my past events, my game will not be dictated by analysis from the past. I unify my past conditioning into the present moment. Many golfers live their game in instructions from the past. They do this at the expense of losing touch with the moment and losing touch with themselves. Here and now, my past golfing knowledge will "forget itself," and I will live this new game in the present moment as it presents itself to me.

There comes a time you have to let go of all the instruction and analysis from the past and live the round of golf as it happens, and not in the predetermined structure of logic that exists outside of the self and outside of the moment. This is the point where your "feel" will take precedence over the rationalism from some other time and space. After all, who paid for this round anyway? Who's really playing this round of golf, you or some ideal concept of how it should be played? Is the golf swing predetermined, in which every golfer tries to fit into some ideal form of a perfect golf stroke that exists somewhere in Plato's heaven or ideal forms? Or are you playing your own game of golf and making the decisions? Are you playing the game, or is some independent concept unattached to any subject playing the game? Would you like to be the robot programmed for the perfect stroke? And if so, who is playing the game, the golfer or the one who programmed the robot? Does such a perfect stroke even exist? I would like to think the game of golf partakes in freedom of choice and is not being predetermined. It is hard to imagine that such an ideal stroke exists, given that every shot in golf is different and is continually changing. The subject is continually evolving as a golfer, while the course and the shot demanded are continually changing. Golf is a dynamic process, in which you have to continually modify and adapt to such changes. Your growth as a golfer should not be targeted at filling the roll or fitting into the ideal or perfect swing. Instead, your golf should be targeted at developing your swing so that it works for you in the given situation. The ideal perfect swing does not exist!

So starting the game, it is advisable to make sure you are in the driver's seat, since you are the prime mover of the club and not some external thing or being. Take control!

Standing on the second tee, I observe the way the sun casts shadows over this well-scalped land, the way the birds chirp and the crickets crack, the way the traffic rumbles in the distance, and the way the leaves rustle and the branches bend. All this, and more, contribute to a scene that may never be identical again. When I notice it is time to tee-off, the scene has already changed. Once the ball has flown, it cannot be driven again, for the moment has changed and it would be a different drive.

Modern physics will tell you that nothing we have found to date is permanent. The only thing permanent is change itself. Everything is constantly changing. Everything from the scene on this golf course to the atoms on this desk I write on. Our bodies and minds are continually evolving. Even the earth we walk on cannot survive when the sun's molten core will unavoidably cool and swell into a Red Giant with a greater circumference than the earth's distance from it. Given that there is no permanence, what does this tell us about knowledge, and in particular the golf swing? If there is no permanence, how can there be any absolute truths about anything that is not permanent? When someone says, "you have to do this or you have to do that," such absolutes don't exist. You really don't "have" to do anything. The best instructors will always "recommend" things to "try."

On the third tee, I recommend to my playing partner a new grip in order to keep a tighter grip without as much wrist movement. My recommendation worked for him, but so could have many of the other methods or techniques. My recommendation was not of an absolute nature, since such absolutes do not exist. He generalized this tip into "his" swing for the rest of the round, and it proved to be a useful tip. The best learners, I have noticed, are those who "try" to incorporate these things into their own subjective golf. Even better, they learn through their own feel, "from their inside out" instead of from the outside in, as instructors try to externally install their own swing into another, like a golfing dictator. In the wonderful book *Golf in the Kingdom*, the character Chivas Irons suggests that when you learn from the inside out, you see how it fits into the whole, bigger picture, whereas when you are fed tidbits of things to do, you may not see how it fits into the big picture.

Standing on the fourth tee, once again I observe the scenic environment. As I notice that it is time to tee off again, my mind is no longer focused on the externals; instead. it is diving deep

into the self in search of the harmony and unity that naturally exists with nature, both the external environment and myself. I co-exist with the external world within nature. We are both within the subset of nature, both part of the same totality. Since we are all part of the same whole, there is no reason to separate us. Without trying to shut off the environment, without trying to swing identically to my previous instructions, I drive the ball, as I feel myself being part of the shadows, birds, crickets, traffic, and leaves, all contributing to the unique situation never to take place again—a once-in-a-lifetime experience.

Unification of everything is a central theme in eastern thought. The good shots and the bad, the ego and the egolessness, the course, myself, the golf clubs, and the ball are all incorporated into the vast unified whole of experience. Please do not separate these! After a bad shot, use the ego while walking to the ball, relax, feel yourself being one with the game that is happening in the passing moment.

On the fifth hole, I notice myself free-floating away from the moment, and I have to remind myself to pay attention and get back into the moment. I do not mean to abandon analysis and instruction. The problem with these is that you have to step out of the moment and the self to objectify matters. This approach may be very useful, but it should not be used at the expense of losing touch with your natural flow of your golf. This steeping outside the self and the moment to analyze is what the eastern philosophers call the "ego." The ego is satisfactory, and even necessary, to make it through your daily activities, including golf. You should learn to incorporate the ego into the natural flow of your golf game and not let it dominate the game.

As I look around at other golfers on the course, I see a great deal of frustration being vented in unhealthy measures. Some are cursing at themselves while walking, raising their blood pressure, and worst of all, causing damage to the golf course. They are hurting their own game, themselves, and the course. In a bad shot lies the seeds of a good shot and visa versa. You cannot find the means of correction through such frustration. It only serves to complicate matters and the swing. After a good shot, forget it. The next shot will be different, and a new experience. The "feel" is what you have saved through practice and staying open to the changing winds, not through memory. Often, when trying to duplicate a good shot, it will prove to be unworthy of patterning.

Sixth hole. Living in the moment may not sound so easy. The moment is gone as soon as it appears. It is a futile effort for many, continually trying to catch up to the moment. Once you try to analyze it, the moment is gone.

Trying to live in the moment and analyze the moment is a self-defeating effort. The ego is activated when you try to live in the moment. This problem is even worse when you try to live in the past or the future. In order to escape life in the ego, do not *try* to live in the moment, nor especially the past or future. You will find the ego has vanished, and hence you will find yourself effortlessly living in the moment in light of beckoning, ready to create.

Though I use the term "moment," I do not intend to imply that these "moments" have a beginning and an end. Life's experiences are so abundant that they mesh into a fluid, continual flow of experiences. Let me use an analogy of the sliding filament theory of a contracting skeletal muscle to explain this better. A single muscle consists of thousands of muscle fibers. Within a single muscle fiber, lie filaments with thousands of myosin heads that stick up and insert themselves into grooves of the muscle fiber. These myosin heads pull the muscle fibers closer together. Each of these myosin head contractions contributes to a very small portion of the entire muscle contraction. With this theory, it would seem that the muscle would contract in a ladder-stepping movement. But the point of my analogy is that there are so many of these myosin heads working, that the muscle contraction seems to be one continuous flow of a contracting muscle, similar to life's experiences flowing into one continual experience. Like a movie seems to be continually flowing, it is actually just a series of pictures. It is one total experience with no beginning and no end.

By the seventh hole, I should have been hinted to the golf course's mood. The same golf course I has been playing for years can take on different moods at a given moment. I try to recognize the course's mood the same way I try to recognize my girlfriend's mood when I get home from golfing. My girlfriend and I speak non-verbally, as do the golf course and I. Sometimes the course is dancing and giggles at me, "are you going to get a birdie today?" Other times she stands and snarls with her arms crossed like a brick wall that murmurs, "you can't get to there from here!" The mood of the course can turn talented golfers into a crying mass of protoplasm that seems to be the only remains of a once soulful and spiritual golfer.

Perhaps earlier than the seventh hole, I greet myself to the nature and mood of the course and let it know that I will not kick her shins or cry on her carpet. Did the ground cordially take my tee? Can it make up its mind whether I need a sweater? Has it endured many divot scares?

As the two of us get acquainted with our moods of the day, we continually evolve our relationship into one entity, similar to that of me and my girlfriend. Her mood and needs are continually changing, as are mine. Our relationship becomes one entity, even though we are very distinctively different. Our love is unified as one being and not as a distinct him-or-her duality. She's the *yin* and I'm the *yang*—and sometimes visa-versa.

Earlier in the round, I referred to a term coined by David Miller. In his book *Philosophy of Creativity*, Miller makes the distinction between knowledge that remembers itself and knowledge that forgets itself.

> It is as reason forgets itself that it discovers and evinces its most creative possibilities. This is forgetting that strips reason of its arrogant tendencies to substitute its powers and achievements for the passing wholeness of experience itself; it is a forgetting that prevents reason from tragically substituting the part or parts for the whole; and it is a forgetting that enables us to comprehend ourselves more fully as creatures of creativity rather than as

creatures of reason, sense perception, work, or some other time-honored perspective. At the deepest levels of experience reason forgets its narrow and ill-conceived plans, and in so doing awakens to its most profound possibilities for enjoying the passing concreteness of experience, as it contributes inescapably to the development and satisfaction of that experience. As reason forgets itself, hope in the present radiates, for creativity has the wherewithal to forge new life-sustaining and life transforming values, stretching indefinitely into the Earth's future.

Knowledge that remembers itself gives rise to absolute truths that are purely an illusion. Knowledge that forgets itself, on the other hand, provides a self-correcting mechanism that will not allow such illusory truths to dominate your natural flow of experience. Miller states these truths are derived via abstract reason and credits people like Plato, Aristotle, and Descartes for providing this "Western Disclaimer to Philosophy," in which reason is the highest power and should dictate your behavior and experience.

Can you see the debilitating nature of such thought, especially with regard to golfing? These philosophers claim that the essence of abstract reason exists outside of the self on a higher plane, of which some of us are gifted enough see and use while it "claims enormous, if not complete, access to reality." This thought strips knowledge of its humanity, subjectivity, possibilities, and free will.

Knowledge that forgets itself and reason should not oppose one another. Reason plays a major role in play, spontaneity, and the like. Reason, besides helping us live, provides us with a foundation from which to be "creative," to enjoy and experience the passing moment, and to guide our free-floating rationality. Knowledge that remembers itself rests on axioms that "stay," organize, and close" while knowledge that forgets itself "moves, penetrates and opens." "If it is harnessed, it will be honored."

The Ninth Hole

Things change, we change
The passing moment we cannot rearrange
The instant is gone as it appears
This brings some folks to tears
Everything is empty

The string of events is not a thing
Time is the string and empty is the thing
When you"re sitting at a movie show
It's an illusion that it's a flow
Everything is empty

The past does not exists
The present does not exist
The future never was
This is true because
Everything is empty

Nothing appears out of nothing
It's all dependent on something
So what is its own identity
If it's not a self-subsisting entity
Everything is empty

This theory can be discomforting to many who tend to cling to the desire for permanence in the world and in their life. Letting yourself open to the free flowing experience that is being described here may not be very easy for many. The theory of nothingness can be useful at this point. From a material aspect, modern physics is showing us how material things are not really things as the old paradigm portrays. Instead, they are combinations of energies that are constantly changing; they are various forms of electrons moving around nuclei that give the empty space a material and impenetrable appearance.

Modern physics is encroaching upon explaining such phenomenon as ghosts, E.S.P., walking through walls, etc. Reality as most of us still in the old paradigm perceive it is about to shift into a material nothingness. From a mental aspect, this nothingness is very useful. If nothing exists, why clutter the mind with substance axioms that are immaterial? While throwing darts, do you throw a precise dart actually designed by the laws of geometry through its arch to its target? Not really. Instead the proficient dart player looks, feels in silence, and waits for the feeling/energy to be right and releases. The same should hold true for the golf stroke.

Even if may be possible for one to *will* the ball to the green, you cannot rely on such drastic phenomena. You still have to practice, articulate, diagnose, use geometry and logic; but most importantly you must use these to help acquire a *feel*. Use the logic to acquire this feel, then forget it.

This correct feeling can arise through nothingness of the mind. Let the mind relax; forget past tidbits of accumulated information that will only serve to clog the mind; be the sole golfer along with the club, the ball, the course, and the wholeness of your experience. Let *"the feeling"* manifest—hit it! The direction of the ball depends on us but after we hit a good shot, forget it, for it is "empty."

Hence we have articulated the Walfords' new axiom:

Do It, Be It, and Forget It.

Appendix: The Rules of Golf

In this appendix, the rules of golf have been organized in chart form for ease of remembering.

Legend

( ) = rule number from *USGA Rules Of Golf*

[ ] = penalty

DQ = disqualified

Def. = definition section of the rules

LH = loss of hole in match play

2STR = 2 stroke penalty in stroke play

1STR = 1 stroke penalty in match or stroke play

Chart 1. What a golfer may and may not do

A. The golfer may not:

1. Influence the movement or position of a golf ball (1-2) [LH, 2STR].

2. Touch the ball in play unless the rules permit (1-2) [LH, 2STR].

3. Waive or ignore any rule of the game (1-3) [DQ].

4. Be in possession of more than 14 clubs during play (4-4) [loss of hole, maximum 2 holes. 2 strokes each hole, maximum 4 strokes].

5. No foreign material shall be applied to club face (4-3) [DQ].

6. No foreign material shall be applied to the ball (5-2) [DQ].

7. Practice during play of a hole (7-2).[LH, 2STR].

8. Give or take advice except from caddie/partner (def./8-1) [LH, 2STR].

9. Stroke ball unless farthest from the hole (10-1,2) [Match- opponent may request replay of shot, no penalty. Stroke play- no penalty].

10. Start play outside teeing ground (11-4) [Match-opponent may request replay of shot, no penalty. Stroke play- 2 strokes];

11. Play an incorrect ball (12-2) [LH, 2STR].

12. Alter lie of ball, area of swing or line of play (13-1) [LH, 2STR].

13. Remove loose impediment in hazard if ball in hazard (13-4c) [LH, 2STR].

14. The ball must be fairly struck and not pushed, scraped or spooned (14-1) [LH, 2STR].

15. Play a moving ball unless moving in water (14-5) [LH, 2STR].

16. Lift ball without marking spot (16-1b, 20-1) [1STR].

17. Test surface of putting green (16-1d) [LH, 2STR].

18. Stand astride or on line of putt to putt (16-1e) [LH, 2STR].

19. Wait more than 10 seconds for ball hanging on cup to drop (16-2) [1STR].

20. Strike attended flagstick or attendant with ball (17-3) [LH, 2STR].

B. The golfer may:

1. Ask advice on distance from a permanent object to green but not on distance of ball to green (8-1).

2. Through the green, ask for line of play to target but must not play shot with marker or mark in place (8-2).

3. In stroke play, player must be correct on score for each hole (6-6) [DQ] but no penalty if score is added incorrectly.

4. Stop play on own decision with threat of lightning (6-8).

5. Nudge ball off tee in teeing ground during address of ball. Ball may be replaced on tee with no penalty (11-3).

Chart 2. Water hazard, lateral water hazard, unplayable lie, lost, and out of bounds

Water hazard	Lateral wat.haz	Unplayable lie	lost/out bound
Rule 26	Rule 26	Rule 28	Rule 27
Yellow stakes	Red stakes	Player decision	O.B. white stake
Play as it lies	Play as it lies	except in water hazard	
Play on extended line of hole and entry of hazard penalty stroke	Play on extended line of hole and entry of hazard penalty stroke	Play on extended line of hole and ball penalty stroke	
	2 club lengths at point of entry of hazard penalty stroke	2 club lengths at point of ball penalty stroke	
	2 club lengths at point of entry of hazard on other side of hazard penalty stroke		
Stroke and distance	Stroke and distance	Stroke and distance	Stroke and distance

Chart 3. Obstructions–artificial/man-made
(Rule 24)

Relief	Movable	Immovable
Examples	Ice cubes, paper cups, sand trap rakes	Rain shelter, fixed bench, ball washer
Through green	Move obstruction no penalty if ball moves - drop. No penalty	Interference with stance or swing only - drop 1 club length. no relief from line of flight.
Bunker	Move obstruction no penalty if ball moves - drop No penalty	Interference with stance or swing but not line of flight - drop in bunker no penalty.
Water hazard lat.wat.haz.	Move obstruction no penalty	No relief without penalty (see water hazard chart)
Lost ball in obstruction		Drop ball within one club length where ball entered obstruction. drop in hazard if obstruction is in hazard.

Chart 4. Lifting and cleaning the ball
(Rules 20 and 21)

	Penalty 1 stroke	No penalty
To determine if ball is unfit for play (21)	If cleaned	No cleaning
For identification (21)	If cleaned	Clean only to identify
Lifting ball which may interfere or assist with play (21)	If cleaned	No cleaning
When lifted because of obstruction (24-1,2)		If cleaned
Relief from casual water, ground under repair and course damage (21-1)		If cleaned
Embedded ball in own pitch mark in closely mown area through green (fairway) (25-2)		If cleaned
Cleaning embedded ball in own pitch mark through green (off closely mown area/ fairway) (25-2)	Loss of hole 2 stroke penalty	If local rules permit
Suspension of play		If cleaned
Embedded ball on green		If cleaned
From water hazards or unplayable lies		If cleaned

Chart 5. Line of putt
(Rule 16)

Touching line of putt on putting green Rule 16	
Penalty: loss of hole or 2 strokes	No penalty
Testing surface of green	In addressing the ball
Repair of spike marks	In measuring
Smoothing Surface	In lifting the ball
Brushing or moving loose impediment with object other than hand or club	Moving loose impediments by picking them up or brushing aside by hand or club with no pressing down on surface
	In pressing down a ball-marker
	In repairing old ball plugs and ball marks
	In removing moveable obstructions

Chart 6. Casual water, ground under repair, hole, cast, or runway
(Rule 25)

	Relief	Procedure
Through the green	Relief from condition only	Drop one club length not nearer hole
On the green	Relief from condition and line of putt	Lift and place on green nearest original position but not nearer hole or in hazard
Hazard	Relief granted	No penalty if dropped in hazard near original lie. may drop out of hazard with penalty stroke
Water hazard lateral water hazard	No Relief	One stroke penalty to play out of hazard under Rule 26. Chart 2
Ball lost in condition	Relief granted no penalty	Drop ball within one club length of point of entry not nearer hole.
Lost in hazard	Relief granted no penalty	Drop ball near point of entry to condition but in hazard. or one stroke penalty to drop out of hazard.
Lost in water hazard and lat.wat. hazard	No relief	One stroke penalty to play under rule 26-1 relief from water hazard. Chart 2

Chart 7. Lifts, drops, redrops, and placing ball
(Rule 20)

	Lifts	Drops	Redrops	Place
Procedure	Ball must be marked before lifting.	Drop ball at arm length and shoulder height. May remove loose impediments before drop.	When ball touches player or equipment	Place ball if ball fails to remain in dropped area after redrop
Penalty	1 Stroke. failure to return ball to correct spot [LH, 25STR] no penalty if marker moves.	No penalty if drop is Corrected before stroke is taken. 1 stroke penalty if drop is not corrected	No penalty	No penalty
Lost and out of bounds		Play at previous stroke. In hazard drop in hazard. If on tee area re-tee ball.		
When	As rules permit. See chart 4	As rules permit	When ball rolls: into or out of hazard. onto putting green. out of Bounds.back into relief Condition. more than 2 club lengths on striking Ground. nearer the hole.	If original lie of ball is altered after ball came to rest then place in similar lie within 1 club length. replace if in hazard. recreate original lie.

Chart 8. Loose Impediments, natural objects

(Rule 23)

On putting green	Removeable	
Through the green	Removeable	
On teeing area	Removeable	
Sand and loose soil on putting green only	Removeable	
Sand and loose soil through the green		Not Removeable
Snow and natural ice	Removeable	Considered as loose impediment or casual water. player choice.
Dew and frost		Not removeable
Stones, leaves, twigs branches, etc.	Removeable if not fixed or growing	
Dung, worms, insects casts or heaps made by them, that are not fixed or growing	Removeable	Not removeable if fixed or growing
In hazard if ball is in hazard		Not removeable
In hazard if ball is not in hazard	Removeable	
Drop area or spot	Removable before drop if desired	
Penalty for breach of rule	Match - loss of hole stroke play - 2 strokes	

Chart 9. Ball moved, deflected, or stopped

Ball moved deflected by:	Ball at rest	Ball in motion
	Rule 18	Rule 19
Outside agency	No penalty - replace	No penalty - replace
Player partner caddie or equipment	1 Stroke penalty - replace includes ball moving after address and ball moving by moving loose impediment through green. No penalty for accidental movement when: measuring; searching for covered ball in hazard, casual water, and ground under repair; repair of ball mark; removing loose impediment on putting green; lifting ball under a rule; placing or replacing a ball under a rule; lifting ball interfering or assisting play; removing a movable obstruction.	Match play - loss of hole stroke play - 2 strokes play as it lies.
Opponent caddie or Equipment match play	During search - no penalty replace. other than search - 1 stroke penalty on opponent.	No penalty - replay or play as it lies.
Fellow competitor	No penalty - replace	No penalty - replace
On purpose	Disqualification	Disqualification
Another ball	No penalty - replace	No penalty - replace except on putting green when putted ball hits another ball. 2 strokes penalty in stroke play only.

Chart 10. Lie, area of swing, and line of play
(Rule 13)

Penalty: loss of hole or 2 strokes	No penalty
Improving lie or position of ball	Play ball as it lies
Improving area of intended swing	Moving, bending or breaking anything fixed or growing and moving or pressing down sand, loose soil, replaced divots, etc., while taking stance, backswing or swing only.
Improving line of play	
Moving, bending or breaking anything fixed or growing	
Removing or pressing down sand, loose soil, replaced divots, cut turf or surface irregularities	
Building stance	Planting feet firmly

Chart 11. Practice

	Match play	Stroke play
Before and between rounds	May practice on course before a round	May not practice on course or test putting greens before round
Practice during round	No practice strokes. a practice swing is not a practice stroke	No practice strokes. a practice swing is not a practice stroke
Between holes	May practice putting or chipping on or near green of last hole played, a practice putting green or the teeing ground of next hole. no practice from hazard and no delay of play. penalty loss of hole	May practice putting or chipping on or near green of last hole played. a practice putting green or the teeing ground of next hole. no practice from hazard and no delay of play. penalty two strokes
Committee	Check with the committee on the practice rules as committee may prohibit these rules for their tournament	

Chart 12. Match and stroke play

	Match play	Stroke play
Winner	By winning the most holes	Lowest number of strokes
Conceding putts	Yes	Disqualification for failing to putt out
Claims/disputes	Must be made before start of next hole, if on last hole then claim before leaving the green. no play of second ball. no claim after match officially announced	If doubtful of ruling may play second ball and inform committee before returning score card. failure is disqualification
Delayed claim	No claims after start of next hole unless based on facts previously unknown or wrong information was given	Check with committee before turning score card in
Player taking penalty	Must inform opponent as soon as possible. failure to do so is considered giving wrong information. wrong information can be corrected before next stroke by opponent. failure is loss of hole	Player must inform marker as soon as possible.
Play out of turn	Opponent may require player to cancel stroke and replay in correct order. No penalty	No penalty If players play out of turn so as to give advantage to a player. Disqualification
Start play outside tee ground	Opponent may require player to replay stroke in correct area. No penalty	Two-stroke penalty

Bibliography

(Including sources and other references)

Chapter 1:

Adrian, M.J. & J.M. Cooper. *Biomechanics Of Human Movement*. Madison, WI: Brown and Benchmark, 1989/1995.

Blake Mindy. *The Golf Swing Of the Future*. New York: W. W. Norton, 1972.

Blake, Mindy. *Golf: The Technique Barrier*. New York: W. W. Norton, 1978.

Brancazio, Peter J. *Sport Science*. New York: Simon and Schuster.1984.

Buttitta, Joe. *The Fire Drill*. Golf Tips.

Cochran, A. & J. Stobbs. *The Search For the Perfect Swing*. Philadelphia: Lippincott, 1968.

Cooper, J.M. & B.T. Bates & J. Bedi & J. Scheuchenzuber. "Kinematic and kinetic analysis of the golf swing." *Biomechanics IV*, R.C. Nelson and C.A. Morehouse (Eds.). Baltimore: University Park Press, 1974.

Croker, Peter & Jeffrey Johnson. "Swing of the Future." *Golf Digest*. April & May 1965.

Fox, Peter. *Golf Reform Is At Hand*. Natural Golf Corporation, 1996.

Hall, Susan J. *Basic Biomechanics*. St. Louis: Mosby, 1995.

Handy, Ike S. *How to Hit a Golf Ball Straight*. Cameron and company San Francisco, 1967.

Hamill, J. & K.M. Knutzen. *Biomechanical Basis of Human Movement*. Baltimore: Williams & Wilkins, 1995.

Heard's Super Swing. Jerry Heard Golf Academy, Florida.

Jensen, C.R. & G.W. Schultz & B.L. Bangerter. *Applied Kinesiology And Biomechanics*. New York, 1983.

Jorgensen, Theodore P. *The Physics of Golf*. New York: AIP press, 1994.

Jones, Ernest. *Swing the Clubhead*. Golf Digest Classic Book, 1952.

Kuykendall, Jack. *Golf Reform at Hand*. Video and Book from Natural Golf. Hoffman Estates, IL 60195.

Leadbetter, David. "Throw the clubhead for a freer release." *Golf Digest*, October 1996.

Lee, David. *Gravity Golf*. Homosassa, FL: Gravity Sports Concepts.

Mann, Ralf. "Shattering the Swing Phase and other Teaching Myths." *Golf Digest*, July 1986.

McLean, Jim. "Widen the Gap (the X-Factor)." *Golf Magazine*, December 1992.

Mullins, Andrew. *Golf Magazine*, November 1985, p. 56.

Natural Golf, 2400 W. Hassell Rd. Suite 370, Hoffman Estates, IL 60195.

O'Meara, Marc. "How To Make The First Move Down." *Golf Digest*, September 1996.

Stickney, Tom & Perer Morrice. "The Keys To Consistency." *Golf Magazine*, December 1999, p.92.

Tomasi, T.J. "The Power V: How to Leverage Your Golf Swing." *Golf Illustrated*, August 1993.

Torbert, Marianne. *Secrets to Success in Sports and Play*. Prentice Hall, Englewood Cliffs, NJ, 1982.

Trahan, Don. "The Case for the Shorter Backswing." *Senior Golfer*. February 1998.

Walker, Alan. *The Relationship Of Distance And Accuracy To Three Golf Grips*. Masters Thesis. Springfield College 1964.

Williams, David. *The Science of the Golf Swing*. Pelham Books, 1969.

Web sites:

Big-Grip Golf. *www.big-grip.com*. 1-800-800-6116

Kuykendall, Jack. "Lever Power Golf." *Kuykendall's Golf Science Magazine*.

Scigolf. Formerly Ideal Mechanical Advantage. Scott Hazledine. *www.scigolf.com*

Chapter 2:

Brumer, Andy. "Revolution in Graphite Shafts?" *Golf Illustrated*, May/June 1995.

Cochran, A.J. & M.R. Farrally., ed. *Science and Golf II: The Proceedings of the World Scientific Congress of Golf* (ISBN 0-419-18790-1). London: E & FN Spon, 1994.

Pelz, Dave. *Putt Like the Pros*. New York: Harper Row, 1989.

Williams, Dave. *The Science of the Golf Swing*. Pelham Books, 1969.

Chapter 3:

Blake, Mindy: *The Golf Swing of the Future (ISBN 0-393-08376-4). New York: W. W. Norton & Co, 1972.*

Chapter 4:

Fitts, P.M. "Perceptual Motor Skill Learning." In A.W. Melton (ed.). *Categories of Human Learning*. New York: Academic Press, 1964.

Fitts, P.M. & M.I. Posner. *M.I. Human Performance*. Belmont, CA: Brooks/Cole, 1967.

Gallway, W.T. *The Inner Game of Golf*. New York: Random House, 1979.

Griffith, Coleman. "An experiment in Learning to Drive a Golf Ball." *Athletic Journal*. Vol, 1. 1913, p10-13.

Harris, D.V. & W.J. Robinson. "The Effects of Skill Level on EMG Activity During Internal and External Imagery." *Journal of Sport Psychology 8, 1986, p105-111.*

Hatfield, B. & Others. "An Electroencephalographic Study of Elite Rifle Shooters." *The American MarksmanI, February 1982.*

Jacobson, E. "Electrical Measurement of Neuro-muscular States During Mental Activities." *American Journal of Physiology 94, 1930, p22-34.*

Jones, J.G. "Motor Learning Without Demonstration of Physical Practice, Under Two Conditions of Mental Practice." *Research Quarterly 36, 1965, p270-276.*

Mead, M. In J.M. Tanner and B. Inhelder (eds.). *Discussion on Child Development. Vol, 3. Tavistock Press, 1958.*

Morley, D.C. *The Missing Links-Golf and Mind*. New York: Atheneum/SMI, 1976.

Nieporte, T. & D. Sauers. *Mind over Golf*, New York: Doubleday and Co., 1968.

Rock, I. & C.S. Harris. "Vision and Touch." *Scientific American 216, 1967, p96-104.*

Singer, R.N. *Motor Learning and Human Performance*. New York: MacMillan, 1975.

Suttie, J.K. "A Biomechanical Comparison Between a Conventional Golf Swing/Learning Technique and a Unique Kin-

esthetic Feedback Technique." *Dissertation Abstracts International 44(3), 1983.*

Walford, G.A. "Vision and Nonvision (Blindfold) Techniques in Learning the Golf Putt." (Unpublished raw data for Doctoral Dissertation). University of Maryland, 1988.

Wiren, G. & R. Coop. "The New Golf Mind." *Golf Digest*, Norwalk CT 1978.

Chapter 5:

Cochran, A. & J. Stobbs. *The Search for the Perfect Swing*. Philadelphia: Lippincott, 1968.

Garfield & Benneth. *Peak Performance: Mental Training Techniques of the World's Greatest Athletes*, 1984.

Herrigel, Eugen. *Zen and the Art of Archery*. New York: Vintage Books, 1953.

Chapter 6

The following two books give an excellent background to the NLP program. The book by Mackenzie gives many techniques for various phases of the game:

Mackenzie, Marlin M. & Ken Denlinger. *Golf The Mind Game*. Dell Trade Paperback, 1990.

Alder, Harry & Karl Morris. *Masterstroke Use the Power Of Your Mind to Improve Your Golf with NLP*. Piatkus Publishers, 1996.

Chapter 7

McLean, Jim. "Widen the Gap (the X-factor)."*Golf Maganize, December, 1992.*

Stickney II, Tom & Peter Morrice. "The Keys to Consistency." *Golf Magazine*, December 1999.

Chapter 8

Faxon, Brad. Comments on CBS television during broadcast of Greater Greensboro Open. April 22, 1989.

Lyle, Sandy. Comments on CBS television during the Masters Golf Tournament. Sunday, April 9, 1989.

Pelz, Dave. *Dave Pelz's Putting Bible*. New York: Doubleday, 2000.

Web sites:

SP Golf Company. "Makers of the Bald Eagle Golf Ball."
1-888-774-6534. *www.spgolf.com.*

Chapter 9

Jones, Ernest. "Swing the Clubhead." *Golf Digest Classic Book*,
1952.

Chapter 14

The grip:

Paul Azinger	*Golf Digest*	8/87 p52
Bobby Clampett	*Golf Magazine*	4/83 p59
Bernard Langer	*Golf Magazine*	1/88 p30
Tom Watson	*Golf Digest*	1/87 p38
Mike Dunaway	*Golf Magazine*	8/85 p33
Al Wagner	Golf Digest	7/81 p18
Charles Owens	*Golf Digest*	2/87 p113

The stance:

Bob Toski	*Golf Digest*	1/83 p52
Whitney Crouse	*Golf Magazine*	12/84 p23
John Mahaffey	*Golf Magazine*	3/84 p31
Jim Flick	*Golf Digest*	6/73 p46
Don Trahan	*Golf Magazine*	6/84 p59
Mike Dunaway	*Golf Magazine*	8/85 p32
Charles Owens	*Golf Digest*	2/87 p114
Tom Weiskoff	*Golf Digest*	6/73 p46
Doug Sanders	*Golf Digest*	12/71 p38
Peter Jacobson/Johnny Miller	*Golf Digest*	7/85 p60

The backswing:

Gretchen Byrd	*Golf Digest*	4/82 p106

Bobby Clampett	*Golf Magazine*	4/83 p59
Gene Littler	*Golf Magazine*	8/74 p43
Don Willingham	Golf Magazine	4/86 p32
Ben Hogan	*Golf Digest*	4/87 p97
Gary Player	*Golf Magazine*	7/81 p45
Charles Owens	*Golf Digest*	2/87 p114
Craig Shankland	*Golf Magazine*	10/84 p60
Bernard Langer	*Golf Magazine*	1/88 p30
Jack Nicklaus	*Golf Magazine*	1/86 p19
Charles Owens	*Golf Digest*	2/87 p114
Peter Beames	*Golf Magazine*	9/82 p71
Johnny Miller	*Golf Magazine*	5/75 p41
Arnold Palmer	*Golf Magazine*	5/75 p41
Andrew Mullin	*Golf Magazine*	11/85 p56

The downswing:

Peter Jacobson	*Golf Magazine*	11/84 p26
Ernie Vossler	*Golf Magazine*	4/78 p88
Joe Nicols	*Golf Magazine*	9/78 p56
Mike Dunaway	*Golf Magazine*	8/85 p114
Ernie Vossler	*Golf Magazine*	4/78 p87
Paul Bertholy	*Golf Magazine*	12/82 p28

Contact:

Scott Verplank	*Golf Digest*	11/86 p70
Phil Rodgers	*Golf Digest*	6/83 p84
Dr. Ralph Mann	*Golf Illustrated*	Summer/1985

Follow-through:

change in follow-through	*Golf Digest*	7/85 p27
Peter Beames	*Golf Magazine*	9/82 p70

Overall Swing:

Desmond Tolhurst	*Golf Magazine*	Yearbook/83
mechanic to magician	*Golf Magazine*	7/85 p50
Joe Nichols	*Golf Magazine*	9/78 p54
Alex Morrison	*Golf Digest*	5/87 p84
Eddie Merrins	*Golf Magazine*	4/83 p87
Tom Purtzer	*Golf Digest*	6/87 p136
Hank Johnson	Golf Digest	8/82 p40
Ben Doyle	Golf Digest	8/83 p81
Manuel de la Torre	Golf Magazine	7/77 p50
three?quarter swing	Golf Magazine	2/86 p38
Henry Cotton	Golf Magazine	7/81 p77
Henry Cotton	Golf Digest	10/73 p42
David Lister	*Golf Digest*	12/75 p51
James Haber	*Golf Magazine*	5/74 p65
Mr. X	*Golf Magazine*	6/74 p55
Oliver Brizon	*Golf Magazine*	10/83 p30
Sam Byrd	*Golf Magazine*	11/74 p58
Desmond Tolhurst	*Golf Magazine*	1/78 p56
result of the equipment	*Golf Magazine*	5/86 p52
Al Barkow	*Golf Magazine*	12/81 p35

The Short Game:

| Dick Farley/Rich McCord | Golf Magazine | 3/86 p3 |

Tom Pullman	Golf Magazine	1/87 p20
Ken Venturi/Isao Aoki	*Golf Magazine*	9/85 p64
Hubert Green	*Golf Magazine*	7/77 p37
Phil Rodgers	*Golf Magazine*	Yearbook/81
Dave Pelz	*Golf Magazine*	12/83 p34

Putting:

Phil Rodgers	*Golf Magazine*	7/82 p52
Dr. Robert E. Kraft	*Scholastic Coach*	1/86 p110
All the theories	*Golf Magazine*	8/87 p32
New putting research	*Golf Magazine*	Yearbook/78

Chapter 23

Suzuki, D.T. (In Introduction to Eugen Herrigel. *Zen and the Art of Archery.* New York: Vintage Books, 1953.

Chapter 24

Yagyu, Munenori. *The Sword and the* Mind. Translated by Hiroaki Sato. Woodstock, NY: Overlook Press, 1986.

Chapter 25

Miller, D. Prologue. In *Philosophy Of Creativity. New York: Peter Lang, 1989, p7-14.*

Murphy, M. *Golf In The Kingdom.* New York: Viking, 1972.

Index

A

abdominal muscles, 20
act as if in control, 151
aerodynamics, 39
aerodynamics of ball flight, 38
agonist, 22
allround club, 97
alternating tension and relaxation, 70
aluminum, 28, 32,
aluminum shafts, 35
ambivalence (the mind), 48
analyzer (the mind), 45
anchor, 57, 58
angular speed, 13
anisotropic, 32
antagonist, 22
anxiety, 106, 109
Aoki, Isao, 123
Aoyama, S., 38
Applied kinesiology and
    biomechanics, 21
approach shot, 97
Aristotle, 160
arm and hand roll, 71
arm roll, 66
art of thinking, 100
attention, 49
automatic stage, 68, 78
automation, 45
average handicap, 41
average hit, 97
axis of rotation, 23

B

backswing, 71, 120
balata, 28, 36
balata ball, 28
Bald Eagle golf ball, 76
bald spots, 76
ball placement, 72
ball's center, 37
Bangerter, B.L., 21
Barkow, Al, 123
baseball grip, 119
baseball swing, 127
basic swing, 70
basketball, 19
Beames, Peter, 120, 122
being natural, 80
bendpoint, 31

Bennet, H, 52
bent elbow, 19
Bent (grass), 99
Bermuda (grass), 99
Bertholy, Paull, 121
Better Golf in Five Minutes, 123
Bibliography, 168-171
Big-Grip Golf Co., 19, 26, 27
binocular vision, 77
biomechanics of human movement, 19
Blake, Mindy, 20, 23, 43
blank chart for distances (table), 89
blindfolds, 49
body activity, 109
body alignment, 128
body awareness, 45, 71
body rehearsal, 45
boron, 32
Boros, Julius, 16
breathing, 151
Brizon, Oliver, 123
bronze alloy, 29
bubble shaft, 34
buldge (on clubhead face), 41
bullwhip, 18, 19
Buttitta, Joe, 16
Byrd, Gretchen, 120, 123

C

carbon-graphite, 33
careless attitude, 108
careless performance, 108
carom shot, 101
carpenters, 30
casual water, 103
CBS television, 80, 81
center, 60
center of percussion, 23.
centerline system, 96
centrifugal torque, 18
centrifugal force, 13, 17, 18, 25, 32, 34,
    57, 61
centripetal force, 13, 17
ceramic, 33
C_g (center of gravity), 40
Chevreul's Pendulum, 68
childlikeness, 150
chip shot, 98
chipping, 77, 88
Chivas Irons, 158

choking, 115
Chou, A., 31
Clampett, Bobby, 120
cleaning (grips), 39
closed eyes, 71
closed stance, 119
club selection, 96
clubheads, 40
clubhead awareness, 48
clubface, 40
club selection, 95
clubface inserts, 28
clubhead mass and speed, 24
coordination, 22, 85
COAM: Conservation of Angular Mo-
    tion, 18
coat hanger, 84
Cochran, A., 17, 23, 25, 51
coefficient of restitution, 28, 38
cognition, 45
cognitive thinking, 44
Compact Golf, 122
compression, 37
concentrating, 49, 69, 100, 114, 126,
concept stage, 78
confidence, 57, 108
confused mind, 80, 108
confused muscles, 79
conscious, 54
conscious movement, 68
consistency, 94
contact, 121
controlled tension, 22
Coop, R., 45
coping strategies, 104
copper, 28
cord (in grips), 40
Cotton, Henry, 122
Crocker, Peter, 15, 17, 84
cross-handed grip, 119
Crouse, Whitney, 119
cut shot, 98
cycolac, 28

D

Dave Pelz's Putting Bible (book), 76
dead grass, 101
Descartes, 160
dimple patterns, 38
Dimple depth on distance (table 2-1), 38

dimples, 36, 38, 39
dispersion patterns, 132
distance by swing length, 87
distance/club chart (table), 90
distance patterns, 132
distractions, 79
do not try, 159
doing process, 53
dollar bill, 88, 102
dominant eye, 99
double overlap grip, 119
doubt, 95
doubting mind, 79
downswing, 121
drag effect, 38
draw, 78
Dunaway, Mike, 118, 119, 121
duranium shafts, 35

E

early modern swing, 44
East, J. Victor, 123
Eastern thought, 158
ego, 134, 158
empty mind, 53, 57
energy, 41
epoxy, 28
equipment, 95
evaluation (of learning), 114
external feedback, 52
eyes closed, shut, 77, 93

F

fade, 78
false assumptions, 96, 98, 107
false confidence, 109
Farley, Dick, 123
fat shaft, 34
Faxon, Brad, 80
fear, 80, 152
featherlight (golf clubs), 30
feedback, 52, 75
fiberglass, 32
figure skater spin, 18
finder finger, 122
Fitts, P.M., 45
five stages of accomplishment, 116
fixation, 45
flexpoint, 31
Flick, Jim, 119
floating shot, 98
fly/roll ratio, 88

flying elbow, 136
focus, 80
focus of attention, 49,125
follow-thorough, 121
four-inch swing, 75
freewheel, 126
friction (on putter face), 76
fried egg lie, 102
full swing, 71

G

Gallwey, W.T., 48
Garfield, C., 52
Geiberger, Al, 48
general rules (green reading), 100
goal setting, 109
golf and life, 149
golf club distances (table), 133
golf balls, 35
Golf Illustrated (magazine), 25
Golf in the Kingdom (book), 158
Golf Reform is at Hand, 25
Golf Magazine, 16, 22, 52, 62
Golf Digest, 16, 84
Golf Swing of the Future (book), 20
Golf – The Mind Game (book), 58
Golf Made Easy (book), 123
Golf Swing of the Future (book), 23
grain, 99
graphite, 32
gravity, 15, 36
Gravity Golf (book), 16
Greater Greensboro Open, 80
Green, Hubert, 123
greens, 98
Griffith, Coleman R., 45, 52
grip, 19, 118, 39

H

Haber, James, 123
handkerchief, 102
Handy, Ike, 17
Harris, C.S., 49
Harris, D.V., 49
Hatfield, Brad, 49
Hazledine, Scott, 26
Heard, Jerry, 26
Heard's Super Swing, 26, 27
heavy sand, 102
heavy grass, 101
here and now, 151
Herrigel, Eugen, 53

Hogan, Ben, 119, 120
    Ben Hogan's secret, 120
hook, 78
Horwood, G.P., 32
how to practice, 93
hypnosis, 114

I

Ideal Mechanical Advantage, 26
imagery styles, 54
imagery, 48, 109, 112
imagery for mental development, 112
imagery for skill development, 112
inertia, 12, 18, 32
integrator (the mind), 45
interlocking grip, 19, 118
internal feedback, 52
Introduction to Zen in the Art of Archery (book), 150
isotropic, 32

J

Jacobson, Peter, 119, 121
Jacobson, E., 48
Japanese swordsman, 154
Jensen, C.R., 19
Johnson, Hank, 122
Jones, J.G., 16, 17, 25, 48, 82
Jorgensen, Theodore P., 14, 19, 121
judging distances (learn to), 95

K

karate chop, 19, 151
keep it simple, 79
Kevlar, 32
kickpoint, 31
Killer Bee "Stinger" Golf Cub Method, 87, 90
kinesthetic, 45, 49
kinesthetic sense, 44, 71, 75
kinetic energy, 38
knowledge of results, 53
Kraft, Dr. Robert E., 124
Kuykendall, Jack, 19, 25, 26, 27, 66,
    Kuykendall's Golf Science Magazine (web site), 19, 26

L

Landers, D., 49
Langer, Bernard, 120

late hit, 17
late modern swing, 45
Leadbetter, David, 15, 17
learn like a kid, 80
learned reflex, 52, 53
leaves, 101
Lee, David, 16
lessening importance of the situation, 108
letting go, 52
Lever Power Golf, 19, 26, 66
leverage, 130
lightweight steel, 31, 33
Lister, David, 122
Littler, Gene, 120
lock in, 53
logic, 157
long fairway shots, 96
long irons, 97
long thumb, 118
loose grip, 22
Loren, Carl, 123
Lyle, Sandy, 81

M

Mackenzie, Marlin, M., 58
Mahaffey, John, 119
management by objectives, 109
Mann, Ralph ,18, 19, 22, 121
Manuel de la Torre, 122
martial arts experts, 19
mass, 24
matched set, 31
McCord, Rick, 123
McLean, Jim, 66, 25
Mead, M., 44
mechanical robot, 157
mechanics, 54, 60, 80
meditation, 115
Melvin, T., 36
mental practice, 48
mental confusion, 94, 95
mental exercises, 109
mental recall, 108
mental skills, 104
mental strategies, 93
mental toughness, 101, 107
Merrins, Eddie, 122
metaphors, 53
middle irons, 97
Miller, Johnny, 119, 120, 129
Miller, David, 159
mind confusion, 92

mind control, 154
mind set, 115
modality synchronization, 30
moment of inertia, 23, 41
Morley, D.C., 45
Morrice, Peter, 22, 62
Morrison, Alex, 122
movement feedback, 52
movement outcome, 52
Mr. X, 123
Mullins, Andrew, 13, 120
multi-layered golf balls, 36
Munenori, Yagyu, 154
muscle memory, 78, 79, 93

N

Natural Golf, 19, 25, 26
natural rubber, 40
negative imagery, 58, 93
negative reinforcement, 107
New Golf Mind (The) (book), 45
Newton, Sir Isaac, 13, 20
Newton's third law of action/reaction, 25, 63
Nichols, Joe, 121, 122
nickel, 28
Nicklaus, Jack, 18, 120, 121
nickle shafts, 35
Nieporte, T., 49
ninety-degree swing angle, 62
NLP (Neuro-Linguistic Programming), 53
no thinking philosophy, 52
no thoughts, 54
non-balata ball, 28
non-radius arm, 75
non-taper grip, 39
nonvisual practice, 71
Norman, Moe, 17,20, 25, 119

O

obsession, 155
off the tee, 95
Olsavsky, T., 41
One Move to Better Golf (book), 123
one-leg stork stand drill, 73
open/closed club face, 96
open stance, 120
over-coaching syndrome, 79
overall swing, 122
overcoming inertia, 24
overlapping grip, 19

Owens, Charles, 119, 120
O'Meara, Marc, 16

P

pace of swing, 77
palm grip (Moe Norman), 19, 24
Palmer, Arnold, 120
parables, 53
paralysis by analysis, 80
Path to Better Golf (Book), 84
patience, 152
Peak Performance: Mental Training Techniques of the World's Greatest Athletes (Book), 52
Pelz, Dave, 24, 37, 76, 124
pendulum, 11, 87
perceptions, 108
performance breakdown, 79
performance phase, 104, 105
performance zone, 51
perimeter weighting, 28
PGA tour, 41
Philosophy of Creativity (book), 159
physical and mental codes (table), 112
Physics of Golf (The) (book), 14
pine needles, 101
pitching, 77
plastics, 28
Plato, 157, 160
Player, Gary, 81, 120, 122
plumb-bob method, 99
polymer, 28
positive attitude, 100
positive perception, 57
positive thinking, 94, 107
Posner, M.I., 45
potential energy, 19
powdery sand, 102
practice stage, 78
practice workbook, 146
pre-programmed, 78
pre-shot routine, 105
preparation phase, 104
pressing, 81
pressure on the ball, 23
prime mover, 156
principle of force, 20
pro-trajectory, 31
problem thoughts, 92
propulsive force, 22
psychological strategies, 104
Pullman, Tom, 123
Purtzer, Tom, 122

push-and-pull action/analysis, 14
Putt Like the Pros, 37
putting, 75, 88, 124
putting distance, 77

R

R&A rules, 36
radius, 60
railers (on sole of club heads), 40
rational thinking, 107
Ray, W., 49
reading the greens, 99
ready position, 120
rebound, 28
reflex, 19
Rehling, Conrad, 13
Relationship of Distance and Accuracy to Three Golf Grips (Masters Thesis), 19
relaxing the body, 22, 112
release, 143
reminiscence, 115
reverse release, 123
rhythm, 12, 77
right brain/left brain, 45
right shoulder problem, 137
Roberts, O.C., 31
Robinson, W.J., 49
robotic stroke, 156
Rock, I., 49
rod and piston, 27
Rodgers, Phil, 88, 121, 123, 124
roll (on clubhead face), 41
rotor method, 121, 122
rough, 101
rough shot, 98
roundhouse swing, 43
routines, 109
rules of golf, 103, 156–167

S

sand shots, 88
sand trap distances (table), 89
sand trap shots, 101
Sanders, Doug, 122
Sanders, Tom, 26
Sato, Hiroaki, 154
Sauers, D., 49
Schultz, G.W., 19
Science of the Golf Swing (The) (book), 16, 17, 39,
Science and Golf II (book), 32, 36, 38, 41
Scigolf, 26

scrambling, 100
scrape the grass, 93
scrape-the-grass drill (with ball), 72
scrape the grass drill (without ball), 69, 70
Search for the Perfect Swing (The) (book), 17, 23, 25
second guess, 106
Second Law of Motion, 13
Secrets to Success in Sports and Play (book), 20
self, 150
self-hypnosis, 115
self-talk (positive and negative), 58, 106
Senior Golfer (magazine), 15
set-up, 22
shaft butt, 34
shaft length, 34
shafts (various materials), 31
Shankland, Craig, 120
short irons, 97,133
short game, 123
shoulder rotation, 66
similarities, 53
single plane, 24
Singer, R., 44
single pendulum, 82
single axis, 24
single-axis/plane swing, 19, 24, 26
size (of golf balls), 36
size (of grips), 39
skipping a stone on water, 130
slice, 78
soccer ball, 19
somatic or body activity, 106, 109
sound barrier, 18
sources of energy, 19
SP Golf Company, 76
spin (on golf balls), 36
spinal column, 62
spirit stage, 149
sport psychologist, 115
spot putting, 124
square dimples, 39
square stance, 119
stainless steel, 31, 33
stance, 119
statistic formulas, 139
Stickney II, Tom, 22, 62
stiff-wrist method, 123
stimulus overload, 79
Stobbs, J., 17, 23, 25, 51
stop learning process, 53
strategies and abilities, 104

string drill, 74
subconscious, 99, 122
subconscious putting, 76
Sullivan, M.J., 36
supersize driver, 41
surlyn, 36
Suttie, James, 45
Suzuki, D.T., 150
sweet spot, 23
swing arc, 25
swing failures, 73
swing problems, 73
swing speed and distance, 86
Swing the Clubhead (book), 17, 82
swing weight, 29, 30
swinging a broom, mop, open umbrella, 143
Sword and the Mind (The) (book), 154
swordsmanship, 154
synthetic compounds, 40

T

Tao (the), 156
tape measure, 76, 88
Taylor Made, 34
teardrop shape (dimples), 39
ten-finger grip, 19, 119
tennis ball, 19
tension, 109
thermoplastic elastomers, 40
thermoplastic shafts, 35
thinking process, 105
third law of motion (action/reaction), 20, 73
Thomas, F.W., 41
thought stopping, 105, 106
three stages of learning, 45
three-lever system, 19
three-piece ball, 38
three-quarter swing, 122
timing of swing, 15
titanium, 28, 29, 33, 34, 40
Tolhurst, Desmond, 122, 123
Tomasi, T.J., 25
Torbert, Marianne, 20
torque, 13, 17, 33, 34
Toski, Bob, 119
total weight or golf club, 30
traditional swing, 24
Trahan, Don, 15, 119
trajectory (high, mid, low), 39
transfer of energy, 16, 19
trap approach shot, 98

Trevino, Lee, 26
trial and error, 80
triggers, 57, 58
trust, 80
trust yourself, 80
try (do not), 159
trying too hard, 81
tungsten carbide, 29
twin pendulum, 20, 82, 84
two-lever system, 19
two-piece solid surlyn cover ball, 37
typing skills, 44
typist, 127

U

unconscious, 54
unconscious concentration, 149
uneven lie, 100
upright swing plane, 24
USGA, 29, 36, 38,
USGA Research and Test Center, 38

V

Vardon grip, 19, 24

Vardon, Harry, 26
Venturi, Ken, 123
Verplank, Scott, 121
vertical swing, 43
visualization, 68, 70, 711
Vossler, Ernie, 121

W

Wagner, Al, 119
Walford, Gerald, 49
walk-through, 122
Walker, Alan, 19
water shots, 102
Watson, Tom, 118
weather, 102
wedges, 29
weight (of golf balls), 36
weight shift, 16, 71
weight transfer, 17
Western Disclaimer to Philosophy, 160
whip, 18, 19
whipping action, 130
Williams, Dr. Dave, 16, 17, 25, 39
Willingham, Don, 120
Wiren, G., 45

wishful thinking, 107
wound balls, 38
wound surlyn 95 compression ball, 37
wound surlyn 105 compression ball, 37
wrist action, 63

X

"X"-factor, 25

Y

yang, 159
yard stick, 88
yesterday's swing, 43
yin, 159
your own par, 103

Z

Zen, 53, 53
Zen golf, 149
Zen in the Art of Archery (book), 53, 151
Zen learning, 150
Zen philosophy, 57, 150
zone (in the), 51, 57